世界语言学与应用语言学研究丛书

U0743377

# Disciplinary Identities:
# Individuality and Community in Academic Discourse

# 学科身份：
# 学术话语中的个体与共同体

Ken Hyland（英） 著

**外语教学与研究出版社**
FOREIGN LANGUAGE TEACHING AND RESEARCH PRESS
北京 BEIJING

**剑桥大学出版社**
CAMBRIDGE UNIVERSITY PRESS

京权图字：01-2019-2755

**图书在版编目 (CIP) 数据**

学科身份：学术话语中的个体与共同体：英文／（英）海亮（Ken Hyland）著. ——北京：外语教学与研究出版社，2020.1
（世界语言学与应用语言学研究丛书）
ISBN 978-7-5213-1550-9

Ⅰ. ①学… Ⅱ. ①海… Ⅲ. ①学术交流－应用语言学－研究－英文 Ⅳ. ①H08

中国版本图书馆 CIP 数据核字 (2020) 第 030039 号

出 版 人　徐建忠
责任编辑　解碧琰
责任校对　陈　阳
封面设计　彩奇风
出版发行　外语教学与研究出版社
社　　址　北京市西三环北路 19 号（100089）
网　　址　http://www.fltrp.com
印　　刷　北京虎彩文化传播有限公司
开　　本　650×980　1/16
印　　张　17.5
版　　次　2020 年 4 月第 1 版 2020 年 4 月第 1 次印刷
书　　号　ISBN 978-7-5213-1550-9
定　　价　69.90 元

购书咨询：（010）88819926　电子邮箱：club@fltrp.com
外研书店：https://waiyants.tmall.com
凡印刷、装订质量问题，请联系我社印制部
联系电话：（010）61207896　电子邮箱：zhijian@fltrp.com
凡侵权、盗版书籍线索，请联系我社法律事务部
举报电话：（010）88817519　电子邮箱：banquan@fltrp.com
物料号：315500001

记载人类文明
沟通世界文化
www.fltrp.com

# Contents

# 导读

　　身份研究一直是应用语言学领域的重要议题。通过语言看身份，或通过身份看语言，我们逐渐了解个体与群体之间的社会关系，也加深了对语言的社会属性的认识。应用语言学的身份研究经历了由结构主义到后结构主义的转变（Block，2006）。前者视身份为一组天生或者非天生的固定不变的特征，后者则认为身份是一种基于人际互动的社会建构；前者解答"我们是谁"的本质问题，后者探索"我们成为谁"的社会互动过程。因此，身份不只体现在作者身上及其文本中，更存在于作者和读者之间的话语活动所产生的社会意义中。Benwell and Stokoe（2006）评论道，身份研究的这一话语转向是革命性的，使人们对身份的认识从解读作者的内心世界转向了阐释话语及各种语言符号的社会意义。身份的社会建构属性及其话语实践建立在语言的对话性和社会文化视角基础之上（Bakhtin，1981；Wertsch，1991），且离不开语言的意义表达功能（Halliday and Matthiessen，2014）。

　　2015 年，《应用语言学评论年刊》（*Annual Review of Applied Linguistics*）就以身份为年度主题，评述身份在语篇分析、外语学习和社会语言学研究中的重要体现。从中，我们不难看出，语篇是身份研究的焦点，在身份的社会建构中起着"中介机制"（mediating mechanism）作用。它不仅反映了作者以话语共同体认可的方式来描述世界，而且呈现出可供作者选择的语言资源（Ivanič，1998）。因此，作者的能动性和社会约束力一直是基于语篇的身份研究的核心议题，即作者在多大程度上能够彰显自我、表达个体的声音，同时又在多大程度上受语境和话语共同体的限制。

这种对立也是个体主观主义（individualistic subjectivism）和社会建构主义（social constructionism）的分歧：前者认为身份就是个体情感的表达，而后者强调社会对个体表达手段的约束力。当前，更为可取的视角是社会构建主义（social constructivism）（Matsuda，2015），因为它既强调社会规约对作者的约束，又不否定作者驾驭社会规约、实现个体身份的能动性。这也正是本书标题所突出的观点：身份是个体与共同体的对立统一体。

在本书中，Ken Hyland 主要以学术语篇为载体，这是因为学术语境在身份研究中常常被忽略。与其他语境不同，学术语境中的身份研究容易令人产生一种想法：作者若在学术语境中表达身份，则会增添学术研究的主观色彩，有悖学术报告的客观性。然而，Hyland 通过考察各类学术体裁，基于语料实证分析不同语言特征，向我们展示事实并非如此。相反，围绕学科话语共同体的话语规约与认知方式，学术作者可以运用各种劝谏策略及语言资源，构建学术立场，令自己的学科身份被共同体接受。在描述作者贴近学科共同体、表达个体声音的话语实践时，Hyland 采用了"亲缘"（proximity）和"姿态"（positioning）这两个概念。此外，他还以表达人际意义和语篇意义的语言特征（如自称语和过渡词等）为指示标记（indexicality），考察"亲缘"和"姿态"的话语实践与修辞策略，进而从不同侧面反映学科身份。

2012 年，本书由剑桥大学出版社出版，拓展并深化了 Hyland 在学术语篇研究领域的理论。Hyland 现为英国东英吉利大学教育学院应用语言学首席教授，曾在我国香港特区及新西兰、巴布亚新几内亚、马来西亚、沙特阿拉伯等地从事学术英语教学与研究工作近四十年，是学术英语领域的旗舰刊物《学术用途英语》（*Journal of English for Academic Purposes*）的联合创始主编。他于 1993 年至 1995 年在澳大利亚昆士兰大学攻读应用语言学博士学位，研究学术期刊论文中的模糊语（hedging in scientific research articles），对学术语篇的人际互动及其语言形式有独到而深刻的理解。此后，他提出了一系列关于人际互动与劝谏修辞的解读视角和分析框架，包括引导类与互动类元话语资源、作者立场、读者带入、文本声音以及词块的结构和功能分类等。截至 2019 年 6 月，他共发表学术论文 230 余篇，出版学术著作 29 部，谷歌学术引用率逾 4.3 万次。Hyland 在学术语篇领域的经典之作莫过于 2000 年出版的《学科话语：学术写作中的社会互动》（*Disciplinary Discourses: Social Interactions in Academic Writing*）、2005 年出版的《元话语：写作中的互动研究》（*Metadiscourse: Exploring Interaction in Writing*）以及本书——《学科身份：学术话语中的个体与共同体》（*Disciplinary Identities: Individuality and Community in Academic Discourse*）。其中，《元话语：写作中的互动研究》已由外语教学与研究出版社于 2008 年引进，出版时书名为《元话语》。可以说，这三本专著是从事学术语篇以及学术英语语料库研究必读的经典文献。它们均基于自建的学术英语语料库，以学术互动的语言和修辞资源为切入点，探索语言与学科知识、体裁规约和话语实践的关系。第一本讲述不同学科话语共同体之间创造知识、构建话语的语言差异；第二本聚焦元话语，讨论其丰富的人际意义与劝谏功能；第三本论述个体与学科共同体对话过程中的人际互动与身份构建。

本书共九章。前两章分别综述身份和学科的概念与表征，第三章评述已有文献中身份的研究路径，第四至八章分别通过不同的学术体裁实证分析学科身份构建，第九章总结身份与学科话语、学术写作的联系及相关启示。本书自 2012 年出版之后，引起了应用语言学界的广泛关注，《应用语言学》（*Applied Linguistics*）、《学术用途英语》、《专门用途英语》（*English for Specific Purposes*）等众多国际权威期刊相继发表相关书评。接下来，我将按章节顺序逐一介绍本书内容。

第一章是"身份：互动与共同体"，旨在阐释身份与学科这两个看似不相关的概念。Hyland 开篇指明，本书的焦点即探索学科共同体语境中的学术身份，考察个人如何通过运用学科话语资源构建学术身份。首先，身份不是一个自然人的属性标签，而是基于人际互动的社会建构。在这个过程中，人们与目标共同体成员联系、交际，展示自我并塑造身份，协商他者对所建身份的认同。可见，身份是一种外在的表现，随着个人的经验积累而逐步形成，同时也是他者对这种身份表现的认可和接受。Hyland 借用了 Goffman（1971）的"印象掌控"（impression management）和"立足点"（footing）概念来刻画这一合作交际的社会建构过程。人具有多重身份，只不过在不同的情境中，一方会通过交际策略凸显或者淡化特定的角色，从而影响交际另一方对其身份表现的印象，即在不同的立足点转换不同的身份和立场。

也就是说，身份来自人际互动过程中的社会意义，体现个人的施动（performative）行为。个人根据经验和实践的积累，建立目标读者能够接受的身份，而个人的经验与实践往往产生于与话语共同体成员的对话和互动。学科恰恰就是学术语境下特定的话语共同体。它是一个抽象概念，体现为一定的、规约的行事、思考和言语方式，也反映共同的信念、价值观、认知方式以及权力关系。可见，学科共同体构成了学术身份构建的话语环境；同时，共同体成员通过使用学科倚重的语言资源和话语实践，与学科保持联结与亲缘关系（affinity），使学术身份得到认可。

对身份的理解从隐含的认知过程发展到社会构建的外在表现，研究者逐渐关注语言，认识到身份是通过文本和语言得以塑造和构建的。Hyland 认为写作不仅是人们使用语言资源描述世界的方式，也是他们运用话语资源呈现自我的方式。他以自称语（self-mention）为例，发现人文和社会科学领域的论文使用自称语的数量是理工学科文章的四倍还多。他评论道，理工科作者少用自称语，旨在刻画一种视真理源于自然界与客观实验的科学家身份；相反，人文学者通过使用自称语来彰显一种论辩者身份，崇尚知识论断的社会偶然性。因此，在身份构建过程中，学术作者一方面通过运用学科共同体认可且共享的语言资源表达自身的学术见解，使自己的研究和观点被学科共同体接受；另一方面，在满足共同体期望和成员身份常规要求的同时注入自身的经验、目的和认知，通过运用学科应允的话语资源来凸显自己的个性和不同。

在第二章"学科：亲缘与姿态"中，Hyland 主要阐释了学科的概念及其与身份的关系，认为学科为学术身份的构建提供参照语境，而成员的学术话语实践在增强学科凝聚力的同时也塑造了个体身份。学科常常被视为机构界限、沟通网络、政治制度、价值领域、研究范式和意识形态的权力基础。相关的"软学科"与"硬学科"、"应用学科"与"理论学科"等分类也是层出不穷。加之后现代主义的多元化以及新兴交叉学科的产生，学者难以给学科下一个明确的定义。Hyland 认为，学科是以成员共同参与的文本产品和话语实践形式存在的，因此学科语境和身份表征相辅相成，并通过语言联结在一起。虽然学科规约像"聚合空间"（affinity spaces），但是它并没有吞噬个人的主观能动性。正如 Hyland 在本书第 45 页所说："我们并不只是鹦鹉学舌般地照搬学科的话语范式，而是有选择地利用恰当的语言资源来映射、推介我们的个性特征。"

学术身份不仅反映在个体与共同体之间的关系上，而且蕴含于作者与所言之事的关系中。Hyland 将前者称为"亲缘"，描述作者与学科共同体之间的隶属关系。它反映语篇的对话性（dialogism），涉及学科的语篇规约、知识建构以及潜在的权力关系。作者通过语言选择实现交际，只有使用学科共同体接受的、符合学科规约的话语资源和意义形式，才能确保知识建构与信息传播，体现作者的学科共同体成员身份。"姿态"则指作者采取特定立场与观点，对话他者并评判所言之事，主要通过立场（stance）和读者带入（engagement）两种修辞策略来实现。立场指作者的文本声音，是以作者为导向的价值判断；读者带入则是指作者引入读者，将其作为话语参与者共同参与讨论和辩驳。在学术语境中，作者在与学科共同体建立亲缘关系的同时表明姿态，在这样一种对立统一的社会互动过程中建立学科身份。

第三章"探究身份"回顾了话语研究中考察身份的常见研究路径。对身份的不同理解涉及对语言和互动的定位、对个体与社会关系的认识，能指导研究范式的择取。如果我们认为身份是在瞬时变换的人际交流中建立的，那么我们需要仔细分析交际对话的详细记录；如果我们认为身份产生于权势话语和不平等的权力关系，那么我们需要分析交际的社会政治与文化语境；如果我们认为身份是自传式的自我抒发，那么我们需要在个人经历叙述中寻找身份的表达轨迹。这些对身份的理解和认识形成了话语身份研究的三个主要路径——会话分析、批评话语分析和叙事分析。

Hyland 指出，这三种路径都是通过语言来探究身份，结合机构及社会语境解释身份，不同之处在于语料的选择、分析的过程和研究的目的。同时，他还分别指出了这三种研究方法的不足。会话分析注重细节。用此方法，研究者在话轮中研究身份，因此只能在"会话"（conversational）层面揭示话语特点，很难看到情景语境之外更为宏观的机构及社会身份。此外，身份会随着话轮而改变，会话分析难以明确何种身份是根本性的，什么是会话者的真实意图。批评话语分析的先验主义语境观难以帮助研究者明确身份是个体遵从共同体的结果，还是个体选择的结果。该研究方法所提及的语境只是分析者带有政治和机构色彩的主观阐释，忽略了身份构建过程中的直接语境以及参与者自身的认知和观点。叙事分析过于依赖诱发环境中的访谈自述，因此对身份的研究不充分、不完全。发话人自己的叙述只是身份构建的一部分，身份在话语中的构建不单纯是发话人自我身份的主观投射，还需要话语依据和对方的认同。Hyland 提出，将语料库与身份研究结合可以有效地弥补以上路径的不足。语料库提供了语言使用规律的证据，研究者可以通过频率表、词汇索引和主题词分析身份构建的学科差异，包括本体论定位（ontological positions）、意识形态立场（ideological standpoints）、论辩风格（argument styles）以及参与者关系（relationships between individuals）等。

在接下来的五章中，Hyland 对学术身份构建中的体裁、学科、文化、性别等因素进行了基于语料库的定量研究，同时辅以主体识解和参与者访谈等定性分析方法。Ivanič（1998）和 Mastuda（2015）认为，基于语篇的身份研究一方面需要实证描写身份构建的语言特征，另一方面需要进行现象学阐释，了解语篇参与者对身份表达和语言选择的认知。因此，正如本书第四至八章所示，只有通过定量与定性研究的有机结合，才能较全面地考察学术语篇中的身份构建问题。

第四章"表现类体裁中的身份"分析语境对作者身份表达的影响。Hyland 表示，每个人身份的呈现和阐释都随语境变化而不同，取决于交际目的、读者、作者与读者之间的关系以及所适用的体裁。人们在互动秩序中协商自己的身份，在语境、共同体和体裁中启用修辞策略。只有当自我表现的方式令学科共同体成员产生共鸣时，学科身份才会被共同体认可，知识论断才会被接受。Hyland 以论文致谢、奖项申请书以及学院教员主页为例，将它们称之为"表现类体裁"（representational genres），重点讨论在这类表现作者自我的体裁中权力和对话者关系是如何对身份构建产生影响的。

针对论文致谢体裁，Hyland 分析了其中的反思语步、鸣谢语步和宣称语步，观察论文作者如何通过上述语步联结业内同行和学术资源，承认论文的不足之处以及致谢家庭贡献，进而展现不同的学术身份。Hyland 关注奖项申请书的评价手段与立场资源，发现在该体裁中，作者常常强调创新性（如 groundbreaking、originality 等）、重要性（如 significant implications、major contribution 等），或突出研究专长（如 my approach、in my own claims 等）。Hyland 认为，这些策略反映出学生在建立自己的学术身份时，其迎合话语共同体的意识在不断增强。对于学院教员主页而言，他观察到，虽然这是一种机构化的体裁，但同时也是重要的传播媒介。教员通过该表现类体裁推介自我，通过自制的页面元素和超链接等手段营造职业上和生活中的不同形象。

在第五章"学术传记中的自我呈现"中，Hyland 将注意力转移到一个常被忽视的"小舞台"——学术论文的作者简介（academic bios）。尽管该体裁中严格的字数限制在一定程度上约束了作者的展示空间，几乎排除了学术以外的个人描写；但 Hyland 发现，作者在撰写简介时常常借助语言的不同表达功能，展现自己与学科共同体之间的亲缘关系，折射自己特定的学者身份。Hyland 自建了含有 600 份作者简介的小型语料库。基于主题内容（themes）与过程类型（process types），他分析了科研经验和学科特点的差异对身份构建的具体影响。

Hyland 发现，资深学者常常提及各种经历，包括工作、科研、出版物和成就，以此展现十分全面的学术身份。此外，他们还运用较多的认同型关系小句（identifying relational clause）来增强修辞效果。相比之下，年轻学者或学生则较多使用关系从句介绍自己，他们往往用个人信息，如出生日期，来充实自己的研究资历和工作情况。理工科学者的简介往往较长，突出教育背景和研究团队，并且常用物质过程描述科研行为；而人文类学者则主要通过研究兴趣和出版物展现学术身份，其简介遵从了以独立研究为主的学科特点。此外，人文类学者使用认知过程的频率远高于理工科学者，进而凸显软学科的知识发现和研究行为倚重主体的认知和思辨这一特点。

在第六章"文化：权威与可见性"中，Hyland 通过分析中国香港学生的英文写作语料，揭示文本语料中用于表达作者立场的第一人称的使用情况，从而考察文化因素和先前学习经历对学术身份构建的影响。自我提及是学术写作中一个重要的语用特征，主要通过第一人称代词体现，它不仅有助于表达概念意义，而且还可以帮助作者增强自身的说服力。但是，本章的实证研究发现，中国香港地区的学生很少提及自我，他们在学术论文中总是对自己的角色轻描淡写，不怎么表现自己的立场。Hyland 指出，作者选择如何报告观点和展示自我受个体认知和社会文化等诸多因素影响，而且也因人而异；而语料数据揭示的是作者群体反复使用的、规律性出现的语言选择，反映的是社会群体的共有实践和意义表达。因此，该研究发现中国香港地区的学生低频率的自我提及与其背后的文化特征有关，Hyland 认为这一点与西方的学术习惯截然不同。

Hyland 借用 Ohta（1991）和 Scollon（1994）的研究结论对此差异进行了解释——亚洲文化传统对第一人称的使用接受度低，因为第一人称过于强调自我和非集体观念。可见，文化在很大程度上影响了沟通实践和身份确立。因此，Hyland 建议教师应该让学生熟悉不同的写作习惯和文化理念，设计各种各样的课堂活动，不仅要增强学生的体裁意识，还要提高他们的目标文化意识，从而协调本国文化与学科文化之间的关系，运用更多的语言资源和修辞手段建立良好的学术身份。

在第七章"威望：个性和遵从"中，Hyland 将视线转移到姿态上，表示资深学者在利用话语资源表达立场和姿态方面比年轻学者更娴熟、更有技巧，因为这些策略和资源是作者在以往话语交际和文本撰写中塑造人际意义的经验积累。不过，结合学科经验形成的身份构建并非完全脱离宏观的社会和文化习俗，因为学者所处的学术共同体常常与不同个体的背景和隶属关系交织着，也杂糅着不同的世界观和语言习惯。

通过对比应用语言学领域两位知名学者 Deborah Cameron 和 John Swales 的学术文章，Hyland 探究了这样的问题：资深学者是如何结合社会背景并在学科共同体接受的范围内选择修辞资源，带动读者，使观点具有说服力，从而折射自身的学术身份的？受英国公共辩论传统的影响，

Cameron 高频使用 not、but、although 反驳对立观点，并运用 it is + ADJ + to 句型（如 it is reasonable to suppose that）和评价型 that 句型（如 it is my own view that）增强观点力度，呈现出积极有力且充满智慧的辩论风格，接近媒体话语中高调的公众人物身份。相比之下，Swales 则更体现一种温和、谨慎且常常自讽的公共知识分子的身份，因为他高频地使用具有人际意义或互动性的反思语言（如 I think、I believe 等）、自我提及（如 my analysis、my argument 等）、模糊语（如 would、suggest 等）和读者带入语言（如 we、our 等）。

在第八章"性别：学科和姿态"中，Hyland 以书评体裁为焦点，探讨了学术话语中性别与身份的关系，因为在这种体裁中书评人必须对所读书目和读者表明自己的立场。基于包含 56 篇独立作者书评的自建语料库，Hyland 考察了不同学科男女作者的元话语特征，发现不同学科、相同性别的书评人的元话语标记并不相同，性别和语言不是一一对应的关系。整体而言，女性作者使用的引导类（interactive）元话语略多于男性作者，但是互动类（interactional）元话语却显著少于男性作者。然而，就具体学科而言，生物学女性作者的引导类和互动类元话语使用频率皆少于男性作者，而哲学女性作者的话语特征与整体趋势保持一致。

正如我们在前面章节中所看到的，学术作者与学科共同体建立亲缘关系、表达个体姿态的话语实践受语境和经验的影响。Hyland 将学术话语中性别和学科之间的关系归为个体与共同体、个人施事与共同体期望之间的关系。他认为学术话语中男性和女性使用语言的方式不是由性别决定，它可以在学科共同体的人际互动中被构建、协商和改变。可见，虽然学科身份构建受性别和民族等各种社会关系影响，但是在学术话语共同体中，人们对于身份的文化理解终究是由学科规约与话语实践来塑造和决定的。

第九章"身份、学科和研究方法"是总结章节。在本章中，Hyland

首先总结了学术身份与学科的关系。学术语篇及写作活动能够充分展示作者的学术身份，使作者在描述世界、报告知识的同时，也在不断表达自我的声音，是一个协商个体与共同体、与学科建立亲缘关系并表达姿态的过程。身份对于学术语篇的重要性体现在它勾画出了话语活动与学科特点之间的关系，以及具体的人类行为与抽象的共同体之间的关联。身份是一个社会化的施动过程，展现个人如何围绕学科共同体的向心力与个体声音的离心力，在二者的交互作用中投射自己并获得他人的认可。这一切又在人们连续反复的话语及修辞行为中得以体现，因此语料库为身份研究提供了语言使用规律的实证，对身份研究具有重要的方法论意义，有助于我们更直接地观察学科特定的认知方式和话语规约。

Hyland 指出，虽然期刊论文是展示学科身份最为突出的体裁，但是诸如项目申请书、审稿答复信、会议演讲等体裁也是重要的身份构建话语。此外，交叉和新兴学科（如护理学、商学等）作者的学术身份构建与协商也可以是今后身份研究的重要领域。此外，Hyland 也强调，以体裁为导向的研究常常过度强调话语实践的共性与相似性，但是我们也需要挖掘个体能动性的系统差异。同时，更加翔实地探索语境相关因素也是身份研究的关键，例如调查作者的体裁网络（genre networks）和活动系统（activity systems）、重视读者的作用、融入多模态分析等。

最后，Hyland 指出，学术身份和学科特点的研究对学术写作教学而言具有宝贵的参考价值，尤其是在学术出版、论文发表以及 EAP 写作方面。

综上，本书清晰地论述了学术语境中学科身份的社会构建属性，能帮助我们更好地理解语言使用的社会情境，充分认识身份与个体、共同体之间的关系。身份不仅表达作者个体的立场与声音，而且也反映作者被共同体成员接纳的程度。同时，身份也体现着作者与读者之间的学术劝谏与人际互动，是作者使用修辞性语言的交际目的。关于学科身份的本体认识对学术写作教学有着重要的指导作用（Cremin and Locke, 2017）。将教学重点从文本创作的认知过程转向写作活动的社会维度，增强体裁与修辞意识，充分了解学术写作的交际目的和学科文化，这些都将有助于学生和年轻学者更好地加入目标话语共同体，构建学科身份。

姜峰

2019 年 9 月 3 日

## 参考文献

Bakhtin, M. (1981). *The Dialogic Imagination: Four Essays* (ed. M. Holquist). Austin, TX: University of Texas Press.

Benwell, B. and Stokoe, E. (2006). *Discourse and Identity*. Edinburgh: Edinburgh University Press.

Block, D. (2006). Identity in applied linguistics. In T. Omoniyi and G. White (eds.), *The Sociolinguistics of Identity* (pp. 34–49). London: Continuum.

Cremin, T. and Locke, T. (2017). *Writer Identity and the Teaching and Learning of Writing*. London: Routledge.

Goffman, E. (1971). *The Presentation of Self in Everyday Life.* Harmondsworth: Penguin Books.

Halliday, M. A. K. and Matthiessen, C. M. I. M. (2014). *Halliday's Introduction to Functional Grammar* (4th edn.). London: Routledge.

Ivanič, R. (1998). *Writing and Identity: The Discoursal Construction of Identity in Academic Writing.* Amsterdam: John Benjamins.

Matsuda, P. K. (2015). Identity in written discourse. *Annual Review of Applied Linguistics*, 35: 140–159.

Ohta, A. S. (1991). Evidentiality and politeness in Japanese. *Issues in Applied Linguistics*, 2 (2): 211–238.

Scollon, R. (1994). As a matter of fact: The changing ideology of authorship and responsibility in discourse. *World Englishes*, 13 (1): 33–46.

Wertsch, J. (1991). *Voices of the Mind: A Sociocultural Approach to Mediated Action*. Cambridge, MA: Harvard University Press.

# Preface

Another book on identity needs some justification. After all, there has been an explosion of talk around the topic in the last 25 years in just about all areas of the human and social sciences. So much talk, in fact, that for many observers, contemporary questions of politics, gender, personal relationships and culture now quickly distil down to issues of identity. Identity is the lens through which contemporary social analysis sees the world, which means that everyone has something to say about it. There is a glut of perspectives and proliferation of definitions. What makes things more complicated is not only that different theoretical approaches generate different understandings of identity, but that these tend to compete with our own folk theories of the self. So while we may refer to our sense of identity as a guiding reference in our lives, the concept is increasingly problematised and disputed among social scientists.

In our everyday lives identity is something that can be stolen, filed away, improved and marketed, and it is widely seen as far more malleable and open to choice today than in the past. Self-help articles, TV make-over shows, advertising campaigns and a burgeoning counselling industry are part of a Zeitgeist which encourages us towards a pick-and-mix view of identity: to believe that we can *elect* who we want to be through therapy, meditation, appearance or consumption. It is a presumption of modern life that our purchases and possessions express who we are so that exposure to international media and communications technologies means that we can shop for our identities at a global 'cultural supermarket' (Mathews, 2000) which makes available a range of identities to be put on and dropped as we like. The mass marketing of lifestyles and of a culture of possibilities persuades us that the self is not a fixed entity but is actively constructed through consumption and display so that we can all aspire to a more attractive self.

In more exalted domains of talk, social theory itself divides over giving precedence to notions of identity as either the active shaping of a self by creative individuals or the regulation by social and institutional forces, and the more academics debate the issue, the more complex it seems to be. Post-modernists suggest that identity has become so important because of the instability and uncertainties created by the rapid changes brought about by globalisation. We are constantly confronted with ever-growing social complexity and cultural diversity which, in turn, offers us more experiences and possible identities than ever before, generating a greater concern with our sense of self and with protecting an 'authentic' identity in the face of insecurity.

I therefore step into this minefield with some trepidation, and my only excuse for doing so is to offer an argument for a largely new view of identity and to address a specific context where the discursive construction of identity has been relatively neglected: the university. In academic contexts identity has often been regarded with some ambivalence: seen as either a contamination of scholarly objectivity or a source of creative subjectivity. Certainly, many students, teachers and researchers feel estranged by the literacy conventions of the academy, and writing as an academic often means the construction of individuals by texts, rather than the other way round. But while they may seem constraining and unfamiliar, these discourses are also *enabling*, allowing individuals to connect with others and participate in new communities. If writing is an act of identity, then it is important to see how this is so and the options open to us as writers.

This volume is, then, an elaboration of these ideas. In it I draw on a range of genres and language features to focus on the ways that identity is implicated in academic writing. Putting these two concepts together draws attention to the fact that identity is, above all, about how we create meanings while engaging with others. It points to the fact that we use language as the raw materials for the presentation of ourselves to the world and that what we say and write aligns us with or separates us from other people and other positions. So while often experienced as something private and personal, identity is very much part of our participation in the routine social encounters of our everyday lives. Here, then, I set out to offer what is a novel, and I hope, interesting, approach to understanding the various ways our participation in academic communities influences the performance of identity and how this performance helps to shape academic communities.

# Acknowledgements

This book argues for a social view of writing and itself as the product of a social process, involving exchanges over many years with colleagues, friends and students. Although the book deals with academic discourse, disciplinary writing and interpersonal aspects of language, all themes I am fairly familiar with, it does so from a perspective that is new to me. Wading into an unfamiliar literature and field of understanding is not possible without substantial help, and I would like to acknowledge those who have contributed to this journey.

First and foremost I would like to acknowledge Susan Hunston and Carol Chapelle, for their painstaking critical reading of my drafts, and particularly to Susan for her intelligent suggestions, penetrating questions and sound advice. The final text owes a great deal to her critical good judgement and sense of reader awareness. I also want to thank Maurizio Gotti, whose invitation to give a paper on identity at a conference in Bergamo in the summer of 2008 got me started on this, and John Swales, Vijay Bhatia and David Block for their texts and conversations, which kept me on the path. I would also like to acknowledge the support, encouragement and photocopied articles I have received from friends and colleagues while writing, particularly Lillian Wong and Carmen Sancho Guinda, and my collaborator on some of the work discussed in these pages, Polly Tse, for her relentless enthusiasm about academic writing. I should also mention Fiona Hyland who has always helped and supported me in my writing.

I am also grateful to John Swales and Deborah Cameron for making their texts and thoughts about writing available to me for the study which appears as Chapter 7. Thanks, too, to those who gave me permission to use extracts from their websites: Ian Howarth, Professor of Astronomy at University College London; Dr Cian Dorr, Faculty of Philosophy at the University of Oxford; Mark Colyvan, Professor of Philosophy and Director of the Sydney Centre for the Foundations of Science and Dr Greg Restall of the Philosophy Department, University of Melbourne. Finally, I would also like to thank publishers for permission to reprint previously published material. An earlier version of Chapter 7 appeared as Hyland, K. (2010). Community and individuality: Performing identity in applied linguistics. *Written Communication*, 27 (2): 159–188. Reprinted by permission of Sage Publications Inc. Parts of Chapter 8 also appeared in Tse, P. and Hyland, K. (2008). 'Robot Kung fu': Gender and the performance of a professional identity. *Journal of Pragmatics*, 40 (7): 1232–1248. Reprinted in revised form with kind permission of Elsevier Ltd.

# Notes on Corpora and Abbreviations

One main source is the Michigan Corpus of Academic Spoken English (MICASE), a collection of 152 transcripts (totalling 1.8 million words) of various academic spoken contexts from large lectures to dissertation defences. A discussion of its creation and categories along with full online access to the corpus can be found at http://quod.lib.umich.edu/m/micase/. There are additional examples of academic speech from the John Swales Conference Corpus (JSCC), a collection of transcripts from an academic conference held in honour of John Swales hosted by the English Language Institute at the University of Michigan in June 2006. JSCC contains both lectures and question-and-answer sessions, amounting to around 100,000 words and is available at https://web.archive.org/web/20120105203003/http://jscc.elicorpora.info. Written corpora are described in the text, but examples in the first three chapters are from the 'Hyland Corpus' – a 1.4-million-word corpus of 240 research articles. The corpus consists of three papers from each of ten leading journals in eight disciplines, nominated by expert informants as among the leading publications in their fields and selected to represent a broad cross-section of academic practice from engineering, social sciences, the science and humanities.

Disciplines from these and other corpora are abbreviated following text and interview examples as follows:

AL          applied linguistics
Bio         biology
BS          business studies
Comm        communications
CS          computer science
Econ        economics
EE          electrical engineering
IS          information system(s)
ME          mechanical engineering
Mk          marketing

| | |
|---|---|
| PA | public administration |
| Phil | philosophy |
| Phy | physics |
| RA | research articles |
| Soc | sociology |
| SS | social sciences |
| TESOL | teaching English to speakers of other languages |

# 1 Identity: Interaction and Community

*Identity* is who and what you are. But while this is a simple enough statement to make, how we experience and manage our sense of self is far more complex. This is because we tend to see ourselves as unique individuals with a 'true', stable identity locked away deep inside us, yet we also recognise that our behaviours, affiliations and even our ways of talking shift through encounters with different people, often creating tensions and conflicts. Added to this there is also a range of different ways of theorising identity, each producing a different definition and way of approaching it. The current centrality of the concept of identity in the human and social sciences, in fact, suggests something of this slipperiness. So for some observers identity is what unifies our experience and brings continuity to our lives; for others it is something fragile and fragmented, vulnerable to the dislocations of globalisation and post-industrial capitalism.

There is, however, general agreement on the idea that there are various forms of identity that people recognise, and so identity involves *identification*. In identifying myself as a man, for example, I am identifying myself with a broader category of 'men', or at least some aspects of that category. At the same time, or more often at other times, I may be identifying myself as a vegetarian, a hiker or a son. No one has only one identity, and for a subset of the population, an important aspect of who they are relates to their participation in academic disciplines: they are physicists, historians or applied linguists. These different identities have to be managed because they impact on each other rather than simply add to each other, so the way I enact an identity as a teacher is influenced by my identity as middle-aged, British and so on. This book explores what academic identity means: how it is constructed by individuals appropriating and shaping the discourses which link them to their disciplines.

This chapter reviews some of the work on identity to set out a view which argues for the importance of interaction and community in identity performance, but I want to begin by presenting some key ideas up front.

## 1.1   Connecting *disciplines* and *identities*

The link between disciplines and identities might not seem immediately obvious. After all, things generally get done in universities without thinking too much about what our activities mean for the way we see ourselves. We go along to meetings, seminars or lectures and write essays or papers with a good enough working sense of who we are and who the others in our lives are, and they in turn seem to relate to us in the same way. People are generally accustomed to seeing themselves as having a nature and an identity which exist prior to their participation in social groups and the roles and relations they establish in these groups. Such a view implies that a discipline is just an aggregate of individuals, something distinct and independent from the people who comprise it.

### Identity and other people

A very different view sees identity not as belonging *within* the individual person but *between* persons and *within* social relations; as constituted socially and historically (Vygotsky, 1978). Identity is not the *state* of being a particular person but a *process*, something which is assembled and changed over time through our interactions with others. Here the self is formed and developed within the structures of understandings, allegiances and identifications which membership of social groups, including disciplines, involves. It emerges from a mutual engagement with others in 'communities of practice' (Lave and Wenger, 1991), the 'ways of doing things, ways of thinking, ways of talking, beliefs, values and power relations' (Eckert and McConnell-Ginet, 1992: 464).

This kind of mutual engagement in community activities is accomplished every day in universities, of course, as in this example from an undergraduate biology tutorial, where a tutor leads a group of students over an extended interaction to construct shared understandings through shared language.

(1)

> **T:** okay you take D-N-ase, mkay that kills D-N-A. and if D-N-ase wipes out the D-N-A do you see transformation occurring?
> **S1:** no
> **T:** no. what about protease that kills the protein?
> **S2:** it still transforms
> **T:** mkay. still transforms, and therefore what did, Avery conclude?
> **S2:** the D-N-A was the uh,
> **S1:** transforming agent

T: mkay, D-N-A is the transforming principle and not protein.

(MICASE: DIS175JU081)

Building on one another's turns, repeating the same words, overlapping and interrupting, the tutor guides the students to the conclusion of the transforming principle as a shared account. By participating in interactions such as this, students learn the practices and beliefs of a discipline. They slowly take on its discourses and understandings to construct a self which gains recognition and reinforcement through use of these discourses. In other words, learning to use recognised and valued patterns of language not only demonstrates competence in a field, but also displays affinity and connection. Identity in this sense therefore refers to 'the ways that people display who they are to each other' (Benwell and Stokoe, 2006: 6) so that *who we are*, or rather *who we present ourselves to be*, is an outcome of how we routinely and repeatedly engage in interactions with others on an everyday basis.

The view taken here therefore frames identity as an ongoing project as opposed to a fixed product and has little to say about any underlying core dispositions. It does, however, draw attention to the importance of language, which is central to our interactions with others and our participation in communities. Seeing identity as constructed by both the texts we engage in and the linguistic choices we make relocates it from the private to the public sphere, and from hidden processes of cognition to its social construction in discourse. Our preferred patterns of language, in both writing and speech, index who we are in much the same way that our clothes and body language index our social class, occupation and age group, making the study of discourse a legitimate means of gaining insights into self-representation. Analysis of disciplinary discourses can therefore complement existing approaches to understanding identity as discursively constructed by revealing something of how they function to articulate the relationship between the self and the world.

## 1.2  Identity and interaction

Current post-structuralist theories are deeply suspicious of the durable, unitary notion of identity summed up in Descartes' aphorism 'I think therefore I am.' While a consciousness of self may provide the basis for the sense that we are the same person from one day to the next, it is also true that identifying ourselves and others involves meaning – and meaning involves interaction.

Agreeing, arguing, comparing, negotiating and cooperating are part and parcel of identity construction, so identities must be seen as *social* identities. Cameron puts this view succinctly:

> A person's identity is not something fixed, stable and unitary that they acquire early in life and possess forever afterwards. Rather identity is shifting and multiple, something people are continually constructing and reconstructing in their encounters with each other in the world.
>
> (Cameron, 2001: 170)

Identity is therefore an ongoing venture, responsive to social stimuli, and created through interaction, a view I will develop in this section.

## Identity as a social construct

Social constructionism is perhaps the best-known view of identity as something created between people (e.g. Berger and Luckman, 1967; Burr, 1995). Shotter (1993), for example, talks of 'joint action' to emphasise that identity is constructed in tandem with others rather than somehow emanating from internal psychic structures. Constructing an identity as a competent academic writer, for example, involves an often protracted dialogic process of socialisation into the expectations of a new community. Something of this can be seen in the responses language teachers make on undergraduate students' essays, as this example from a recorded protocol suggests (Hyland and Hyland, 2001) (italics = student's text; bold = teacher's written comment; other = teacher's self-talk):

(2)

> *In a free market economy there are more productive efficiency than in a planned economy and consumers are happier for they can choose and get the goods they want and are willing to buy most by themselves.* Ha ha she clearly knows which one she wants, but a very sudden end – OK – **the conclusion is a bit abrupt – you need to re-state some of the main points – the essay is rather** – it's way too much – **middle heavy. The conclusion is the place in an academic essay where you reinforce your main point and bring the reader round to your ideas.**

Here the teacher is responding to a student writer rather than to a student text, engaging with her as a novice writer in a dialogic process of instruction. Behind the feedback comments is an assumption that the student is learning to identify with the community and that this is aided through interactions of this kind with experienced members.

Social constructionism's view of identity as a form of social action rather than a psychological construct is not really new. Its seeds are evident in the symbolic interactionism of Mead (1934) and Cooley (1964) who saw identity as produced through socialisation, and then made and remade in people's dealings with others throughout their lives. We form our individual identities by seeing ourselves as other people see us, the image we get of ourselves that is reflected back from other members of our communities. Seen from this perspective, the self is thoroughly a social product, an emergent ongoing creation that we construct over time in our attempt to form a consistent orientation to the world.

In this Symbolic Interactionist work, there is therefore a close link between self and society, but the link seems altogether too smooth and unproblematic, as if the self is simply the product of others' approval. The use of language allows individuals to become self-conscious agents acting in their communities by taking on its values, roles and norms, but there is no space here for other elements of experience. Not only does this view neglect individual desires and aspirations, but it conflates the personal and social to a degree where social control seems to actually constitute identity. In other words, it is difficult to see how conflicts might arise between the self and one's community and how individuals might cope with exclusion.

## Managing an impression

Erving Goffman's (1971 and 1981) well-known work on 'impression management' follows Mead (1934) in seeing the self as situated in everyday life but represents this as an altogether more strategic enterprise. Goffman argued that the self consists of the individual's awareness of the many different roles that are performed in different contexts. These roles involve individuals in continually monitoring the impressions they make on others from behind a public mask, consciously stage-managing how they engage with them in order to achieve particular goals. People move relatively effortlessly, for example, between contexts which demand either highlighting or downplaying occupational, family, gender, class and ethnic roles, and perform these seriously, playfully, self-consciously or ironically at different times. Identity in this view is the outcome of collaborative interactions in particular situations where performances are treated as if they represent the real person.

At the centre of Goffman's detailed analysis of process and meaning in interaction is the relationship between performance and front stage. An actor performs in a setting which is constructed of a stage and a backstage, using

5

parts of the physical context as props (such as a wall of books in an office) and watched by an audience at the same time as the actor is an audience for the plays of that audience. The actor's main goal is to maintain the coherence of a performance and to adjust to different settings. The process of establishing social identity is therefore closely linked to the concept of 'front', or 'that part of the individual's performance which regularly functions in a general and fixed fashion to define the situation for those who observe the performance' (Goffman, 1971: 22). The front acts as a vehicle of standardisation, allowing others to understand the individual on the basis of projected traits.

A clear example of this is the conference presentation, where the speaker seeks to achieve rapport through informality and an explicitly interactive stance while meeting expectations of competence associated with an academic presentation. In this (slightly edited) extract, we see a speaker seeking to diffuse potential criticism of her research by establishing an identity as a junior academic (up to the third round of audience laughter), then presenting the purpose and method of her research in a way which meets the audience members' definition of what they expect to find in this genre:

(3)

**Speaker:** hi. uh good morning. uh it's a great pleasure to be here to give a talk uh, in front of all these people, um. I, uh have to acknowledge the great work of John Swales um, he used to I think he is the first scholar to introduce, uh citation analysis into applied linguistics. his paper appeared in applied linguistics in 1984 I think. and, uh, I didn't read it when it was published, but I later I read it.
**Audience:** 'laugh'
**Speaker:** it was very useful I it was a huge sort of field. my appeal to me to get into this citation analysis but to me it was very useful for my dissertation so I very briefly touched on citation analysis then later I was very, interested to do more then I applied for this Morley scholar and then they kindly gave me but unfortunately when I came in 2001 um, I was really overwhelmed by the amount of data so I did just photocopying all the time
**Audience:** 'laugh'
**Speaker:** and I felt a bit guilty of giving a kind of short um showed uh, I'm going to say, I didn't give him a well I didn't do things which I was supposed to do so now I'm trying to pay the debt in instalments
**Audience:** 'laugh'
**Speaker:** okay. I'm going to start. so citation analysis is a very useful view and I was very interested in the difference between English speakers' writing and Jap-because I'm Japanese um I thought there might be some well lots of difficulties

for Japanese. so I was comparing the differences between Japanese writing and, um English speakers' writing. and because I did my dissertation in the UK I interviewed the British academics and of course no Japanese and I compared. Then now, when citation analysis came in, I thought oh maybe I can compare sort of papers highly cited sort of very well known written by very well known established scholars, possibly. so I created three categories one um highly cited papers and another one papers written by English speakers, and the other one is papers written by uh Japanese. and then I tried to see some differences …

(JSCC06)

To present a compelling front, to effectively engage in 'impression management', the actor needs to both fill the expectations of the social role and consistently communicate the characteristics of the role to others. In addition to content selection, the use of 'contextualisation cues' (Gumperz, 1982) such as changes in voice quality, intonation, gesture and so on can signal in-group bonding and engagement with an audience, thereby indicating particular identity positions (Archakis and Papazachariou, 2008). The audience, in turn, verifies the honesty of the performance through monitoring these unconscious non-verbal signals which are inadvertently 'given off' rather than given. Although we cannot know with certainty how our signals will be interpreted, we attempt to present an 'idealised' version of the front consistent with the norms of the group.

## Roles and performances

Impression management therefore draws attention to the *performative* aspects of identity and to the fact that individuals consciously pursue personal goals in attempting to be seen as a certain kind of person. It would be wrong to take the dramaturgical image too far as this is not a pre-learnt and delivered 'script'. Rather, individuals are socialised through habitual experience to 'fill in' and manage the positions they adopt so that actions derive from 'a command of an idiom' which they enact from one moment to the next and become more comfortable with over time. In other words, we consciously *improvise* performances to assume identities as good students, hard-working lab technicians, Nobel scientists, contentious researchers or whatever. We need to enact and re-enact our selves again and again:

A status, a position, a social place is not a material thing to be possessed and then displayed; it is a pattern of appropriate conduct, coherent, embellished and well articulated. Performed with ease or clumsiness, awareness or not, guile or good faith, it is none the less something that must be enacted and portrayed, something that must be realized.

(Goffman, 1971: 75)

The question obviously arises about where this leaves our sense of a single coherent self. Is there a 'real me' hidden on the inside which views these performances with a coherent and unifying eye? Goffman (1975) flatly denies the existence of a character behind the performer and sees the self as 'a stance taking entity' of shifting alignments, strategically adjusting to different communicative events. So by focusing on the analysis of interaction, Goffman avoids the trap of seeing roles as normatively determined behaviour patterns where individuals automatically become the role they play. Roles can be played with more, or less, attachment or antipathy, and actors can conform to or resist the roles that are situationally available to them. Many students, for example, resist taking on the kind of objective, author-evacuated stance their academic writing asks of them. In other words, self-conscious decision-making allows actors to distance themselves from expected conventions so that they can 'play at' rather than 'play' a role or bring other aspects of their experience to style the role in their own way.

Goffman (1981) coins the term *footing* to describe the different ways people can take up recognised identities. The choice of footing depends on the combination of three speaking roles available at any moment in talk: the *animator* is the one who speaks or writes the words, the *author* is the one who originates them and the *principal* is the one who believes them. Usually, there is congruence between the three roles, but speakers can make delicate shifts in epistemic or affective stance, changing their commitments and articulating different identities or positions. Such changes capture something of the sparky qualities of interaction and suggest how actors can inhabit roles in individual ways to perform distinct identities so that in a lecture, for example, a speaker may reframe a serious utterance as irony or move from a formal delivery to a personal aside by a change in footing.

One option speakers have is to manipulate the tenor, or interpersonal attitude, they take to their audience. In this extract from a MICASE undergraduate presentation, for example, the speaker seeks to display knowledge and a presentational competence to the tutor for a class grade and also to speak directly to a group of classmates who may be critical of the academic literacy conventions the genre requires. He does this in a way which avoids the ideologically inscribed identity the discourse makes available by separating the *animator* from the *principal*, the presenter from the believer, by mixing the authorised discourse with a more conversational style of delivery:

(4)

> Okay we just went through that. Alright so basically how is this all found out? They um, did a lot of work on mice and rats obviously and they're they have O-B O-B mice which um are lacking the O-B gene and these mi- so these mice they don't produce um, a lot of leptin and they were found to be obese as um, was hypothesized by the researchers. So then they went and they took out the gene that makes neuropeptide Y as well as the gene that makes leptin. And these mice so they thought okay since we're taking out both these genes there's not gonna be any leptin, but there's not gonna be any neuropeptide Y to stimulate feeding. So they thought that these mice um, should show decreased um decreased weight like, lower than normal or like about normal. But what actually ended up happening was these mice were, heavier than the normal mice, but they were, lighter than the mice that were lacked in leptin altogether.

(MICASE: STP175SU141)

While footing is often communicated prosodically, we can see that the speaker's alignment, or projected self, is at issue here as he is animating a message while keeping some distance from it. Although he takes responsibility for selecting the words and ideas as an author, he frames information about the methodology of obesity experiments as a narrative. By foregrounding the actions of scientists rather than the wider concerns which drive the work, and by adopting conversational features of anecdote, hesitations, repetitions, fillers, projected quotes and vagueness, he separates himself as a *speaker* from the *institution* whose position is represented.

The idea that identity is generated in concrete and specific interactional occasions has been picked up by those who emphasise its *performative* nature. Thus Judith Butler (1990) famously theorises gender identity as endlessly played out in discourse, while Brubaker (2004) shows how an apparently stable identity category such as ethnicity is a product of identification, rather than something people can be said to have. Both reject essentialist models of identity so that Butler, for example, asserts that there is no gender identity behind its expression in actual performances. For post-modern theorists such as Laclau (1990), this transient view of identity suggests that individuals have multiple or hybrid identities and that they can switch between them at will. I would want to argue, along with Butler, however, that identities are not limitless but are constrained by the authority of historical repetition. The ways that we perform our particular identities involve a considerable accumulation of unconscious practices which allow for new elements in each new iteration, but which also structure how we project ourselves in interaction.

# 1.3   Identity and community

The accumulation of these practices is continually co-constructed and re-constructed in interactions with others in social communities. The idea of *community*, and of some collective identification with a community, is vital to understanding both disciplines and identities. This adds the dimension of routine engagement to identity construction, as it is through relationships with significant others that we identify similarity and difference and so generate both group and individual identities. Behind every individual's engagement in a professional existence lies an institutional identity constructed through countless interactions. Community, in fact, helps us not only to better understand language use but also to appreciate the ways it works in the construction of identity.

## The individual and the group

Some theorists believe that group membership is central to identity because it offers a basis for marking out differences and similarities with others through social comparisons. The social psychological perspective of Social Identity Theory or SIT (Giles and Coupland, 1991; Tajfel, 1982), for example, distinguishes between personal identity and social identity and sees both as constructed through processes of categorisation. *Personal identity* refers to the unique personal attributes which differentiate us from others and which are generally based on a sense of self-continuity and uniqueness. S*ocial identity*, on the other hand, is an individual's perception of himself or herself as a member of a group, particularly in terms of value and emotional attachment. Social identities imply that we invest in the identity positions which our groups make available and build a self based on a dichotomy between *us* and *them*, creating in-group identification and out-group discrimination (e.g. Tajfel, 1982).

SIT therefore suggests that group membership provides actors with ways of categorising both others and themselves so that they can perform a recognisable identity, but it also sets up a tension between personal and social identities. This is because awareness of a personal identity inhibits the perception of in-group similarities, while a social identity limits the perception of individual differences among group members. We need to be cautious in creating an arbitrary division between personal and social identity, but this is nevertheless a potentially useful distinction. Both similarity to and difference from others, or assimilation to the group and differentiation from it, are central to identity, but they need to be seen *together* to understand how identities are shaped in interaction. An overemphasis on individuality can easily underestimate the reality and significance of our communities to us, and so how we relate meaningfully and consistently to other members, while too great a focus on similarity can encourage a slide into conformism.

The fact that we generally experience a continuity and coherence in our sense of self makes it important to account for the dual presence of personal and social identities and avoid privileging one over the other (Alvesson et al., 2008). Goffman, Mead and the Symbolic Interactionists attempted to resolve this duality by exploring the relational aspects of identity and foregrounding the ways we adopt consistent alignments to others. It is, for example, difficult to experience oneself as an inspiring supervisor or teacher without a group of devoted students. However, SIT's neglect of interaction in favour of experimentation leads to a narrow concentration on the individual who seeks to construct an identity outside of community pressures and isolated from the repeated influences of others. It is therefore unable to show how identification emerges through participation in community discourses.

Cohen's (1985) notion of community as a 'symbolic construct' is perhaps a more helpful account of how individuals create a sense of themselves as belonging in a particular setting of relationships and interactions. For him, notions of similarity and difference are at the heart of people's awareness of their culture, so community is a potent symbolic presence in our lives, allowing us to see that others do things differently. This view stresses the cognitive rather than the structural importance of communities and emphasises the role of a group culture as experienced by its members. Communities are therefore extremely powerful imaginings upon which individuals draw rhetorically and strategically, encompassing notions of inclusion and exclusion and carrying a normative dimension of 'how things should be'. As Jenkins (2008: 23) observes: 'Solidarity, once it is conjured up, is a powerful force.'

## Community and discourse

The idea of community draws attention to the idea that we do not use language to communicate with the world at large, but with other members of our social groups, each with its own beliefs, categorisations, sets of conventions and ways of doing things. It therefore unites aspects of context that are crucial to the production and interpretation of spoken and written discourse and therefore to language choice and identity. These aspects include knowledge of a cultural and interpersonal situation, knowledge of interlocutors, knowledge of the world and knowledge of texts and conventions for saying things. In particular it follows Faigley's (1986: 535) claim that writing 'can be understood only from the perspective of a society rather than a single individual' and Geertz's (1973) view that knowledge, talk and writing depend on the actions of members of local communities. 'Community' therefore offers a way of bringing interactants and texts together into a common rhetorical space, foregrounding the conceptual frames that individuals use to organise their experience and get things done using language. It provides a schema which allows individuals to process and evaluate each others' social performances effectively.

Engaging in a community's discourses thus provides security for individuals by making the world meaningful and populated by others who have similar understandings and ways of sharing ideas. This is not something achieved overnight or picked up easily, but something that is learnt both formally and informally through engagement. Conventional modes of expression help reinforce a sense of self by eliminating ambiguity and promoting similarity. Vološinov (1973: 87) put this well:

> Each and every word expresses the 'one' in relation to the 'other'. I give myself verbal shape from another's point of view, ultimately, from the point of view of the community to which I belong. A word is a bridge thrown down between myself and another. If one end of the bridge depends on me then the other depends on my addressee. A word is territory shared by both addresser and addressee.

Community is therefore a potent notion for mobilising values and images for members, although these might be different for different people, particularly as symbols are abstract and often vague and imprecise. So while members may *aggregate* around certain practices and ways of thinking, they do not necessarily *integrate* (Cohen, 1985: 20). Differences of opinion are normal and natural, but often hidden by a veneer of agreement and a common symbolic discourse which constructs a boundary to outsiders. Although Cohen overemphasises the importance of thinking over doing, it is clear that it is through the *products* of thinking that individuals produce and reproduce communities. Thinking and actions are accomplished through talk and working together in common pursuits, and the patterns of this talk, developed through countless encounters in corridors, conference halls, seminar rooms and research papers, both formal and informal, planned and ad hoc, contribute to the community's distinct interactional identity. It is not only a shared belief but also the sense of organising their lives with reference to it that make communities real for individuals.

## Reflection and dialogue

Community participation therefore involves at least some command of relevant cultural and social practices. If identity is *performed*, then actors need to have some understanding of the events in which they perform and what *counts* as performing a competent identity in those events. Both Goffman (1971) and Giddens (1991), for instance, argue that reflexivity, as a sense-making facility, allows us to read and monitor social contexts, actions and wider cultural signs and to change our behaviour in response to these readings, so changing the events themselves. But while knowledge of the practices of our communities is important, it is not decisive. Of course the ways we engage with others say something about who we are, or how we would like to be seen, but identities are more than mere performance. They need to be ratified in the identifications of others and this, in turn, has consequences for how we see ourselves. In other words, we are not simply whoever we want to be, but continually develop and contest others' identifications of us within our social groups.

Views of the self such as that proposed by Goffman suggest a view of the individual freely exercising rational choice in pursuit of self-interested goals, but this seriously underestimates the exercise of power in social relationships. In fact, we have to see individual identities as emerging from the synthesis of internal self-definition and the external definitions of oneself by others, particularly powerful others. As I have been arguing, this is an interactive process and the connection between them is recoverable through analysis of the ways individuals engage in community discourses.

To adequately theorise social identity, then, we need to acknowledge the dialectic between how we see ourselves and how others see us. The self is dialogic – a relation – as we take an active and responsive role to language, we get our sense of self from others (Bakhtin, 1981). For Bakhtin, all text is produced in relation to previous texts and, as writers appropriate and transform them, they textually construct social identities in the sense of representing themselves in alignment, or dissonance, with those discourses. Lemke (1995: 24) observes that

> we speak with the voices of our communities, and to the extent that we have individual voices, we fashion these out of the social voices already available to us, appropriating the words of others to speak a word of our own.

In any context, however, one discourse is likely to be dominant and hence more visible so that individuals, consciously or unconsciously, tend to take up the identity options this privileged discourse makes available (Wertsch, 1991).

## Power and identity inscription

Powerful discourses, such as those authorised by academic disciplines, certainly help define any situation and act to restrict what identities can be performed. Some theorists go even further and argue that our identities are not co-constructed by the processes of identification, but actually inscribed in the discourses which are available in a context. Foucault (1972), for example, sees identities as the product of the dominant discourses which are tied to institutional practices. The subject, in fact, is brought into being through language: identity here is merely the effect of discourse (Laclau and Mouffe, 1985).

This is, however, something of a one-sided and deterministic model of identity which downplays the creativity of human action and ignores the impact of emotions on behaviour. As Elliott (2007) points out, it is discourse that produces human experiences for Foucault rather than experiences producing discourse: the individual is therefore merely an artefact of discourse and not an initiator of action. Clearly, however, some kind of reflexive choice making is important to human behaviour so people can resist, negotiate or refuse the restrictive subject positions which are available (e.g. Caldas-Coulthard and Iedema, 2008).

While authoritative discourses limit the identities we can adopt, they do not exclude the possibility of agency. Bakhtin (1986), for example, talks of a process of 'becoming' as we develop an awareness of our tacit choices and habits of meaning-making to gain control over our projections of self in speaking and writing. We draw on a repertoire of voices as we communicate, bringing to the task our own experiences, purposes and conceptions of self to recombine the options offered by the genre to perform a community identity. Our diverse experiences and memberships of overlapping communities, including those of class, ethnicity and gender, influence how we understand our disciplinary participation and how we interact with our colleagues in the performance of this academic identity. All these present us with discoursal alternatives, or what Ivanič (1998), borrowing from Foucault, calls 'available subject positions', which allow us, potentially, to represent ourselves in different ways.

## Continuity and integration

To sum this up, while identity may be personal and unique, it is constructed through socialisation into communities so that internal self-definition and external definitions by others eventually form a synthesis which is the self (Jenkins, 2008). This emphasis on the surface malleability of identity, however, leaves open the question of what lurks beneath as a foundation for human activity and ignores some important ontological issues (Bendle, 2002: 8). Consistency is a concerted accomplishment of social actors and a key element to how we understand and conduct ourselves, creating a self 'as a sensible, accountable, rational, reliable, human being' (Edwards and Stokoe, 2004: 501). It is the recurrence of the opportunities to enact identities, the access we have to particular situations, genres, material resources and rhetorical affordances, which links the long- and short-term performance of our identities and shapes our sense of self. A sense of identification with others in a community therefore 'often comes to feel enduring, even though it is a process never completed – always "in process"' (Hall, 1996: 2).

The longer-term aspects of our identity are therefore not created in a single performance but are crafted and managed across time and across situations. We experience a certain continuity in who we believe we are, a coherence from one day to the next, and we call this capacity to integrate and hold our varying experiences together our *identity*. We can therefore see the self at the centre of a Venn diagram of overlapping experiences in various domains – at the heart of negotiated intersections with other simultaneously held 'identities'. In other words, our identities are the product of our lives in different communities, and we learn to interact with different kinds of people in those communities, building both a cumulative repertoire of roles we can play along with an attitude to those roles and how we want to play them. Our identities are built through discourse and linked to situations, to relationships, and to the positions we adopt in engaging with others on a routine basis.

# 1.4 Identity and academic discourses

This idea that identity is constructed by negotiating performances in engagement with others over time suggests that identity is not just about being male, Chinese, a parent or whatever, but importantly for many people, also about being a classicist or physicist, an engineer or an archaeologist. Discourse is central here because taking on a voice associated with a particular field of study involves aligning oneself with its knowledge-making practices: the topics it believes are worth talking about and how it talks about them. Acting as academics, individuals attempt to embed their talk in a particular social world which they reflect and conjure up through the discourses which others anticipate and understand. Discovering how individuals perform academic identities therefore involves the study of disciplinary discourses.

## Disciplinary discourses and identity

To project an identity as an academic means buying into the practices of a discipline and handling its discourses with sufficient competence to participate as a group member. How individuals exchange information, build alliances, dispute ideas and work together varies according to the group they belong to, so each discipline might be seen as a distinct academic *culture* (Hyland, 2004a) or *tribe* (Becher and Trowler, 2001), each with its particular norms and practices. As Wells (1992: 290) observes:

> Each subject discipline constitutes a way of making sense of human experience that has evolved over generations and each is dependent on its own particular practices: its instrumental procedures, its criteria for judging relevance and validity, and its conventions of acceptable forms of argument. In a word each has developed its own modes of discourse.

Disciplinary discourses thus allow us to communicate in ways that others can see as 'doing biology' or 'doing sociology' or, more importantly, as 'being biologists' or 'sociologists'. Their conventions both restrict how something can be said and authorise the writer as someone competent to say it. They comprise what Gee (2004) calls the 'affinity spaces' where people interact through shared practices in a common endeavour.

Choices in language affect not only the ideational meaning of the text, or what is being talked *about*, but also the impression of the writer which is conveyed. To be a scientist, for example, involves reworking experience through a range of technical terms which are ordered to explain how things happen or exist. Example (5) is typical, where the writer replaces common-sense ways of seeing the world with specialised concepts and complex noun phrases to describe the results of a process:

(5)

> Cavity nucleation occurs as a consequence of stress concentrations developed at, for example, GB carbide particles, where GBS is inhibited by these particles so that the rate of sliding depends on the rate at which diffusion or plastic strain accommodation can occur through or around particles. This inhibition of sliding leads to local stress concentrations, which are dependent on the spacing, and the size, of the GB carbide particles (i.e. the reciprocal of Equation 7).

To be a philosopher, on the other hand, an individual must use abstraction rather than technicality, moving from instances to generalisations by gradually shifting away from particular contexts. In example (6) the writer begins with a narrative, rather than the scientist's exposition, to provide a fictional scenario that leads logically to a question that he himself has posed, introducing the abstract from the concrete:

(6)

> Doris has just driven her car into a tree. She's unconscious, slumped over the steering wheel. Perry comes upon the scene. He looks around to see if anyone can help, but there's no one else there. Visions of wrecked cars catching fire and exploding into boiling balls of flame fill his mind, and he feels that he must rescue the driver now or else she'll surely die. So, with considerable trepidation, Perry rushes in and quickly drags Doris free from the wreck, thinking that at any moment both he and she might get caught in the explosion. As it happens, the car does not explode. Soon after, some emergency vehicles screech to a halt. Paramedics jump out. The paramedics take a look at Doris, and they arrive at a chilling conclusion: Perry has paralysed Doris. Is Perry morally responsible for what he has done? That depends. One thing it depends on is whether Perry acted freely in paralysing Doris.

Because identities are only successful to the extent that they are recognised by other people, these ways of using language tend to encourage the performance of certain identities and to exclude others, limiting what a person can bring from their past experience and constraining what they might take from the current situation. How we chose to express ourselves must resonate with colleagues, examiners or teachers, and this means finding a balance between accommodating ourselves to, and appropriating the language of, our disciplines (Bakhtin, 1986). The study of disciplinary discourses therefore informs the study of identity: it reveals how actors understand what it means to be a philosopher or physicist, how far particular individuals decide to take on these identities and how they perform them. For some, this will not form a central part of who they see themselves to be, while for others it will be a core part of their self-representation.

Academic writing, and speaking, is thus an act of identity. The two are linked because writing is not just about conveying 'content' but about the representation of 'self': how we portray ourselves to others in our disciplines. As the examples above suggest, writing inscribes particular versions of ourselves at the same time as we present our versions of reality, using available discourses to both position ourselves to others and talk about the world.

## Negotiating self-representation: The case of self-mention

One example of how academics and students use the resources of their disciplines to negotiate a self-representation is the preference for the use or avoidance of self-mention. Examples like these, from applied linguistics and electrical engineering articles, are commonplace and reflect the fact that explicit reference to the author is over four times more common in humanities and social science articles than those in the hard sciences (Hyland, 2001b):

(7)

**I bring to bear** on the problem **my own** experience. This experience contains ideas derived from reading **I have done** which might be relevant to **my puzzlement** as well as **my personal contacts** with teaching contexts.

(AL article)

**This paper presents** results of work performed to investigate the effects of area reduction, friction and material hardening models on the deformation behaviour in the extrusion of an aluminium alloy. **In the paper,** the effects of the extrusion process parameter on defect formation during extrusion **is investigated** and the effects of friction in extrusion processes on defect formation **are considered**. The influence of friction on defect formation during extrusion processes **is established**.

(EE article)

Such differences not only suggest how writers seek to portray themselves and their work to readers in different domains, but how they construct legitimate and recognisable identities as applied linguists and engineers. The use of an impersonal scientific discourse, for instance, implies that the writer has a commitment to universalistic knowledge motivated by conceptual issues. It helps construct an identity as someone who sees truth as originating in direct access to phenomena in the external world and who believes this truth is recoverable through controlled experiments (e.g. Whitley, 1984). We recognise here an individual who has confidence in methods of explaining the world through familiar procedures and relatively clear criteria of acceptability. By downplaying his or her personal role in the research, then, he or she not only highlights the phenomena under study and the generality of the findings, but his or her credibility as a scientist. The avoidance of first person strengthens the objectivity of interpretations by suggesting that research outcomes would be the same irrespective of the individual conducting it. One of my respondents expressed this view clearly:

(8)

> I feel a paper is stronger if we are allowed to see what was done without 'we did this' and 'we think that'. Of course we know there are researchers there, making interpretations and so on, but this is just assumed. It's part of the background. I'm looking for something interesting in the study and it shouldn't really matter who did what in any case.

(Bio interview)

In contrast, academics who work in the soft fields see knowledge as altogether more socially contingent and employ a discourse which projects a very different identity. Their language choices recognise that variables are generally less precisely measurable and less clear-cut than in the hard sciences, and so they need to adopt a form of argument that puts a real writer in the text. Here then, self-mention can help construct an identity as an intelligent, credible and engaging colleague with the desire both to strongly identify himself or herself with a particular argument and to gain credit for an individual perspective:

(9)

> The personal pronoun 'I' is very important in philosophy. It not only tells people that it is your own unique point of view, but that you believe what you are saying. It shows your colleagues where you stand in relation to the issues and in relation to where they stand on them. It marks out the differences.

(Phil interview)

The first person therefore assists authors to make a personal standing in their texts and to demarcate their own work from others. It helps them distinguish who they are and what they have to say. Focusing on interpersonal features of language such as this has been particularly productive for analysts elaborating how writers position themselves in relation to their work and their readers. I will take up the issue of first person in identity construction again in Chapter 8.

## Appropriation and alienation

When academics or students sit down to write an essay or research paper, they take on the words and roles that the discipline makes available and so lose something of their 'individuality'; trading isolation for involvement and separateness for membership. As I have mentioned, these discourses influence individuals by restricting the available subject positions they can occupy and encouraging identities based on an autonomous and impersonal observer (e.g. Ivanič and Simpson, 1992). This is not to say that the conventions are fixed and monolithic – they change over time in response to changing circumstances – but individual discursive innovations are unlikely to be readily accepted.

Some theorists stress that these discourses make it possible to reconfigure our experiences and to discuss complex issues with precision and subtlety (Halliday, 1998). They are resources that can be used to categorise, quantify and evaluate according to the perspectives of a discipline. It is a discourse which carries authority and commands esteem, allowing individuals to engage with others in ways they find convincing and persuasive. Other theorists, however, see these literacy demands as alienating and restricting, forcing users to portray themselves as something they think they are not by adopting a rational, anonymous persona which can seem pretentious and false. Students, in particular, often feel manipulated by the impersonality and abstractness of academic discourses into presenting themselves in ways which they don't recognise and which perhaps they don't much like.

Novice researchers and students from non-mainstream social, cultural and linguistic backgrounds, in particular, often find their familiar ways of making meaning marginalised and dimensions of their personal knowledge denied. As one of Ivanič's subjects noted:

> The thing about me is I cannot just write as an ordinary person, I have to have … to say, look this person when you read it you've got to know that I'm a black woman.
>
> (Ivanič, 1998: 314)

The fact that specific forms and wordings are marked as more, or less, institutionally appropriate means that writing is a complex negotiation of a sense of identity and the institutional regulation of meaning-making, and students are not always willing to drop their everyday lives to take up this new, institutional identity.

This means that negotiating a representation of self from the standardising conventions of disciplinary discourses is often, perhaps always, going to be rather fraught as actors manage the tension between shared norms and individual traits. This is interesting simply as a skilled accomplishment, but more generally it is worth studying for what it can reveal about the ways individuals carve an independent self from personal experiences created around shared practices.

## 1.5   Conclusions

Identity amounts to a subjective achievement to sustain a coherent self alongside cultural messages and discursive practices which our communities offer us. While it may be a 'performance', and so subject to change and reinterpretation, identity is a performance which is informed and reinscribed in us over time, constituting dispositions to behave in certain ways and make particular discourse choices in routine situations. Mediating between enduring social structures and the routines of our everyday interactional experiences, identity helps characterise both what makes us similar to and different from each other. For academics, it is how they simultaneously achieve credibility as insiders and reputations as individuals.

However, while academic discourses seek to limit the ways we enact our membership through rhetorical positioning and by constant monitoring and evaluation of our performances, we are not merely the product of these available stereotypes. As Richards (2006: 5) notes:

> Those involved in the talk are not actors on a stage whose every word is predetermined. Responsibility for the dialogue that eventually emerges falls to them, and although the process of construction must be based on a shared understanding of the interactional business in hand, (the conventional features) are not determinants of the talk so much as resources on which the interactants can draw.

The unique amalgam of experiences that we bring from participation in other communities sets us apart from any one of them and allows us greater space to pursue our own agendas and, within limits, to craft a distinctive way of occupying any role.

So while the gaze of others places limits on how far individuals can opt in or out of prefigured roles or subject positions, they are by no means simply the products of disciplinary discourses. They learn to be the people they are through the meanings they give to their interactions. They gradually understand community expectations through the ways others respond to their discourse and behaviours. At the same time, however, they chart a course between their unique feelings and dispositions and the off-the-peg identities provided by a discipline, finding a voice that makes use of local conventions but which says something about who they believe they are. These, then, are the themes of this book: how our language choices position us and others; how individual agency and community expectations interact in discourse; and how our engagement with others contributes to our sense of self. In the next chapter I look more closely at these issues by focusing on disciplines more directly and the ways identity is rhetorically constructed through proximity and positioning.

# 2 Discipline: Proximity and Positioning

In the previous chapter I tried to show that we produce and reproduce an identity through our repeated interactions as members of social groups. Identity is a person's relationship to his or her social world: it is a joint, two-way production, and language allows us to create and present a coherent self to others because, over time, it ties us into webs of common sense, interests and shared meanings. *Who we are* and *who we might be* are therefore built up through participation and linked to situations, to relationships and to the language we use in engaging with others on a routine basis.

Communities based around occupation, recreation, family and so on thus provide meaningful reference points and so help shape collective definitions of identity within their frameworks of understandings and values. In academic contexts, disciplines provide such reference points. They are places where participation involves communicating, and learning to communicate, in appropriate ways, and membership depends on displaying the ability to communicate as an *insider*: using language to represent ourselves as legitimate members. But while individuals enact who they are only in their dealings with others, they all bring different experiences, inclinations and proclivities to their performances as academics, teachers and students. Disciplinary membership, and identity itself, is a tension between conformity and individuality, between belonging on the one hand and individual recognition on the other. In this chapter I introduce the terms *proximity*, to refer to the first of these, the relationship between the self and community, and *positioning* to talk about the second, the relationship between the speaker and what is being said, as a way to begin unpacking these tensions. First, though, I want to establish the idea of discipline as a rhetorical community and site of identification.

## 2.1 What is a *discipline?*

Discipline is a common enough label, used to describe and distinguish topics, knowledge, institutional structures and individuals in the world of scholarship.

While emergent multi-focused and practitioner-based fields may challenge conventional notions of academic disciplines, students and academics themselves typically have little trouble in identifying their allegiances (Becher and Trowler, 2001).

## Definitional difficulties

Although less controversial than the idea of identity, *discipline* is, however, no easier to define. Disciplines, in fact, have been seen in numerous ways: as institutional conveniences, networks of communication, political institutions, domains of values, modes of inquiry and ideological power-bases. Kuhn (1977) identifies them according to whether they have clearly established paradigms or are at a looser, pre-paradigm stage; Biglan (1973) and Donald (1990) draw on faculty perceptions and Kolb (1981) on learning-style differences to provide categories which distinguished hard from soft and applied from pure knowledge fields; Storer and Parsons (1968) oppose analytical to synthetic fields; and Berliner (2002) distinguishes 'hard' and 'easy-to-do' disciplines in terms of the ability to understand, predict and control the phenomena they study. Others, writing from post-modern positions, predict their imminent demise, arguing that the fragmentation of academic life has resulted in the death of disciplines (e.g. Gergen and Thatchenkery, 1996; Gilbert, 1995).

Clearly, the term needs to be treated with caution. As a gloss on the complexity of how research and teaching is socially organised and conducted, the concept of *discipline* has its limitations. Some writers, in fact, see it as little more than a convenient shorthand for practices that are less distinguishable and stable than we usually suppose (e.g. Mauranen, 2006). It is certainly true that the boundaries of scholarship shift and dissolve, aided by institutional changes such as the emergence of practice-based and modular degrees and the fact that research problems and investigations often ignore disciplinary boundaries. New disciplines spring up at the intersections of existing ones and achieve international recognition (biochemistry, gerontology), while others decline and disappear (philology, alchemy). Similarly, there are cultural and geographic variations among disciplines as different education systems, levels of economic development and political ideologies come into play (Podgórecki, 1997). It is, however, important to recognise that centripetal as well as centrifugal forces are at work, with increased global information flows and resource networks counteracting the influence of nation-states and local cultural practices.

## Divergences and differences

Nor do all disciplines exhibit the same degree of cohesiveness and internal agreement. Some (such as modern languages and biochemistry) are convergent and closely knit in terms of their ideologies, awareness of a common tradition, research methodologies, allowable topics, standards of quality and so on. Others (perhaps geography and literary criticism) are more divergent and loose, where members lack a clear sense of group cohesion, where disciplinary borders are ill-defined, and where ideas cross boundaries more readily. Disciplines also often embrace a spectrum of specialisms, of theory, methods or subject matter, which seem to fragment cohesiveness. As Becher and Trowler (2001: 65) observe, 'there is no single method of enquiry, no standard verification procedure, no definitive set of concepts that uniquely characterizes each particular discipline'. In some contexts, in fact, it is more accurate to see communities in the overlapping subsidiary domains within disciplines (Hyland, 2009). Instead of uniformity, then, we find fluid and permeable entities impossible to pin down with precision.

There are also difficulties in reconciling how large, amorphous and dispersed groups of individuals defined by common bonds of discourse practices and conventions can be matched up with groups of individuals who typically work together and subscribe to common work practices and patterns of communication (e.g. Killingsworth and Gilbertson, 1992). Everyday local practices of teaching, supervision, research, marking and committee work can often seem removed from a wider involvement in publishing, networking and conference attendance. Killingsworth and Gilbertson themselves argue that membership in 'global communities' now dominates the activities of Western academics and that this 'tends to be regulated exclusively by discourse-governed criteria (writing style, publication in certain journals, presentations at national conventions, professional correspondence, and so forth)'. Local communities, on the other hand, have largely been characterised in terms of shared practices and the engagement of individuals around some project which fosters particular beliefs, ways of talking and power relations (Swales, 1998).

In fact, how far realms of knowledge come to be accepted as *disciplines*, rather than remaining as, say, *approaches*, seems largely a matter of institutional recognition. International significance is a key measure, particularly the extent to which leading universities recognise the independence of an area and give it the status of a department with professorial chairs, budgets and degrees; whether a distinct international community has appeared around it with the professional paraphernalia of conferences, learned societies and specialist journals; and whether the wider populace generally see it as having academic credibility and intellectual substance. All this points to the contextually contingent nature of disciplines and the fact that they are not monolithic knowledge-generating apparatus but are very much dependent on local struggles over resources and recognition. In other words, a discipline is as much determined by social power and members' categorisations as it is by epistemological categories.

## Disciplines as sites of identity

Disciplines, however, are not mere chimera. They have a very real existence for those who work and study in them, who attend conferences, supervise students, manage programmes, read journals, write books, sit through lectures and take exams. Although they work day to day in local *institutions*, members have a sense of being part of a *discipline* and of having a stake in something with others. In fact, one often has more to do with people one meets occasionally at conferences or corresponds with by email than with those on the next floor of the same building (e.g. Swales, 1998). It is in disciplines, rather than particular physical sites, that the important interactions in a professional's life occur, bringing academics, texts and practices together into a common rhetorical locale. Group membership, in other words, implies some degree of group identification and this, in turn, presupposes that members will see themselves as having some things in common and being, to some extent, similar to each other (e.g. Turner, 1987).

Identity is about who the individual is, and an academic identity is who the individual is when acting as a member of a discipline. This clearly involves a range of practices, understandings and values in which familiarity with a common literature, knowledge of accepted and topical theories, fluency in arcane research practices, and awareness of conferences, journals, leading lights, prestigious departments and other paraphernalia of daily academic life are important. However, individuals identify themselves, and are identified by others, largely through their use of a language, a language which interprets and reports these activities and beliefs in specific ways and which simultaneously helps distinguish insiders from others. There is an essential and integral connection between identity and the cultures of disciplinary groups, which is mediated by distinctive patterns of language so that, to put it crudely and no doubt a shade polemically: we are what we write. An engineer is an engineer because he or she communicates like one and the same is true for biologists, historians and linguists.

Because social groups objectify in language certain ways of experiencing and talking about phenomena, these come to influence the self-perceptions and presentations of group members. Conditions of homogeneity tend to be created within communities defined by that language so that texts help evoke a context where the individual activates specific recognisable and routine responses to recurring tasks. Whether this context is a face-to-face lecture, an online supervision, an exam board meeting, or a research report to anonymous others around the world, it involves actors constructing themselves in terms of how they understand reality and want to be seen. All this, in turn, increases the social distance between members and outsiders and works against cross-community cooperation:

> As the work and the points of view grow more specialised, men in different disciplines have fewer things in common, in their background and in their daily problems. They have less impulse to interact with one another and less ability to do so.
>
> (Clark, 1987: 273)

The idea of interdisciplinarity, almost universally held to be a positive aspect of knowledge and research, actually often amounts only to the accumulation of knowledge gleaned from more than one field. Relentless diversification and specialisation appear to be more common, leading to the growing mutual incomprehensibility of academic communities.

The concept of discipline thus helps explain how individuals identify themselves and act to persuade others of that identification. Discipline helps apparently heterogeneous individuals form first-year undergraduate classes, departmental committees and research groups. It helps concretise, in specialised textually encoded knowledge, the 'invisible colleges' which span the globe through webs of journals, symposia, conferences, Skype chats, pre-print circulations and email exchanges. In short, the notion puts each individual's decision-making and engagement at centre stage and underlines the fact that academic discourse involves language users in constructing and displaying their identities, both moment by moment and over extended periods, as members of *disciplines*. This membership, however, implies both similarity and difference, conformity and individuality, and I turn to these issues now, recasting existing work on academic discourse to show its relevance to the study of disciplinary identity.

## 2.2    Proximity: Hegemony, solidarity and convention

I have been arguing that actions that we perform routinely, and particularly routine *rhetorical* actions, are central to the performance of self. This is particularly the case in the performance of a *disciplinary* self where language ties actors into webs of association and allows them to become part of the collective, to identify with others and, as Mead (1934) has it, to 'take on the role of the other'. Seeing others as similar or different allows members, for practical purposes, to create a sense of self through consistent engagement with those like them. Over time, they construct a recognisable and valued identity through competent participation in the common genres and discourse forms of a discipline. I use the term *proximity* to refer to a writer's control of these practices to manage themselves and their interactions with others; it is *the use of a disciplinary-appropriate system of meanings*.

### An orientation to readers and discipline

Proximity implies a receiver-oriented view of communication and is closely related to Sacks's (1995: 438) notion of 'recipient design', or how talk is shaped to make sense to the current interactant. In fact, talk has figured far more prominently than writing in identity research as analysts have established that gender (Butler, 1990), ethnicity (Day, 1998), family role (Wortham and Gadsden, 2006) and so on are performed through verbal interaction. Writing is no less important in constructing identity, however, as lexical choice, topic selection, conventions of argument and so on also display an orientation and sensitivity to co-participants.

The particularities of any situation therefore connect with wider norms and practices. This is not because members rationally decide these norms are sensible, but because constant exposure to this discourse leads them to work out what norm the group favours. Choices are narrowed to the point where we do not have to decide on every option available. In academic contexts this means that the process of writing involves creating a text that we assume the reader will recognise and expect, and the process of reading involves drawing on assumptions about what the writer is trying to do. Skilled writers are therefore able to create a mutual frame of reference and anticipate when their purposes will be retrieved by their audiences. This is not to claim anything new, of course: a considerable literature supports the fact that individuals are socialised into disciplinary membership. But the use of preferred discourse patterns has not usually been seen in terms of proximity or identity construction.

Proximity ties the individual into a web of disciplinary texts and discourses, recalling Bakhtin's (1981) influential notion of *dialogism*, mentioned in Chapter 1. This suggests that all communication reveals the influence of, refers to or takes up what has been said or written before and at the same time anticipates the potential or actual responses of others. Utterances exist 'against a backdrop of other concrete utterances on the same theme, a background made up of contradictory opinions, points of view and value judgements' (Bakhtin, 1981: 281). Most obviously, this means talking to others by explicitly responding to a disciplinary literature, and in some cases with long-dead thinkers (examples from my corpus of 240 research articles in eight disciplines):

(1)

The first is derived from Durkheim's (1938) notion that there is a general ...

(Soc)

However, both Piagetian and Vygotskian thinking involve constructivist ...

(AL)

Wittgenstein insists that what is true or false is what people say ...

(Phil)

Matthei's equations [17, 19] were first used as a starting point in the scale model.

(EE)

But it also involves anticipating other viewpoints and positions, as yet perhaps unstated, talking to readers and drawing on a knowledge of what particular interlocutors might find contentious, unexpected or limited:

(2)

Some readers will want to argue that this is a comparative analysis of neighbourhood associations more than social movements.

(Soc)

These results were surprising in that they showed that a $Ca2+$ influx apparently is not required for a low level of increase in the rate of transcription from flageltar genes following acid shock.

(Bio)

> Readers who feel sceptical about this argument should consider its pedigree, or perhaps find better examples of their own.
>
> (AL)

More generally, individuals present and represent themselves by locally managing their use of argument conventions to engage in such dialogues, immersing themselves in the reservoir of meaning options that constitute a distinctive culture. Who we identify with therefore contributes to who we are and says something to others about us, but this reliance on a common, authoritative discourse also points to the fact that a lot of what happens in the field of identity is done by others, not by oneself, as those we interact with can validate who we claim to be, refute it or impose an alternative. In other words, as I shall return to below, power and authority are critical in determining whose definition counts. Socially competent individuals therefore learn to bring their self-presentation into line with the ethos of the group, both to be understood and to be recognised. Proximity, then, involves both identification *with* and *by* others.

## Hegemony and ideology

An individual's proximity to his or her discipline is built on language, but our displays of who we are and what we are doing as members of particular groups always involve more than language. Following Foucault (1972), Gee (1999), for instance, talks of Discourse (with a big 'D') to refer to a hegemonic system of thinking and seeing the world specific to particular groups which encompasses an entire interlocking network of practices, structures and ideologies. This is the language we use to enact our identities and get things done in the world:

> Such socially accepted associations among ways of using language, of thinking, valuing, acting, and interacting in the 'right' places and at the 'right' times with the 'right' objects (associations that can be used to identify oneself as a member of a socially meaningful group or 'social network'), I will refer to as 'Discourses' with a capital 'D'.
>
> (Gee, 1999: 17)

This, then, is discourse as form-of-life: the stuff of our everyday world of activities and institutions which is created by our routine uses of language, together with other aspects of social practices. It is through discourses, for example, that we build meanings for things in the world such as meetings, shopping and drugs, and in academic contexts such as lectures, journal impact factors and research. Discourse is how we foster group mythologies, solidarity and social control; how we distribute prestige to people and value to ideas; and the ways we make connections to the past and to the future. Discourses consist of the basic assumptions, vocabularies and values of group members which form the shared and standardised frameworks for acting in and making sense of social settings and interactions. Displays of proximity thus help to ring-fence disciplines by identifying their users as insiders and excluding others. They create both group and individual identities.

Identities are therefore anchored around sets of norms that regulate values and behaviour, and particularly language-using behaviour, so that identity construction necessarily involves perceptions of 'correctness' and 'appropriateness'. But proximity does not imply regimented conformity or slavish rule observance. Just as gender identities allow degrees of masculinity and femininity, it is also possible to negotiate nearness or distance from a discipline. The neophyte and the Nobel Prize winner have different commitments to the epistemological values and social practices of a discipline and different investments in creating and sustaining a disciplinary identity. Individuals, in other words, can be more or less 'proximate'.

## Disciplinary ideologies and collective practices

Proximity underlines the fact that appropriate language choices do not just offer a view of the world but reveal what writers and speakers see as important, how they believe they should select and present material, and what these selections imply about disciplinary values and practices. In other words, specific linguistic realisations represent disciplinary ideologies and help individuals to identify themselves as members.

Rhetorical strategies which highlight a gap in knowledge, present a hypothesis related to this gap, and then detail experiments and findings to test this hypothesis, for example, construct a scientific 'objectivity' and the view that knowledge emerges in a linear step-wise fashion, each new finding building on the last and leading inexorably towards the truth (Prelli, 1989; Rorty, 1979). This appearance of objectivity is further strengthened by suppressing any reference to the fact that experimental observations depend on personal interpretation or that experimenters are committed to specific theoretical positions (e.g. Gilbert and Mulkay, 1984). Reporting excludes the role of the interpreting scientist and the symbolic construction of papers as Introduction – Methods – Results – Discussion scaffolds an ideology of inductive procedure. Truth, in Knorr-Cetina's (1981) words, is 'theory impregnated'. Form is ideological.

This abstract from a letters' journal in physics is unremarkable, but in reporting experimental procedures in a dispassionate, impersonal and expository style, it mimics inductive research practices and so helps to reinforce an empiricist ideology:

(3)

> The influence of the quantized centre-of-mass motion on the dynamics of a one-atom laser with a quantized field is investigated. Both the atom-field coupling and the decay channels depend on the motional state. It is demonstrated that sideband cooling can prevent the atom from heating up while laser action is maintained. Furthermore, the discrete nature of the motion is reflected in multiple vacuum Rabi splitting.

(Lage, et al., 1991: 6550)

Writing as a physicist means accepting certain scientific precepts, or at least behaving in that way. It means acting as if truth were built on non-contingent pillars of impartial observation, experimental demonstration and replication and as if the text were merely the channel which relays them.

Research in the humanities employs equally formal conventions although they are generally more explicitly interpretive and less abstract, with less 'exact' data collection procedures. Here we find discourses which recast knowledge as sympathetic understanding in readers through an ethical rather than cognitive progression (Dillon, 1981; Hyland, 2004a). Readers expect that authors will display more of a 'reflexive self, unable to write with the classic detachment of positivism' (Starfield and Ravelli, 2006). Cultural studies is just one discipline where we expect to find this kind of reflexivity, where the involvement of the writer is an essential element in the credibility of the account:

(4)

> It is always something of an out-of-body experience to read other people's readings of my own work. One of the ironies of the academy is that although we are always happy to accept there is no 'right' reading of a text, there are in general two categories that always remain an exception: first, those theorists whose work we find most important to our own; and second, our own work. I remember, for example, early in my career, reading a critique of my work in which the author claimed it was obvious, from what I wrote, that I did not like rock music. To say that that blew my mind and sent me into shock would be an understatement!

(Grossberg, 2011: 425-426)

Arguments thus involve a more personal stance and exploration of specific cases, but disciplines vary both in the kinds of problems they address and in the forms of argument they adopt. All humanities disciplines are *reiterative*, for example, in that they are obliged to revisit and reinterpret material already studied, but historians and literary critics persuade readers to accept their reinterpretations of the familiar in very different ways. One difference worth mentioning is that literary critics use the *it is* + ADJ + *that* pattern (e.g. *it is clear that*) to include previously introduced aspects of the writer's argument far more than historians, who are more likely to use it to emphasise the empirical grounding of claims (Groom, 2005). Proximity is also evident in the extent to which knowledge is attributed to individual scholars, schools of thought or conventional wisdom, or whether it is expressed in a non-attributed canonical form. Here economics textbooks are apparently more like those in physics than sociology, with the latter containing far more references to social actors and processes, perhaps because sociology has failed to establish clear agreement among its members about how the world is seen and how research issues are to be tackled (Moore, 2002).

The most obvious expression of proximity to a disciplinary discourse, however, is an orientation to a topic recognised as current and relevant. Topics, in fact, are more than just a research focus as they represent resources of joint attention which coordinate activities and mark out co-participation in disciplines. Selecting a topic and arguing for its novelty and significance are critical in securing colleagues' attention and in displaying the speaker's right to be taken seriously as a disciplinary member. Whether discussing xylem embolisms, motherese or Collective Consequentialism, academics are staking a claim to be a certain kind of person, drawing on the themes of their fields and the vocabularies of their trade in the careful management of identity.

## Situating research and constructing novelty

Topics, however, must also be handled appropriately so that local research is situated in the broader concerns of the discipline in order to establish novelty and value. The pursuit of novelty, in fact, is often seen as the driving force of disciplinary activity. As Foucault (1981: 66) observes, 'for there to be a discipline, there must be the possibility of formulating new propositions, ad infinitum', while Kaufer and Geisler (1989: 286) refer to academic communities as 'factories of novelty, encouraging members to plod towards their yearly quota of inspirational leaps'. Creating novelty is, however, also a demonstration of identity as novelty is seen differently across disciplines.

As my corpus data suggest, in the sciences constant innovation and progress are expected, and practitioners look for new results to develop their own research (5), while engineers construct a practical, applied orientation by combining novelty with the utility of their research to the industrial world (6):

(5)

Analyzing a Xenopus liver CDNA library, we identified a CDNA encoding a new HNF4 gene.

(Bio)

In this paper a new coherent transient effect is reported: a two-pulse stimulated echo observed via the angular distribution of anisotropic gamma-radiation from oriented nuclei under axial GE.

(Phy)

(6)

In this work, a novel inductive sensor system has been realized using an arrangement of planar microcoils that allows for a precise measurement of the wheel position, independently of speed and target distance.

(EE)

To handle design problems with conflicting objective functions, a novel procedure has been developed for pruning the design space iteratively that is based on identification of relative significance of design factors on different objectives.

(ME)

To write in the humanities, on the other hand, means situating novelty as having a disciplinary-internal relevance, so it is new only as a contribution to current theories and issues (Hyland, 2004a):

(7)

It offers a new way of theorising ageism itself, as a contingent and negotiated interactional practice.

(AL)

On this new account, we have a pluralist story, not just about morality, but also about benevolence.

(Phil)

Novelty has to be sold to peers as a valid contribution, and this is most obviously achieved by establishing explicit intertextual links to existing knowledge through citation and the marketing of the newsworthy in the structure of research papers. It is apparent, for instance, in abstracts where writers seek to gain readers' attention and selectively highlight what they are likely to find new. Similarly, the introduction assembles claims for novelty by reference to what the discipline knows and believes is worth knowing. This is more carefully elaborated in the literature review, which seeks to justify the value of the current research and persuade the reader that it links into a coherent chain of disciplinary activity. Finally, writers urge the value of their research onto the reader in results sections through a series of rhetorical moves designed to justify the methodology and evaluate their findings (e.g. Ruiying and Allison, 2003).

In short, persuasion can be effective only if the author has correctly identified the opinions and expectations of his or her audience and the culture of his or her community. The semiotic resources which our disciplines put at our disposal are so rich and complex that we have only a limited conscious awareness of them, and we can never second-guess colleagues with absolute precision. Through conversations with peers, attending conferences, reading the research and by generally engaging with the interdiscoursal paraphernalia of the discipline, we discover not only which topics and theorists are currently hot, but also the kind of arguments and warrants that are ideologically appropriate. Proximity to the conventions of a discipline thus allows individuals to engage with peers to construct effective knowledge claims while performing a competent insider identity.

## Proximity and identity

Observations on disciplinary differences have been made before, but their links to identity have not been previously established. The idea of proximity, however, not only suggests how individuals display an alignment with the group, making connections to the cultural models which are the discourse of a discipline, but also draws attention to the symbolisation of this discourse. Proximity helps reinterpret this earlier work to indicate that discourse can be seen as both an attitude *toward the another* and *of the other*, building and occupying a body of dispositions in the context of a social group. The idea underpins the constructivist conviction that scientific papers are not persuasive because they communicate independently existing truths about the external world, but because they appeal to community-grounded and subjectively shared beliefs of members. Focusing on the language of the disciplines thus reveals how the epistemological and social assumptions of the author's disciplinary culture help to form academic identities discursively.

Claiming a disciplinary identity involves collusion, at least to some extent, in community discourses. This is not to say resistance is impossible or that constraints are immutable. Hegemonic discourses are blueprints which are always changing and changeable; they are not determining or controlled by any particular individual or group. In fact, they are constantly recreated in every act of communication so that the identity claims that individuals make through a disciplinary performance simultaneously re-make these discourses. To study the social interactions expressed through academic talk therefore reveals something of the sanctioned social behaviours, beliefs and institutional structures which underpin both disciplinary and individual identity.

## 2.3 Positioning: Diversity, appropriation and stance

The idea of proximity highlights the importance of disciplinary discourses in performing identity work by focusing on the shared social representations which provide broad templates for how people see and talk about the world, but it is not the whole story. The stress it places on what is 'shared' among members tends to emphasise a structuralist notion of discipline and a deterministic view of identity, downplaying personal creativity and what the individual brings to the context. While processes of identity formation draw heavily on these disciplinary schema to both shape and enable particular 'speaking positions' and disable others (Baynham, 2006), how individuals actually occupy these positions is more variable.

Academics, like anyone else, pursue individual as well as collective goals and interests. They want to 'be somebody', to make a name for themselves and stand out from the crowd, and while this involves engaging with others in ways they understand and value, it also means staking out a distinctive territory. So while we become who we are only in relation to others, adopting the modes of talk that others routinely use, identity also means assembling the elements of a communicative performance from our backgrounds, which shapes our interpretations of these discourses. Positioning refers to the fact that while we might recognise 'the ways things are done', we also see these as the enabling conditions for individuality.

## Positions and positioning

P*ositioning* is a bridge between identities and discourses, referring to how people locate themselves in discourse when interacting with others. Essentially, I am using it here to refer to how we experience and construct identities by appropriating the discoursal categories of our communities as our own.

The literature on positioning has become extremely diverse, embracing post-structuralist feminism (Norton, 2000), cultural theory (Hall, 1996) and Critical Discourse Analysis (Fairclough, 1992); however, it concerns the fact that an individual emerges in interaction not as a relatively fixed product, but as one continually reconstituted through the various discursive practices in which they participate. Davies and Harré (1990) argue that our experiences and sense of self can only be expressed and understood using the categories made available by discourse, which acts as a kind of dynamic conceptual schema through which meanings are actively achieved. Central to acquiring a sense of self and interpreting the world from that perspective is learning the categories which our communities make available (male/female, student/supervisor) and then participating in the practices that allocate meaning to those categories. We position ourselves as belonging to certain categories and in relation to the 'story lines' that are articulated around those categories (student not teacher, good student not plodder).

Thus, disciplinary contingencies guide language use through the positions they make available to speakers and writers, and individuals come to invest in particular positionings so that they act like someone in that position and 'become like that kind of person' (Wortham, 2000: 166). Foucault (1972) sees this as the potential denial of agency, but while actors *are positioned* in terms of what disciplinary discourses allow, individuals can also *position themselves* in terms of personal stance and interpersonal alignments. Davies and Harré (1990: 46) capture the dynamic like this:

> Once having taken up a particular position as one's own, a person inevitably sees the world from the vantage point of that position and in terms of the particular images, metaphors, storylines and concepts which are made relevant within the particular discursive practice in which they are positioned. At least a possibility of notional choice is inevitably involved because there are many and contradictory discursive practices that each person could engage in.

Identifying ourselves as an undergraduate student, research assistant or lecturer, for example, does not involve stepping into a pre-packaged self. It always entails negotiating overlaps with other simultaneously held aspects of identity (such as being a single, working mother postgraduate student) and making meaning in interaction with the people and the events around us (a celebrated, high-status professor). The ensemble of selves influences how we play any one of them and thus helps shape a particular identity. For Davies and Harré (1990: 47), it is the experience of contradictory positions which provides the dynamic for understanding both ourselves and the world because we can negotiate new positions by posing alternatives. So while we all 'ventriloquate' (Bakhtin, 1981) the voices we encounter in a community to demonstrate our claims to membership, the demands of dominant discourses do not form a closed and determining system. Instead, they can be seen as patterns of options which allow us to actively and publicly accomplish an identity through discourse choices. There is, in other words, always potential for transformation as well as reproduction in academic discourses.

## Collective identity and possible selves

Positioning is made possible by proximity and the cognitive routinisation, or habitualisation of behaviour which regular participation in a community enables (e.g. Bourdieu, 1977; Berger and Luckman, 1967). Not only do familiar patterns of discourse, values and other practices get laid down through repeated experiences so that individuals display membership through their proximity to them, but also this routinisation opens up space for deliberation and innovation so that every situation does not need to be reconsidered as novel. Proximity thus creates a secure and relatively enduring context of the 'way things are' and so facilitates positioning and reflexivity, while positioning contributes to the intersubjective agreement which sustains proximity.

Clearly texts can be read as a desire to shape an individual identity which resonates with the writer's perceptions of the collective identity of a discipline. Actors fashion genres using conventional rhetorical forms to claim membership, but these language choices are also ways of making sense of personal experiences and understandings of themselves. We claim affiliation to any number of groups at different times and with varying degrees of commitment, and so who we portray ourselves as being changes with interactants, settings and life-stages. Importantly, however, we also bring residues of these diverse experiences of group memberships to our participation in each of them. Gender, social class, religion, race, ethnicity, age and geographical region are the most obvious of these; but other communities like school, family and the workplace also shape our perceptions and understandings (e.g. Bondi, 2004). Collective identifications are not just masks we put on and take off; they are real for us and have real consequences.

Helpful here is the idea of *possible selves* (Markus and Nurius, 1986), which provides a conceptual link between cognition and motivation by representing individuals' ideas of 'what they might become, what they would like to become, and what they are afraid of becoming' (ibid., 954). An individual is able to create any variety of possible selves, yet the available pool derives from the categories made salient by the individual's particular sociocultural and historical context and from the models and symbols provided by immediate social experiences. Possible selves are therefore personalised, but they are also distinctly social as they result from previous comparisons to salient others and so provide an evaluative and interpretive context for the current view of self. We develop an idea of what is possible, a motivation to *be* and *become* someone.

Every discipline is therefore composed of individuals with diverse experiences, backgrounds, expertise, commitments and influence, all differing in how far they subscribe to its various goals and methods, participate in its activities and identify with its values. Collective identity emphasises similarity but not at the expense of difference. The idea of positioning helps reveal the creative, local nature of identity construction as part of the shaping forces of social processes and ideologies, what I have called proximity. Together they offer a way of seeing how language acts as both a constraint and a resource: how discursive practices represent people in particular ways and, at the same time, how they offer the means for people to negotiate new positions. In speaking or writing, we are not just mimicking others in a similar position but imprinting our own unique take on it as a result of the experiences we bring to it.

## Positioning in spoken interaction

Positioning is perhaps most evident in spoken contexts where the formal normative 'defaults' are more easily overridden by individual proclivities and personal style. The constraints of the essay or research paper are relaxed in the lecture hall and seminar room as the immediacy of a co-present audience and the need to impart information in an engaging and effective way give individuals the licence to take explicitly personal positions towards their material.

This extract from an undergraduate lecture on the Holocaust, for instance, shows the extent of individual positioning while displaying proximity to the conventions of an academic genre:

(8)

> and um, I want to start with, um, with the essay that I recommended you read and and uh which you can, refer to, after the class if you, um if your interest, has been, um peaked. um, the essay, from the, the uh the book *The Imaginary Jew*, in which he examines his, the development of his own, Jewish identity it's a it's an essay that um, I find particularly resonates with my, my own experience and I I find it um, really um, thoughtful and um, and um, and thought provoking. um ... I I must say that I share myself um his own development from a, um an unexamined, uh pride of um, of being, um, of descending from one from a family that was affected by the Holocaust, to a more, reflexive stance and and um, a more self-conscious, stance on, on uh the place of the Holocaust in my own identity and that's one of the reasons why, um, I told you, that it was with mixed feelings that I, that I had um, revealed to you where, where I come from. but um, Alain Finkielkraut, he's a French philosopher, writes about this, um, this identity. and uh I just wanna quote to you, from page seven in the, in the essay. um he's talking about this this um, new Jewish identity that's uh that's a privileged, identity a privileged identity as, as a victim. um and he says 'I Inherited a suffering to which I had not been subjected. for without having to endure oppression the identity of the victim was mine. I could savor an exceptional destiny, while remaining completely at ease. without exposure to real danger I had heroic stature. to be Jewish was enough to escape, the anonymity of an identity indistinguishable from others, and the dullness of an unevent- uneventful life'. and I think the observation is um is is uh accurate.
>
> (MICASE: LEL542SU096)

Within this enactment of an academic register there is an explicit positioning of the speaker. The numerous framing constructions (*I want to start with, I just wanna quote to you*), organising metadiscourse (*I must say that, he's talking about*), evaluative commentary (*I find it really thoughtful, I think the observation is accurate*) and quotation from a source text are typical of lecture discourse (Mauranen, 2001; Swales and Malczewski, 2001). The extract also contains the colloquial features typical of much impromptu lecturing such as hesitations, false starts, fragments, repetitions, contractions and so on (Biber, 2006). Most striking, however, is the identity work going on here. This is not simply the way the speaker positions himself in relation to the quote, how he agrees with and values the idea it expresses, but how he positions himself as a person: '*the place of the Holocaust in my own identity*'. So while conveying proximity to the conventions of an academic lecture, he takes a very personal position on the issues and moves beyond the role of lecturer to present a personal and intimate characterisation of himself to his students.

## Positioning in academic writing

The ability to take a position is also apparent in the collaborative negotiations of written academic arguments. While some observers see disciplinary discourses as agonistic and aggressive (e.g. Belcher, 1997; Salager-Meyer et al., 2003), explicit confrontation and the destruction of an opponent's standpoints tend to actually be quite rare in published texts in most fields. The systematic avoidance of conflict is an important aspect of disciplinary competence, and while fast-moving science fields may be more competitive and potentially more confrontational than the individual philosopher working to his or her own rhythms (Becher and Trowler, 2001), antagonism tends to be kept below the surface. Debate involves negotiating difference in disciplinary-defined ways. Of course, academic reputations are based on saying something new, by staking a claim to a novel idea or seeing things in an original way, and this often involves disputing previously held truths and challenging positions perhaps cherished and nurtured by others. Effective argumentation requires a display of proximity to the community's collaborative practices, so while it often involves genuine disagreement, it also maximises opportunities to find common ground.

This is clear in the fact that it is crucial for writers to establish a common position at the outset, recognising the importance of a topic and the value of exploring it. The starting point of an academic paper is typically the identification of a gap or shortcoming in earlier research (Swales, 1990), but in establishing this gap, writers largely attempt to respond to a general body of more-or-less impersonal literature (9) or particular theories (10) rather than individual authors:

(9)

> Some commentators have, on the basis of the emerging survey data, argued that drug use among young people is no longer regarded as a deviant activity by them. They claim that drug use is becoming normalized. We wish to challenge this view and contend that far more has been read into the survey data than is warranted.
>
> (Soc article)

> Some authorities believe the permanent conidiogenous cells in Ascochytato to be

annellidic, but this is difficult to interpret in many species, especially with light microscopy.

(Bio article)

(10)

Critical linguistic studies have tended to be 'fragmentary' and 'exemplificatory'. Analyses have generally focused on isolated segments of texts to demonstrate how linguistic theory and categories provide a method for examining the constitutive and ideological character of texts.

(AL article)

Detailed two-dimensional (2-D) physical models have been reported (for example [4] [5]) which provide a valuable insight in to the physics behind the operation of HBT's. However, there are a number of issues that still need to be addressed to obtain good quantitative correlation between these physical models and measured data.

(Phy article)

What emerges from academic argument is a reformulation of the original position in a way that brings members onside rather than results in head-to-head confrontation.

Positioning of this kind enables writers to project an identity which is both disciplinary-oriented and personally committed. Within the constraints of this collaborative environment, the use of various evaluative and engagement features enables writers to construct a distinctive stance, or disciplinary performance.

## Stance and engagement

In academic writing, positioning is largely accomplished through stance and engagement (Hyland, 2005b). *Stance* refers to the writer's textual 'voice' or community-recognised personality, an attitudinal, writer-oriented function which concerns the ways writers present themselves and convey their judgements, opinions and commitments (Biber, 2006; Conrad and Biber, 2001). This includes the use of hedging and boosting devices to express an epistemic attitude, conveying either tentativeness and possibility or assurance and certainty (Hyland, 1998a), authorial self-mention to give prominence to the role of the author in the text (Hyland, 2001b) and attitude markers, which indicate the writer's affective attitude to propositions, conveying surprise, agreement, importance, frustration and so on. This example, from a philosophy paper in my corpus, illustrates how clear such a stance can be:

(11)

> **No doubt** there are a number of criticisms that adherents to the justice-based paradigm <u>might</u> make of the moral model Dworkin proposes. Still, **I believe that** Dworkin's investment model has **remarkable** resonance and **extraordinary** potential power. **The worry I have** about Dworkin's proposal arises from inside his model. **It is interesting** right off the bat to notice that ...
>
> (Phil article)

Similarly, writers can position themselves towards other views through their choice of reporting verbs (Hyland, 2004a; Thompson and Ye, 1991) and other references to external sources (Hyland, 2005b). Verb selections, for example, can ascribe an epistemic status to information, evaluating it as true, doubtful or false (Hyland, 2004a) or marking it as 'received knowledge' (Hunston, 1993). Tadros (1993) argues that some choices allow writers to detach themselves from a proposition and so position themselves to deliver their own viewpoint. In this example, the writer frames his argument in relation to a currently accepted view, drawing on a range of intertextual markers in a way which most effectively supports his own argument. His position thus emerges from the contrast he makes with earlier studies:

(12)

> **Her reading** of Twiggy as an oppressive icon **is consistent with** many popular press analyses **that render** the Twiggy phenomenon as a culturally important manifestation of the 'ideology of thinness' that is, in turn, **widely associated with** eating disorders (see Lague 1993; Leland 1996); hence, the 'waif' look exemplified by supermodel Kate Moss and the so-called postwaif look embodied by the newly controversial model Trish Goff are **commonly characterized** as a regressive turn toward to this oppressive ideal (e.g., Goodman 1996). **This revisionist interpretation** of Twiggy **overlooks** historical research **indicating that** the Twiggy phenomenon represented an intersection of class and gender politics.
>
> (Mk article)

*Engagement*, on the other hand, is more of an alignment function, concerning the ways that writers rhetorically address their readers to actively pull them along with the argument, include them as discourse participants and guide them to interpretations (Hyland, 2001a; Martin and White, 2005). These include the ways authors try to involve readers in the communication process through the use of addressee features such as questions and second-person pronouns (Hyland, 2001a, 2002b). These identify the reader as someone who shares similar understandings to the writer as a member of the same discipline and invite dialogic involvement, encouraging curiosity and bringing interlocutors into an arena where they can be led to the writer's viewpoint:

(13)

> In other words, **we** are facing a dilemma: Wilson's natural theory fails to explain many observations, while cultural theories provide mere verbal explanations of them. **Is it, in fact, necessary to choose between nurture and nature?** My contention is that it is not. A very simple example shows that **we** do not need to evoke any moral sense, or cultural conditioning, to explain familiar moral reactions.
>
> (Phil article)

A different and slightly more risky strategy is for writers to position themselves in relation to their readers with directives (Hyland 2002a). Mainly expressed through imperatives and obligation modals, these instruct readers to act or see things in a certain way:

(14)

> **It is important to** recognize the complexity of mycorrhizal systems, and address the appropriate scale when assessing mycorrhizal function.
>
> (Bio article)

> It must be understood, however, that there are wide variations in applications that describe themselves as 'interactive multimedia'.
>
> (Comm article)

Together these resources enable writers to adopt positions, both towards their material and towards others who hold positions on the topic. They contribute to the writer's ability to take a stand on something and dialogically refer to the positions of potential readers, signalling competent academic engagement and performing a disciplinary identity.

Disciplinary arguments are therefore both an affiliative resource and a mechanism for professional recognition, a display of proximity to community norms and the performance of individual positioning. Academics use these resources to chart a course between critique and collegiality, minimising personal threat while demonstrating a critical expertise. Identity is a representation of ideas as a cooperative accomplishment, presenting a viewpoint while engaging with others' ideas in agreed-upon ways. Ultimately, disciplines are the contexts in which disagreement can be deliberated and identities constructed.

## 2.4 Conclusions

In this chapter I have tried to flesh out the idea of discipline and its connections to identity, exploring the view that members' participation in academic discourses contributes to both disciplinary cohesion and individual identity. The difficulties involved in identifying disciplines in terms of purely academic criteria mean that we have to see them as the collective engagement of individuals in certain discourses and practices so that identity and discipline can be understood only by reference to each other. Each is emergent, mutable and interdependent. The key feature of these processes is language, for while we do not simply parrot the words of our disciplines, we index who we are in the ways we selectively draw on and negotiate the linguistic repertoires they make available.

Individual identity is a unique complex of different group and personal experiences. It is locally constructed along two main discoursal paths: through relationships between the self and community, what I refer to as *proximity*, and through relationships between the speaker and the message, or *positioning*. The former concerns the interactive character of the talk represented through the social and discursive conventions of a discipline and the underlying power relations these draw upon; it means using language to adopt a disciplinary voice to establish the writer as someone competent to engage as an insider, but also creates the potential for positioning and agency through broadly agreed meanings and correspondences of expectations. *Positioning*, on the other hand, means adopting a point of view both to the issues discussed in the text and to others who hold points of view on those issues, including actors' individual evaluations and stances towards what they discuss.

Together these terms help to show how disciplines can be seen as cultures and not merely institutional designations. They are enacted and constructed by social actors. At the same time these actors are also enacting and constructing identities for themselves as disciplinary members and individual academics. An orientation to proximity and positioning is therefore an orientation to disciplines and those we encounter within them, a context where individuals shape a writer–reader dialogue which situates both their research and themselves. The academic is not a victim of his or her discipline or a puppet of its discourses, for while these routinely patterned uses of language help make the world predictable and interactions relatively straightforward, they do not eliminate choice. Our particular biographies, with experiences of different relationships, understandings and interactions, and with varied social, educational and professional affiliations, mean that we fill the positions we occupy with unique experiences of other positions and discourses.

The constructs of proximity and positioning also inform methodology and suggest how we might investigate identity empirically. These features can be studied systematically by investigating the everyday discoursal activities of academics, students and teachers. In the next chapter I turn to look at the methods that applied linguists currently use to investigate identity and to argue for a more empirical and linguistic approach using corpora.

# 3 Investigating Identity

In the first two chapters I have introduced the key notions of identity and discipline and elaborated something of their complexities and connections with each other. I have discussed how discourse, the ways we use language to interact with those around us, is a significant marker of both who we are and the groups we belong to. The question arises, however, of how we actually unpack this: what methods best reveal the processes that *make people who they are*? All discoursal approaches regard texts as evidence of identity – they see people representing who they are to each other through language – but each understands this in different ways.

Benwell and Stokoe (2006: 29) point out that a discursive view of identity can be viewed as a construction in interaction or as a historical set of regulatory structures. In current practice, these broad distinctions translate into three main approaches to the study of identity: Conversation Analysis (CA), Critical Discourse Analysis (CDA) and Narrative Analysis (NA). All three agree that identity is available for investigation through language and that individuals draw on understandings of institutional and social contexts to shape and interpret their interactions. They diverge, however, on what counts as data, on the interpretive activities of the analyst, and on whether it is legitimate to assume the influence of any particular role or relationship unless it is taken up in the talk. In this chapter I explore these key issues and illustrate what each approach brings to the study of identity. I will then go on to show how corpus techniques, by providing evidence for both collective proximity and individual positioning, contribute something new to this picture.

## 3.1 Negotiating identities: Conversation Analysis

Conversation Analysis follows Garfinkel's (1967) insight that social life is a continuous display of people's local understandings of what is happening. Analysts therefore reject any a priori categories to data and argue that everything we need to know about how identity is accomplished in talk can be discovered by studying the fine detail of everyday interaction. Identity is part and parcel of talk and not something that analysts impose through their interpretations of it. This links to social constructionism, discussed in Chapter 1, as individuals continuously engage in making sense of the world with others and so create that world. It is a 'bottom-up' methodology which sees identity as 'the set of verbal practices through which persons assemble and display who they are while in the presence of, and in interaction with, others' (Hadden and Lester, 1978: 331).

## Membership categorisation

This theoretical stance means that CA scholars closely analyse transcripts of conversation to search for categories of identity membership that are relevant to participants in the local context (e.g. Antaki and Widdicombe, 1998; Sacks, 1995). These categories are features that speakers and hearers 'orient to' in their interaction in working out who they are talking to and which help guide the course of interaction. Identities are therefore put to local work while speakers are engaged in other activities. Widdicombe (1998: 191) puts it this way:

> The important analytic question is not therefore whether someone can be described in a particular way, but to show *that* and *how* this identity is made relevant or ascribed to self or others. The analytic task is to delineate the descriptive devices, the properties of categories in talk, the technical skills of conversation which are employed in the service of mobilizing identities.

Such a position rejects the traditional view of identity as a descriptive label and attempts to treat it 'as a resource for the participants rather than the analyst'.

To 'have' an identity as a speaker, hearer or someone being spoken about is to be assigned membership of a category, and this category will have certain characteristics and certain consequences for the talk. The notion of *category* in the CA literature is very broad and can include 'family' or 'race' as well as 'cancer patient', 'cyclist' or 'failing student', but the point is that these categories help order otherwise disparate characteristics into an identity label that can be worked with for the purpose at hand. So once an identity-category has been made relevant, then we see people visibly reacting to it, or to its implications – accepting, resisting or modifying its meaning. Categorisation is thus a routine and necessary contribution to how we make sense of, and attribute predictability to, complex human interactions, and in this way it is similar to 'proximity' in that it offers a way of seeing how language represents people as group members.

As an example of what it means to categorise someone, consider this extract from Hester (1998: 145) of a teacher in a British school describing a difficult pupil to an educational psychologist:[i]

(1)

> MT: Errm (0.5) at the moment I've taken (along his classroom) down in the gym waiting for Jeremy to come down hhh but its reached such a stage with me that errm (.) you know that I find that the boy's completely uncooperative (1.0) now I've been teaching now for something like twenty five or thirty years (0.5) an never have I had to (0.5) to: call on the help of a year tutor or anybody else to assist me with a child but in this one I must admit that I just don't know what to do to handle him.

Here the teacher invokes a category, the 'experienced teacher', of which he claims membership. A feature of this category is generally being able to handle difficult pupils, but his expertise is insufficient in the case of this boy. Together with categorising the pupil as 'completely uncooperative', the contrast this categorisation sets up with the normal competence of the 'experienced teacher' marks the seriousness of the problem and presents an extreme case of deviance which needs special measures. Insider understandings are not available to these interactants, and the teacher is forced to draw on categorisations that are recognisably appropriate for the psychologist, using an 'extreme case formulation' (Pomerantz, 1986) to anticipate possible objections to his designation of deviance while supporting his identity construction as an 'experienced teacher'.

Analysis therefore involves searching for relevant membership categorisations and markers of 'category-bound' identity descriptors, such as 'teacher expertise' and 'pupil deviance'. In addition to content features of talk, however, analysts also tend to look at signals such as pauses, repetitions, descriptive adjectives and so forth, or the function of longer stretches of talk such as anecdotes (Holmes, 2006) and 'reported' dialogue (Mishler, 2006). The role of 'indexicality' and how pronouns, locatives and time expressions help speakers relate to the here-and-now production of an identity are also key aspects of analysis (e.g. Antaki and Widdicombe, 1998).

## Analysis and identity

The 'identities' called up by such indexical features tend to be interactional roles, such as questioner, answerer, hearer, etc. rather than social identities. In fact, the notion of identity is a very flexible term for many of these writers as it can also refer to the moment-by-moment 'discourse identities' assumed by participants in organising the sequential procession of talk (e.g. Goodwin, 1987; Zimmerman, 1998). Georgakopoulou (2006), for instance, believes that individuals' actions as participants in a discourse (initiating, following-up, questioning, etc.) are identities which can lay a platform for social identities (teacher–student, layperson–expert, etc.). While we might see participant roles are tied to adjacency pairs such as questioner–answerer, current speaker–listener, or to discourse activities such as repair-initiator, storyteller, etc., this implies that identities can change between, or even within, turns at talk, making problematic how we might recognise what identities are 'foundational' to the talk at hand.

CA brings a sensitivity to identity research by highlighting how it is negotiated in an unfolding interaction. The idea that identity categories must be *available for use*, however, is a demanding analytical stricture as we can be confident that a category is 'live' in the interaction only if something happens: when we can see the effects. The fact that the analyst is unable to bring wider institutional contexts into play as a tool for understanding disciplinary identities therefore makes it difficult to see how participants are able to invoke 'larger social identities' which 'reach beyond the participants' talk' (Greatbach and Dingwell, 1998: 130). CA thus has an uncomfortable time with political factors which impinge on the discourse to explain how actors may be orienting to physical or cultural symbols which originate outside the immediate context. These may be crucial to the intersubjective categorisation of identities, but they are unavailable to the Conversation Analyst.

Prevented from investigation of the wider context, however, analysis can reveal only the 'conversational' aspects of talk, not those that are constitutive of the institutional tasks and setting (Lynch, 1985). The undergraduate lecture, the doctoral supervision and the corridor conversation are all ways in which the social is incorporated into the self, but if context can only be determined from talk, then there is essentially no difference between conversation and institutional discourse (ten Have, 2007). So while the Conversational Analyst's methodological restraint seems commendable, the researcher cannot avoid trading on his or her cultural knowledge in recognising the activities that interactants are engaged in. Interpretations are unavoidable, in ordinary life as well as in the academic analysis of discourse.

## Institutional identities

These issues have generated considerable debate in CA regarding whether institutional (and thus disciplinary) identities are located in the setting or in the talk. Recognising that some interactions have an institutional purpose, many analysts have moved away from this strict 'pure CA' doctrine to suggest that *talk is shaped by context as well as shaping it* (Drew and Heritage, 1992). While remaining committed to a bottom-up approach to data and to the idea that institutions, and institutional identities, are recoverable from the sequential unfolding of interaction, this more 'applied' approach (ten Have, 2007) recognises that the analyst needs access to register features (patterns of talk in similar contexts) and the ways participants understand these in the local interaction. This position remains controversial, however, as some see it as incompatible with CA's ethnomethodological principles, undermining the view that institutional identities are emergent properties of talk (Hester and Francis, 2001).

Drew and Heritage's (1992) more 'applied' perspective does, however, offer greater opportunities to explore the ways that regular interactions between members of a given community or group will lay down and reinforce particular ways of communicating which make sense to insiders. Recent CA research into organisational environments has therefore begun to open up new understandings of how spoken interactional practices can help sustain social identities in this way (e.g. Heritage and Clayman, 2010). Patterns of turn-taking, the distribution of speaking rights and turn types, and category-bound obligations help show how institutions and identities are produced and oriented to by participants in the talk. However, without a systematic appreciation of the ways in which interactional choices relate texts to contexts, CA has been able to offer only a partial view of the processes of identity construction in professional settings. It is precisely these aspects of identity research which CDA tries to address.

## 3.2 Representing identities: Critical Discourse Analysis

Critical Discourse Analysts advocate a shift away from observation and deduction to consider the role of ideology in public discourses. This means that the relevant context for understanding the enactment of identities is expanded beyond the immediate site of interaction to wider social and institutional contexts.

In a student–lecturer supervision session, for example, the fact that one participant has greater knowledge, higher institutional status and an instructional role all contributes to and reflects a power dynamic which underpins how the interaction unfolds:

(2)

> Tutor: you need to catch these sentences that just, uh go off in random directions that that don't that don't show us the logic of what you're doing. and you should think of you should think of punctuation if you th- if you're thinking of punctuation at all you should think of it as a system, of of signs and pointers to your reader, that that allows that person to see your logic and to anticipate your logic. [...]
>
> Student: oh yeah I I understand. I um, my question is though I just wanna know like what what do you want me to do with it? do you want me to like redo it?

(MICASE: OFC300JU149)

The tutor's language choices, particularly his unhedged assertions and repeated use of the obligation modals *need* and *should* together with the student's rather hesitant and unassured request for guidance, help construct local identities. But these participants are orienting to and playing out identities which are endorsed and sanctioned by their understandings of institutionally defined inequalities. In seeking to understand these orientations and reconstruct how talk functions to create participant identities and so give meaning to interaction, we need to make connections to these wider constraints from text itself.

Much of the CDA literature reflects the theoretical position of Foucault (1972), introduced in Chapter 1. For Lin (2008), Skeggs (2004) and Wodak et al. (1999), for example, identities are often imposed on individuals and groups through dominant discourse practices and ideologies. Identity therefore tends to be seen as something *represented* in interaction rather than *negotiated*. So CDA reminds us that much of what we observe in interaction between people is not a matter of freedom or creativity but is constrained by normative practices shaped by the inequalities of the wider social context. The ways we can represent ourselves and be recognised as possessing a competent institutional identity are limited by the power structures which exist in any situation.

## Power and inequality

Critical Discourse Analysis accounts for identity by starting from the premise that individuals have differential access to particular communicative resources as a result of their education, class backgrounds, social position, ethnicity, gender or social experiences. It implies, then, that there is differential access to valued 'contextual spaces' (Blommaert, 2005) where specific conventional forms ratify the meanings associated with particular expert identities. In academic contexts, the limited repertoires of many students contribute to the fact that only a small proportion achieve distinctions, while most academics never publish a paper in a leading international journal. So the published articles and monographs which allow writers to claim expertise are regulated by disciplinary gatekeepers who monitor ways of making meanings and signalling disciplinary credibility.

There is a tension between agency and constraint in this approach, but it is important to point out that CDA underlines how attending only to what can be observed in the talk means ignoring the ways power operates to constrict and frame what goes on in any interaction (e.g. Fairclough, 2003). Language, in fact, is seen to construct social and political life and, at the same time, is constituted by it in a dialectical relationship. This is a domain of 'invisible contexts' which influence language choices long before it is produced (or not effectively produced) as situated utterances. Context, or at least selected aspects of the context, therefore becomes a crucial element of analysis for CDA. A central methodological challenge is to bridge the gap between language and context, to understand how discourse connects micro instances of identity construction with social and ideological macro structures without reducing one to the other.

## Analytical techniques

To do this, CDA operates with a more systematic model of language than CA. While analysts do not subscribe to any single method, leading figures such as Fairclough (1992, 2003) and Wodak (Wodak and Chilton, 2005) draw on Systemic Functional Linguistics (SFL). This is a useful model for CDA as it views language as a system of semiotic choices which *realise* elements of context such as power and social organisation.Young and Harrison (2004: 1) claim that SFL and CDA share three main features:

1   a view of language as a social construct, or how society fashions language

2  a dialectical view in which 'particular discursive events influence the contexts in which they occur and the contexts are, in turn, influenced by these discursive events'

3  a view which emphasises cultural and historical aspects of meaning.

But while SFL offers CDA a sophisticated means of analysing language and social contexts, Wodak (Wodak and Chilton, 2005) notes that a 'mixed bag' of linguistic theories has been used in CDA, and certainly not all analysts employ SFL or employ it consistently.

Aspects of the systemic model which CDA analysts have found useful, however, are:

- vocabulary – particularly how metaphor and connotative meanings encode ideologies and beliefs.
- transitivity – which can show who is presented as having agency and who is acted upon.
- nominalisation and passivisation – how processes and actors can be repackaged as nouns or agency otherwise obscured.
- mood and modality – choices between declarative, interrogative and imperative utterances can indicate discourse roles, while modality denotes speaker attitudes, commitments and obligations.
- theme – how the first element of a clause can be used to foreground particular aspects of information or presuppose reader beliefs.
- intertextuality and interdiscursivity – the effects of other texts and styles on texts – leading to *hybridisation*, such as where commercial discourses colonise those in other spheres.

Benwell and Stokoe (2006: 116) see identity in CDA as a *representation* in the ideational function of language (expressing ideas), a *position* constructed through interpersonal choices of mood and modality (expressing relationships) and through *alignments* with particular political and evaluative positions through the expressive dimension of language. Generalisation from situated occurrences of talk to wider sociopolitical issues, or accounting for how a stretch of discourse represents particular identities, is achieved in CDA by moving between theory and data. There is, however, always a tension in this work between seeing identity as something we are compelled to adopt through dominant discourses, and regarding it as a rhetorical construction accomplished through our discoursal choices.

## Problems with context

This haziness between compliance and choice in much CDA research is largely a result of an approach to context which often amounts to little more than employing a priori statements on power relations as perspectives on discourse. Context is rarely analysed in its own right and is usually taken for granted or defined impressionistically. It often forms a backdrop of self-evident categories used to interpret features of the language which are cherry-picked for analysis in the text (e.g. Widdowson, 1998).

In classic CDA studies such as Wodak's (1997) paper on doctor–patient interaction and Fairclough's (1995) study of undergraduate prospectuses, context is really the *analyst's* interpretations of events and not, as in CA, those of the *participants*. This privileging of the analyst's viewpoint is often reinforced by appeal to a level of social theory which sits above any analysis of the text itself. There is little dialogue with real readers, and interpretation becomes a black box rather than a product of analysis. As Blommaert (2005: 53) notes:

> In a lot of CDA work, context is often a mere background to rather orthodox (linguistic or interactional) discourse analysis, with some connections running between text and context, while both 'blocks' remain distinct units. Critique thus becomes too often and too much a matter of the credibility of the researcher, whose account of power in contextual narratives is offered not for *inspection* but for *belief.*

This creates a bias in which context is not discursively produced in features of interaction but something projected onto the discourse itself as a set of untheorised and unquestioned 'facts'.

CDA therefore privileges political and institutional contexts over immediate encounters in researching questions of identity, but the links between discourse and context are often tenuous. We cannot see context as a cluster of static variables that surround language use, however; we have to see it as socially constituted, interactively sustained and time bound (Duranti and Goodwin, 1992). The writer who types out a book review or research article is conscious of the purpose of the activity, the expectations and needs of readers, the conventions of the discipline in that genre, and something of the creative boundaries which are operating. He or she has a pragmatic view of context as a resource for accomplishing certain ends most effectively. This is how Van Dijk (2008: vi) understands the term:

> It is not the social situation that influences (or is influenced by) discourse, but the way the participants **define** such a situation. Contexts thus are not some kind of 'objective' condition or direct cause, but rather (inter)subjective constructs designed and ongoingly updated in interaction by participants as members of groups and communities. If they were, all people in the same social situation would speak in the same way. Contexts are participant constructs.

So while we might see power, status and institutional conventions as ever present in interaction, we are not dominated by them. Precisely how individuals define the contexts in which they find themselves, however, is never fully resolved in CDA.

# 3.3 Recounting identities: Narrative Analysis

A third discoursal approach to the study of identity sidesteps the issues of power and institutional constraints to see identity as socioculturally constructed in peoples' narratives. As Daiute and Lightfoot (2004: xi) suggest, 'narrative discourse organises life-social relations, interpretations of the past and plans for the future'. While analysts have used published autobiographies and naturally occurring stories, this data is largely gathered through interviews.

## Narrative and identity

The use of biographical interviews has become the preferred method of data collection for researchers in the social sciences interested in the connections between history and sociology and between structure and agency (e.g. Block, 2006; Wengraf, 2001). The idea is that identity can be explored through the stories we tell about ourselves, tapping into the accounts that individuals select, structure and relate at appropriate moments. The underlying emphasis is on reflexivity and the belief that storytelling is an active process of summation, where we re-present a particular aspect of our lives. Bruner (1997), for instance, observes that self-narratives help sustain a sense of stability and predictability for individuals and provide a frame for explaining disruption and change.

A leading proponent of this approach is Giddens (1991) who argues that self and reflexivity are interwoven so that identity is not the possession of particular character traits, but the ability to construct a reflexive narrative of the self. Identity comprises many narratives that the person constructs for himself or herself and others, which can vary with time and occasion, whereby individuals attempt to give meaning to their lives by constructing a socially recognisable self. In this extract from a 'life story' interview with the Nobel scientist Francis Crick, for instance, there is a (re)construction of the self through a critical moment in childhood:

(3)

> I think I was always interested in science as early as I can remember. I don't think it was due to my parents. My father was a businessman. He never went to the university. My mother had been a teacher but she really didn't know about science. Whereas I wanted to know what is the world made of. And because I asked so many questions they bought me something called Children's Encyclopedia. And that covered all subjects. It covered history and literatures and music as well as science. And it had articles about the nature of the galaxy and chemistry and how things were made of atoms and so on. And I absorbed this with great enthusiasm and I think I must have at that stage decided to be a scientist.

Autobiographical reconstruction allows actors to reconceptualise their actions as representing a coherently motivated picture of continuity and sameness without implying an unchanging essentialism.

## Analysing narratives

While most narrative work adopts a constructionist perspective, whereby stories are seen to be 'constitutive of reality', there are several different versions of narrative analysis, each corresponding to a different view of data and what it can be said to reveal. Analysts generally begin with interviews to collect data on how individuals explain and understand their lives; how they highlight some identities and marginalise others. Typically, they then look at the structure and progress of the narrative, the kinds of stories that are told, and the strategies used to make identity claims.

Riessman (2008) suggests three main ways of analysing narratives which she calls *thematic, structural* and *performative*. The first largely involves focusing on the content of what is said and trying to identify specific themes which might be linked to each other or related to a wider 'master narrative' or cultural story lines, of which it is part. Structural analyses, on the other hand, look at how the story is told and the ways it is developed and sequenced in particular ways. Many analysts focus on linguistic features such as the use of subject pronouns, hedging and lexical choices which can point to shifts of alignment and affiliation, or on the way the storyteller assembles a story through particular functional moves. A significant aspect of a performative analysis is a focus on the 'telling' of the story and how it relates to the 'told'. So here the interview is an interaction in its own right and researchers ask who an utterance is directed to, where it occurs and what its purpose is. Data may include different moments of interaction, such as between the speaker and other interactants and between the interviewee and the interviewer, or instances of uncertainty, confusion and contradiction.

The analyst therefore begins with the immediate context of the utterance and the features of interaction and works up through the social setting to wider social categories which relate to institutional and cultural meanings. An appealing feature of narratives is that they must always be considered in terms of an audience, for an individual's inner thoughts and outward expressions are addressed to others and are the product of a relationship between a speaker and listener, a writer and reader. Narratives are often combined with positioning theory to explore the processes by which narrators adopt, resist and occupy subject positions, such as passive or active, powerful or powerless, etc. that are made available in discourses or by master narratives. This explores how individuals interpret 'who they are' by adopting subject positions set up for us as a consequence of our social class, ethnicity, gender and so on and which we shape with our own interpretations and experiences. Like CDA, however, the analyst has to access wider cultural influences to make sense of what is being said.

## The limitations of narrative analysis

Narrative theorists argue that by analysing the stories people tell about themselves, we can understand how they make their lives coherent and meaningful, so making identity salient and available for analysis. The purposes of interviews is to engage people in conversations about their experiences as members of particular social groups or categories. Often they involve some kind of dislocation in their lives, such as coping with breast cancer (Murray, 2003) or becoming teenage fathers (Wortham and Gadsden, 2006). In more commonplace circumstances, Block (2006) conducted life-story interviews with members of different language groups who had migrated to London, exploring the subject positions they adopted in their everyday social interactions. What is important is that the interviewee self-presents, or gives meaning to the world and organises his or her experiences in it.

Clearly this approach is profoundly social and emphasises the subject's continual interpretation and reinterpretation of experience through a cultural lens. Stories produce particular versions of identity framed by social context to represent a gloss on events which reconstructs the past to resonate with a current conception of one's self. But narrative can only ever be a partial representation of who we are. It is a one-sided self-construction which underplays the fact that our interpretations must accord with, and be validated in, the narratives of others and with the facts of actual events: we cannot claim to be whatever and whoever we want. Indeed, when a gap is seen to exist between semblance and substance, or doing and being, then a person is likely to be accused of pretension or fraud. This is a deception which leaves us feeling cheated and is epitomised in the press by the imposter, the conman and the 'evil' neighbour with bodies under the floorboards (e.g. Lawler, 2008).

More directly, we might question the extent to which research interviews relate to notions of identity theorised as a situated practice. The teller socially displays a language that presents a sense of self which is socially recognisable and socially validated. But these narratives are a self-conscious and reflective assembling of experience for the purpose of constructing an identity, usually for a complete stranger from the local university. They have few consequences for the subject and are produced in a relatively formal and contrived context. But most of the time we are not performing identity work by narrating stories of ourselves into a researcher's digital recorder, but claiming identities while engaged in doing something else. If identity is really a *performance* and not an *interpretive recounting*, then we need to find ways of capturing what people routinely do with language that is similar or different from what others do with it. This is what corpus studies bring to the table.

## 3.4 Performing identities: Corpora and convention

CA, CDA and autobiographical approaches all contribute to our understanding of identity in important ways and each raises key issues about the discoursal study of identity. Corpora offer an important missing ingredient to the empirical study of identity, and particularly to how individuals represent themselves as academics. The way actors understand both the here-and-now interaction (the context of situation) and the broader constraints of the wider community which influence that interaction (the context of culture) is crucial to comprehending both disciplines and identities. By offering evidence of actors' orientations to scholarly communities and the ways they stake out individual positions, corpora are able to show how disciplinary identities are performed and recognised as legitimate.

## Identity and corpus evidence

CDA emphasises that identity is a significant aspect of the relationship between individuals and institutions, and corpus approaches reveal how it is publicly accomplished through community-approved discourses. In Chapter 2, I argued that disciplines are not merely sociological abstractions, but the product of collective practices created through identifications of similarity and difference. This is because we don't just say what we mean and get it over with but take care to design a text for particular recipients, for people like us, so that as far as possible, it meets the rhetorical expectations, processing abilities and information needs of our social groups. Whenever we speak, we do so from within a specific 'regime of language' (Kroskrity, 2000), and this is often not a matter of conscious individual awareness, but of routine and habit, accumulated, acquired and changed through myriad repeated interactions. This is what Bourdieu referred to as 'habitus' and Foucault as our 'archive': the partially visible discursive systems which we take for granted and operate within.

Texts, essentially, are about *solidarity*, about pulling communities together in a collective endeavour of meaning-making. Even when disputing, disagreeing or participating in the bitterest academic catfights, arguments are conducted within boundaries which make sense to disputants and onlookers alike. Identity thus involves proximity: it depends on *identification with* something, and this group identification is most clearly understood through a study of the 'cultural repertoires' (Somers, 1994) or symbolic systems one's discipline makes available to talk about the world and engage with peers. So while we all have different experiences of the world and of language, the cumulative effect of our encounters with particular words, collocations and meanings in our communities contributes to our expectations about how words will be used and what they mean. Individual identities are created out of these collective identifications, and it is in the commonplace and routine texts of the academy, in its everyday, mundane repetitions of preferred ways of saying things, that we should look for them.

In other words, disciplinary discourses are evidence of mutual recognition and preferred patterns of alignment, and we can recover something of these alignments and preferences through the study of collections of texts. Corpora are important here as they represent a speaker's experience of language in a restricted domain and so provide evidence of typical choices in that domain. This is a method which highlights representativeness rather than the uniqueness of texts. It approaches texts as a package of linguistic features employed by specific groups of users to reveal interaction as a collection of rhetorical choices rather than as specific acts of writing (e.g. Biber, 2006; Hyland, 2004a).

The significance of corpora in academic identity research is that they can reveal the impact of discipline on writing and speech and the cross-cutting effects of potential identity characteristics such as seniority or gender. They can also show how specific individuals construct an identity through consistent language choices and rhetorical preferences. Corpus analysis therefore looks past the claims made about identity in interviews or the decisions made by individuals on particular occasions of writing. Instead, it explores the regularity and repetition of what is socially ratified and independently variant and in so doing offers insights into the preferred practices of both individuals and collectivities.

## Bringing corpora to identity studies

While slow to inform identity research, corpora have been used in related areas which attempt to say something about writers on the basis of their linguistic choices. In stylistics, for instance, they have helped reveal what is distinctive about a particular author's work (e.g. Mahlberg, 2007; Stubbs, 2005). In authorship studies analysts have distinguished the plays of Shakespeare, for example, from those of Marlowe, Oxford and other Elizabethan pretenders by identifying their repeated use of language features (Elliott and Valenza, 1991). Methods such as Principal Components Analysis (PCA) have helped determine the likelihood of a particular author having written a piece of work by examining other works produced by that author, identifying sets of features that remain relatively constant over a corpus of texts.

Authorship attribution also has a forensic aspect and has been accepted in British courtrooms by helping to settle legal cases of disputed authorship (e.g. Olsson, 2004). Winter and Woolls (1996), for example, employed average sentence length and lexical richness as markers discriminating the work of two authors. Corpora have also been used to profile writers according to sets of sociolinguistic attributes such as gender (Koppel et al., 2002), language background (De Vel et al., 2002) and education level (Juola and Baayen, 2005). Generally, this work recognises the plausibility of identifying a 'stylistic profile' or 'linguistic fingerprint' (Hanlein, 1999) from the consistent patterns of choices authors make, so that if choice is constant, then it is seen as an individual style marker.

While only indirectly related to identity research, these approaches nevertheless point to the value of corpora as a basis for comparison between an author and his or her peers, or how writing in one discipline differs from that in another. Even simple frequency comparisons, for example, have shown that features such as questions, hedges, imperatives and self-citation differ markedly across disciplines (Biber, 2006; Hyland, 1998a, 2002a, 2002b). So by 'dematerialising texts' away from actual concrete instances, a corpus approach provides linguistic evidence of consistent rhetorical choices. Mapping typicality, it shows what is usual and what is deviant in collections of texts and so helps to reveal both underlying discourses and individual preferences. It brings to identity research evidence of how individuals, repeatedly and routinely, position themselves in relation to their readers so that in constructing knowledge and relationships, they also construct themselves.

In sum, the analyst works from the assumption that texts tell us something about how *writers understand readers*, and how they carry traces of underlying discourses. Interrogating corpora can make transparent the connections between the particular communities and the local interactions in which members are participating. It can show us how individuals collectively and repeatedly assemble markers of 'who they are' through interaction. In this way we can take seriously the idea that identity is *performed* through discourse. In the next section, I put some flesh on these bones by outlining some of the corpus techniques I employ in researching identity in the remainder of this book.

## 3.5   Identity and corpus analysis

As I have argued, a central question in identity studies is: how do we achieve identity, under what circumstances and in what contexts? These constraints and contexts matter, and we need to see the local performance and negotiation of identity as part of wider systems of discourse. The value of a corpus approach is, then, that it helps reveal these constraints and contexts in the repeated patterns of everyday language use. In this section I will consider how corpus linguistics can be used in the study of academic identity.

### Disciplinary data: Texts and transcripts

The textual data for the studies reported in this book are selected from the domain of academic communication: the ways of using language in the academy. The analyses in the following chapters are based on some 1,400 texts from eight genres in disciplines covering a broad cross-section of academic practice from the hard sciences and engineering to the social sciences and humanities. Table 3.1 gives an overview of the texts and features examined in these studies.

This is a range of genres which enact complex social activities like educating students, demonstrating learning, disseminating ideas, evaluating research and constructing knowledge. Research articles, textbooks, dissertations, theses, essays, book reviews and reports are among the most visible written examples and the very stuff of education and knowledge creation. The domain, however, also includes activities leading to publications, promotions, prizes and positions and so embraces more peripheral or 'occluded' genres (Swales, 1996), such as peer review correspondence, promotion recommendations, applications, acknowledgements and posts on specialist bulletin boards. Together these are genres which simultaneously construct academics and students and which sustain the universities, the disciplines and the creation of knowledge itself. Through them, individuals understand issues, build careers and engage with others in ways specific to particular groups, and in doing so they form social realities, professional institutions and personal identities.

By allowing us to abstract away from any specific writer to examine recurring features in a large number of texts, corpora allow us to see that repeated patterns of language are not personal and idiosyncratic, but widely shared in a community (Stubbs, 2001: 215). Individual examples help to concretise general patterns, and there are many of these in the chapters that follow, although all names have been slightly altered to disguise authorship where necessary. Despite the advantages of having large numbers of words to work with, however, corpora are simply collections of texts and do not, by themselves, provide facts. Corpus evidence informs interpretations, but these can be strengthened by triangulation, using multiple methods or sources of data. My own preference is to interview subject specialists concerning their communication practices in order to recover how individuals understand writing as socially situated practice. In some of the chapters, I therefore report the use of one-to-one semi-structured and discourse-based interviews (Chapter 5) and focus groups (Chapter 6).

Academics generally need little encouragement to talk about their work and are happy to comment on texts and their impressions of disciplinary practices. Students are often more difficult to coax, typically requiring the scaffolding and support of focus groups to encourage participation. Both focus groups and interviews are more productive, moreover, with detailed examinations of text extracts, using what Odell et al. (1983) call a 'discourse-based interview'. This requires participants to respond to features in selected texts as either writers or members of the community for whom the texts were composed. The method seeks to make explicit the tacit knowledge that writers and readers bring to acts of composing, allowing them to interpret meanings, reconstruct writer motivations and evaluate rhetorical effectiveness. These discourse-based sessions then move to a semi-structured, open-ended format to explore participants' social and ideological perspectives of their disciplines and how they see themselves as writers.

**Table 3.1  Texts studied in the book**

| Chapter | Genre | Number of texts | Disciplines | Features examined |
|---|---|---|---|---|
| 4 | Student acknow-ledgements | 240 | Applied linguistics<br>Biology<br>Business studies<br>Computer science<br>Electronic engineering<br>Public administration | Move structure |
| | Prize applications | 70 | Education | Move structure<br>Evaluative lexis |
| | Homepages | 100 | Philosophy<br>Physics | Images, design, hyperlinks<br>Content |
| 5 | Research article bios | 600 | Applied linguistics<br>Electrical engineering<br>Philosophy | Move structure<br>Process types |
| 6 | Undergraduate reports<br>Research articles | 64<br>240 | Biology<br>Economics<br>Information systems<br>Mechanical engineering<br>Public administration<br>TESOL<br>Business studies<br>Social sciences | Self-mention |

*(to be continued)*

| Chapter | Genre | Number of texts | Disciplines | Features examined |
|---|---|---|---|---|
| 7 | Books | 3 | Applied linguistics | Topic keywords |
| | Research articles | 35 | Applied linguistics | Verb *to be*, dispute terms, *if*-clauses, self-mention, hedging and attitude engagement |
| 8 | Book reviews | 56 | Biology Philosophy | Metadiscourse |

In keeping with normal ethical considerations, such as the Social Research Association's Ethical Guidelines (2003) (https://the-sra.org.uk/), both the interview data and the corpora have been anonymised. This means that the names of all the people quoted and any person names appearing in the interviews or the text corpora have been changed. Names of places, however, have been retained in their original form. There are two main exceptions to this process of anonymisation. The websites quoted in Chapter 4 are ascribed, with permission, to their actual subjects. The two linguists whose discourse is discussed in detail in Chapter 7 are, for obvious reasons, identified by their real names.

## Assumptions and features of analysis

There are various ways of conducting corpus research, but Tognini-Bonelli (2001) makes a distinction between *corpus-based* and *corpus-driven* studies. The former use a corpus as a source of examples to check the researcher's intuitions; the latter are more inductive: the corpus is the data and the basis for any discovery of patterns of use. The studies in this book are a mixture of the two, each informing the other. In most cases I have started by focusing on potentially productive items based on my reading of the literature, from interviews with writers, or from my previous research in the area. On other occasions, as in Chapter 7, for example, I have delegated the task of identifying features to the computer, generating lists of high-frequency lexical items and keywords for further study. Items identified from either of these starting points then provide the basis for further study through collocation, cluster analysis and demographic comparisons to see how particular academics and disciplinary communities used these features in the expression of social identities.

It is worth emphasising here that analysis always involves some focus of attention and selectivity. The two constructs of *proximity* (essentially the rhetorically constructed relationship between the self and community) and *positioning* (the rhetorically structured relationship between a speaker and what is being said) point to the importance of the interpersonal function of language in realising identity. In Halliday's (1994) systemic functional model, this aspect of language, in contrast to the ideational mode which organises our reasoning and experiencing of the world, refers to the ways we use language to acknowledge, construct and negotiate social relations. It embodies the idea that disciplinary texts are sites where academics do not just offer a view of the world but negotiate a credible account of themselves and their work by claiming an affinity with readers.

Interpersonality, then, concerns the ways that writers use language to negotiate the self and relationships with others by telling their readers what they see as important, how they believe they should select and present material for them, and how they feel about what they write about. While others may adopt a different position on identity and search for other features of language which seem promising, this is what informs my understanding of the concept. Identity is most profitably explored through interpersonal features as a way into the interactions which express and sustain it.

Interpersonal aspects of a text therefore relate it to a given context and convey the writer's personality, credibility, audience-sensitivity and relationship to the message (Hyland, 2004a). While not synonymous with identity, these features perhaps provide the most immediate access to its rhetorical construction because they focus on what individuals do to project themselves within a shared professional context. They reveal most clearly how writers, in pursuing their personal and professional goals, embed their writing in a particular discipline through approved discourses. Both systemic functional and social constructionist frameworks have sought to elaborate the ways by which interpersonal meanings are expressed, describing resources such as *evaluation* (Hunston and Thompson, 2001), *appraisal* (Martin, 2001; Martin and White, 2005), *stance* (Biber and Finegan, 1989; Hyland, 2005a, 2005b) and *metadiscourse* (Hyland, 2005a, 2005b). Features which link text participants as *interactants* therefore allow writers to adopt a persona and a tenor which is consistent with the norms of the field, and so offer a starting point for identity research. They indicate some of the ways that texts carry traces of wider participation frameworks and inform the corpus-based studies in these pages.

## Analysis and frequency

While the items listed above were generated prior to the study of the corpora in this book, their productivity for identity research is often a result of their high frequency in academic texts. Whether adopting a corpus-based or corpus-driven approach, frequency is a good starting point for studying identity as it provides evidence of non-randomness. It can tell us what regularities, and exceptions, exist in the language use of a group of people when engaged in a particular activity. High-frequency items, in other words, represent repeated, taken-for-granted choices in academic writing. User-choice is central here as of all the different ways of saying roughly the same thing, members of individual disciplines select the same items again and again. In-group abbreviations, acronyms, argots, special terms, shorthand names for methods and theories, preferred argument patterns, repeated collocations, predilections for author visibility or anonymity and so on all help define and identify disciplines, and these can be recovered by using a corpus.

Frequency can therefore lead us to what is worth discussing as it often indicates what is *salient* for groups of language users. While statistics are helpful from a hypothesis-testing perspective (e.g. Hunston, 2002), writers and readers do not employ tests to make sure they are observing or deviating from conventions, but simply work with what they are familiar with from repeated experience. Hoey (2005), for instance, argues that words are mentally 'primed' for use with other words through users' frequent experience of them in particular contexts. Everything we know about a word is a result of our encounters with it, so that when we formulate what we want to say, our wordings are shaped by the way we regularly encounter them in similar texts. This helps to explain why it is, for example, that of all the different ways of expressing thanks, over a third of all gratitude in PhD acknowledgements is expressed as nominals (*My sincere thanks to*; *My gratitude to*) (Hyland and Tse, 2004b). Frequency also offers insights into non-standard use and so points to examples of individual positioning. It is possible to see, for instance, how Deborah Cameron is able to present an assertive and clear stance in her writing through a relative absence of modals and an exceptionally high frequency of *to be* (Chapter 7).

In addition to individual words, the frequency of specific *lexical bundles* (or commonly occurring word sequences) in particular fields helps reveal the diversity of disciplinary conventions and how writers signal proximity in performing academic identities. Such bundles (Biber et al., 1999) are familiar to writers and readers who regularly participate in a particular discourse so that their very 'naturalness' signals competent engagement in a given community. Thus, the presence of extended collocations like *as a result of*, *it should be noted that* and *as can be seen* helps identify a text as being written in an academic register, while *with regard to, in pursuance of* and *in accordance with* are likely to mark out a legal text. Despite this register similarity, however, studies point to considerable variation of bundles in different academic genres (e.g. Biber, 2006) and disciplines (Hyland, 2008).

Thus, over half the items in the top 50 most frequent four-word bundles in any discipline do not occur at all in the top 50 of any other (Hyland, 2008). Interestingly, writers in the science and engineering fields use significantly more bundles which refer to the research itself, a feature which helps to convey a greater real-world, laboratory-focused sense to writing in the hard sciences. Most of these are used to show the ways that experiments and research are conducted:

(4)

The DNA was precipitated *in the presence of* 2.5 volumes of ethanol and 0.1 volume of 3.0 M sodium acetate pH.

(Bio)

Transmission phase angle modulation *can be used to* increase the stability of the system, by maintaining the angle at a low value.

(EE)

All of the precipitate *was added to the* cells in a 100 mm culture plate or 300 mm of the precipitate to a 60 mm culture plate.

(Bio)

In contrast, bundles in social science disciplines, such as applied linguistics and business studies, are dominated by text-oriented strings, which reflect the more discursive and evaluative patterns of argument in the soft knowledge fields. Here, persuasion is more explicitly interpretive, and so many bundles frame arguments by highlighting connections, specifying cases and pointing to limitations:

(5)

The term 'linguistics' might be too narrow *in terms of the* diverse knowledge-base and expertise that is required in the applied linguist's job.

(AL)

However, *in the case of* Kodak's KIOO, which is an intricate piece of film, words are kept minimum to keep the viewer's attention.

(BS)

The levels are connected *in the sense that* it is impossible to appreciate the functioning at any one level without taking account of the other levels.

(AL)

Choices such as these, repeated for a range of features, comprise the repertoires of individuals which both constrain this performance and, at the same time, make it possible. Frequency counts, then, are useful, but their main value is in directing the identity analyst's attention to aspects of use which reveal consistent linguistic choices.

## Analysis and concordances

Frequency lists tell us something about the *focus* of a collection of texts, how they represent a particular disciplinary context for identity construction, but they do not tell us how words are actually used within that discourse. Concordance analyses provide information about users' preferred meanings and *positioning* by displaying repeated co-occurrence of words. This method prioritises lexis as the basis for analysis by bringing together all instances of a search word or phrase in its local co-text, revealing regularities in its use that might otherwise be missed. By reading along the lines, we see examples of actual use, and reading down through the examples gives insights into systematic patterning, revealing repeated associations. This patterning provides insights into both word meaning and how communities or individuals use words. As Stubbs (1996: 172) points out, 'words occur in characteristic collocations, which show the associations and connections they have and therefore the assumptions they embody'. In other words, collocations show how words and expressions take on specific meanings for particular individuals and in given communities.

We can see something of this in the ways that the first person is used by novice and expert writers. In a corpus of research articles, for example, half the occurrences of *I* collocated with the presentation of arguments or claims, while this was the least frequent use in undergraduate reports, where writers were reluctant to make such strong personal commitments and instead mainly used *I* to state a purpose (Chapter 6). Similarly, collocation allows us to see differences in the ways that senior academics and graduate students refer to themselves in the bios accompanying research articles (Chapter 5). So, by checking the frequency of definite, indefinite and 'zero' articles in a corpus of bios and then looking at concordance lines for each, we find that professors are far more likely to use naming terms that collocate with definiteness (*she is professor of, he is the author of*) and which serve to uniquely identify them. In the bios of students and non-professorial faculty, on the other hand, such attributive choices signal class membership rather than a unique identity (*she is a PhD student, he is an editor of*).

We also, of course, see differences in disciplinary preferences. By comparing the collocates of the most frequent hedges in different disciplines, we can see how language choices signal identity through both disciplinary competence in argument and epistemological beliefs about the role of the researcher. Scientists, for example, often believe that research findings emerge from the controlled and direct observation of natural phenomena, so part of what it means to be a scientist is to downplay one's interpretive role to suggest that results would be the same whoever conducted the research. Scientists are looking for replicable generalisations rather than individual contributions, and this is achieved by reporting results as facts and disguising the interpretive activities of the researcher.

Thus, frequency counts show that in a corpus of 240 articles, hedges are more than twice as frequent in philosophy, marketing and linguistics as in physics and engineering. Concordance analyses further show that research claims more often collocate with modal hedges (*it could be interpreted that, it may be argued that*) which downplay the role of the author. In the social sciences, on the other hand, the explicit interpretations of the writer are a source of the credibility of the argument, and so claims are more personally softened using epistemic verbs which more easily combine with personal subjects (*I think that, we suspect that*).

Perhaps more obviously, we can see how collocation can be used to understand identity by studying how disciplinary membership implies preferred meanings of the same words. Thus, *process* and *analyse* almost always occur in disciplinary-specific compounds (such as *constant volume combustion process* or *neutron activation analysis*) to create new conceptual objects, while there are overwhelming disciplinary variations in the preferred uses of common words such as *volume, consist, credit, abstract* and *offset* (Hyland and Tse, 2007). The display of an insider identity crucially depends on the ability to use words appropriately in this way, signalling familiarity with a discipline's conceptual as well as semantic practices. In sum, these preferred word choices, collocates and fixed phrases colour everyday uses of words with more particular discipline-specific meanings, reflecting how writers represent themselves and their ideas through a locally appropriate framework.

## Analysis and keyness

A final analytical method used in the approach to identity what I am proposing in this book is *keyness*. The basic idea is that a word form or cluster of words which is common in a given text is *key* to it, it is what the text is 'about' or 'what it boils down to … once we have steamed off the verbiage, the adornment, the blah blah blah' (Scott and Tribble, 2006). The text analysis program *WordSmith Tools* (Scott, 2007) identifies keyness by comparing frequencies in one corpus against those in another to determine which ones occur *statistically* more frequently using a log-likelihood calculation. This gives a better characterisation of the differences between two corpora than simple frequency comparison as it identifies items which are most prominent and not just common. Identifying keywords thus requires a suitable 'reference corpus' against which a comparison is made. The program carries out a statistical test on each word and reports whether the strength of a word's presence in one corpus results from chance alone or is due to authorial or disciplinary choices.

The program throws up three main kinds of words (Scott, 2007). First of all, proper nouns which are unusual and infrequent, such as the name of the city where students have conducted a survey in a set of essays. Then there are the open-class lexical words which characterise a text, so that a comparison of applied linguistics books on undergraduate reading lists with a wider sample of university coursebooks, for instance, shows *language, speech, interaction and communication* to be far more frequent (Hyland, 2006). Finally, keyword lists contain high-frequency grammar words which indicate the style of the texts in the corpus. So, at a broad level, we find the keywords which distinguish spoken from written English in the British National Corpus are almost all grammar words, with *you, I, its, that's, that, it, got* and *what* occurring significantly more often (Scott and Tribble, 2006).

Keywords are therefore useful for investigating a specialised corpus as they provide a way of identifying which words best distinguish the texts of a particular author or group of authors from another. Comparing different disciplines, for example, Scott and Tribble (2006) found the most frequent keywords in humanities to be *of, the, in, early, war, theory, as, century* and *between*; in medicine to be *clinical, patients, treatment, disease, of, study* and *diagnosis*; and in the natural sciences to be *are, Fig, shown, observe, sequence, obtained, surface* and *analysis*. The lists begin to suggest features of the domains in terms of what they are about and their style of argument. Keyness therefore reveals a kind of interdiscursive similarity and helps build a picture of particular disciplines and how they are distinctive from each other. It therefore offers ways of characterising individual writers who are members of those disciplines and provides a starting point for *corpus-driven* investigations of academic corpora by generating list of items which can be further explored in more detail using concordance analyses.

## 3.6    Conclusions: Identity and methods

Different ideas about identity correspond to different perspectives on language and interaction, different understandings of the relationship between self and society, and different views of the nature of research itself. So, if we see identity as negotiated in the moment-by-moment unfolding of interaction, then we will closely analyse transcripts for its traces in talk; if we see it as the imposition or appropriation of authoritative discourses and unequal power relations, then we will look for its working in the sociopolitical contexts of interaction; and if we see it as the individual's sense of autobiographic continuity, then we might search for it in the reconstruction of experience in personal narratives.

I have argued that identity can be seen as an individual's constructed display of group membership: the ways people make discourse choices to express their similarity and differences to others. To see identity in this way means that corpora become central to understanding the ways individuals construct themselves and their groups through language. By providing evidence for repeated patterns of language, they suggest disciplinary preferences for particular ontological positions and ideological standpoints, encoding different points of view, argument styles, attitudes to knowledge, and relationships between individuals and between individuals and ideas. Simple corpus linguistic procedures such as frequency counts, concordances and keyword analyses can reveal sanctioned community practices and therefore the intersubjectivity of group practices. What constitutes appropriate argument involves a community-sensitive deployment of linguistic resources to represent a coherent view of not only the world, but also writers and their readers. The patterns that corpus studies highlight suggest the rhetorical conventions which are the shared templates of professional life.

The features of academic texts, both their repetition and variation, can only be fully explained when considered as the actions of socially situated writers. While individual factors no doubt contribute to the choices made by particular writers in the moment-by-moment creation of a research paper or term assignment, meanings are ultimately produced in the interaction between writers and readers in specific circumstances. What we see on the page as an author's decision to urge acceptance, solicit solidarity or counsel caution, or as an option to step back and encourage cold judgement and an objective consideration of facts, reflects clear interactional and institutional understandings. The ways writers choose to express their arguments tell us something of how they see their readers and themselves; how they participate in the disciplinary contexts which are the sites of identification. In the remaining chapters of this book, I illustrate something of these ideas through a series of studies focusing on different genres and writers.

## Notes

i  Like most CA transcripts, the conventions here follow Jefferson (2004): (.) = micropause; (0.5) exactly timed pause; (words) = analyst's guess of unclear talk; : = elongated sound.

# 4 Identity in Representational Genres

Up until now I have been discussing disciplinary identity in fairly broad terms, raising issues of conceptualisation and methodology while introducing some key concepts. In particular, I have argued that we take a *position* as a particular kind of person only in *proximity* to a community. How we choose to express ourselves must resonate with group members so that our claims to membership are visible in the repeated patterns of language choices and acknowledged by insiders. While all identities are a negotiation of a self which is coherent and meaningful both to oneself and to others, disciplinary identity seems particularly dependent on this kind of acceptance. It crucially involves the *identification* with some community of others, taking on and shaping its discourses, behaviours, values and practices to construct a self both distinctive from and similar to those of its members. Identity, then, is a two-way street in that our identities are successful only to the extent that they are recognised by others.

In this chapter I want to begin to explore this relationship between the self and others more specifically by looking at particular communicative contexts – what I am calling 'representational genres'. Clearly all genres are 'representational' in the sense that they express a performance of the actor in some way, but this is usually while he or she is doing something else, such as reviewing a book or speaking at a conference. 'Representational genres' are atypical in that they involve the direct assertion of identity claims and have the self-conscious expression of self as their primary purpose. Here academics are required to project themselves explicitly as competent individuals, using valued language forms and attributes.

Thesis acknowledgements, prize applications and academic webpages all offer a particularly clear and obvious illustration of the role of language in disciplinary identity construction, but they also relate to identity in very different ways. Acknowledgements and applications are concerned with self-aggrandisement, either explicitly or implicitly, and a graduate's claim to a self with the attributes, understandings, experiences and values of a disciplinary member. Academic websites, in contrast, also explicitly present a version of the self, but this is often assembled by institutional functionaries to contribute to the branding and prestige of the employing university. In these representational genres, then, we begin to find something of how disciplinary identity claims are structured and communicated in the power-saturated contexts of academic institutional practices.

# 4.1　Academic acknowledgements in theses

I want to begin with a relatively unsung and disregarded genre, and one which initially might seem to have little to do with identity: academic acknowledgements in theses. This example is brief, but fairly typical:

(1)

> Many people have helped me with this dissertation. First of all, I am very grateful for the supervision of Professor Watkins. Without his valuable guidance and great patience I would not have completed my dissertation. Secondly, I am thankful to the staff of the Run Run Shaw Library for their considerable help. Finally, I am indebted to my elder brother and sister-in-law, for their unfailing encouragement during my study.

Such acknowledgements are commonplace in a range of academic genres and are part of the background interactions that oil the wheels of scholarly communication. They are particularly central to students as they not only offer an opportunity to give credit to institutions and individuals who have contributed to their thesis in some way, but are also a means of establishing a claim to a scholarly identity. So while acknowledgements can act as a means of recognising debts and achieving a sense of closure at the end of a long and demanding research process, they also make a favourable impression on readers by revealing the writer as someone with disciplinary contacts and credentials.

## Acknowledgements and self-representation

Acknowledgements are common in published articles, particularly in the sciences where their high frequency reflects the engagement of scientists in highly developed webs of mutual pre-print circulation, materials exchange and financial dependency (Cronin, et al., 1993). But they are more than a simple catalogue of scholarly interdependence, and the expression of thanks to others is not entirely altruistic. Ben-Ari (1987), for example, comments on the strategic role of acknowledgements in 'careering', and the potential of the genre for flattery and self-promotion has attracted criticism for the 'twin vices of fawning and vanity' (*The Economist*, 1996). Overall, however, acknowledgements are 'formal records of often significant intellectual influence' (Cronin and Overfelt, 1994: 183) which point to strong networks of association between researchers. In so doing, they represent a rhetorical construction of the self through scholarly connections and achievements.

The opportunities acknowledgements offer for constructing a professional identity are not lost on graduate students. A corpus of 240 student acknowledgements accompanying 20 master's dissertations and 20 doctoral theses from each of six disciplines shows that authors sought to manage their relations to the discipline, affiliations to particular figures and orientations to an academic self. The texts were written by students from five universities in Hong Kong of China, totalling 35,000 words and anonymised for publication. The length of texts ranged enormously between 38 and 1,085 words, with an average of 160 words. Table 4.1 shows the importance of acknowledgements to PhD students in particular, with virtually all theses containing one.

**Table 4.1 Acknowledgement corpus (20 dissertations in each discipline)**

| Discipline | Master's | | | Doctoral | | |
|---|---|---|---|---|---|---|
| | Texts | Words | Average | Texts | Words | Average |
| Applied linguistics | 18 | 2,402 | 133.4 | 20 | 7,718 | 385.9 |
| Biology | 15 | 1,825 | 121.7 | 19 | 3,864 | 203.4 |
| Business studies | 6 | 810 | 135.0 | 19 | 2,512 | 132.2 |
| Computer science | 18 | 1,483 | 82.4 | 20 | 3,470 | 173.5 |
| Electronic engineering | 20 | 1,427 | 71.4 | 19 | 2,771 | 145.8 |
| Public administration | 19 | 3,289 | 173.1 | 20 | 3,594 | 179.7 |
| Totals | 96 | 11,236 | 117.0 | 117 | 23,929 | 204.5 |

I coded the texts according to what thanks was allocated for, developing categories inductively through recursive passes through the texts and entering them into *WinMax Pro* for cross-referencing. A sample of texts was coded independently by a second rater for inter-coder reliability, with 96% agreement. The text data were supplemented by interviews with two MA students and two PhD students from each discipline to get an understanding of what the genre meant to the students and their thoughts on disciplinary practices (Hyland, 2003, 2004c).

The analysis revealed a three-move structure consisting of a main 'thanking' move sandwiched between optional 'reflecting' and 'announcing' moves. The structure followed the sequence given in Table 4.2.

**Table 4.2  Move structure of dissertation acknowledgements**

| | |
|---|---|
| **1 Reflecting move** | Introspective comment on the writer's research experience |
| **2 Thanking move** | Mapping credit to individuals and institutions |
| 1 Presenting participants | Introducing those to be thanked |
| 2 Thanking for academic assistance | Thanks for intellectual support, ideas, analyses feedback, etc. |
| 3 Thanking for resources | Thanks for data access and clerical, technical and financial support |
| 4 Thanking for moral support | Thanks for encouragement, friendship, sympathy, patience, etc. |
| **3 Announcing move** | Public statement of responsibility and inspiration |
| 1 Accepting responsibility | An assertion of authorial responsibility for flaws or errors |
| 2 Dedicating the thesis | A formal dedication of the thesis to an individual/individuals |

Just 12 texts contained all three moves. Only the thanking move was obligatory, comprising 90% of all the acts in the corpus, and most writers omitted an announcing move.

## Identity as personal connection

As Jenkins (2008: 71) points out, the elaboration of self-identification draws upon 'a wide palette of accessories in the human world', suggesting that who we express a connection to says something to others about us. The study showed that supervisors were mentioned in every acknowledgement, revealing the intellectual, and often emotional, obligation writers feel towards them:

(2)

> Thank you very much, Prof. Fu, for sharing with me your wisdom and experiences in science and daily life. It certainly benefits me in the rest of my life. You are my teacher, my friend, my example and my idol.
>
> (Bio PhD)

The thanks offered to supervisors often extended to other academics, some only peripheral to the research, indicating associations which not only acknowledge help, but establish a public connection and perhaps anticipate a relationship which the student might call upon in the future:

(3)

> I also wish to thank all the academic staff of Department of Biology and Chemistry, City University, for their on-going advice and support during the course of my PhD study over the last two and a half years.
>
> (Bio PhD)

> My special thank goes to Prof James Morse for sending me his valuable papers and to Dr. R. Dorning for her kindness and patience in answering questions about her excellent research by email.
>
> (PA PhD)

The acknowledgement of senior professionals was far more prevalent in the PhD texts in the sciences and engineering where, because of increasing specialisation of both research and funding, the mentoring tradition seems stronger. Here winning the protection and goodwill of established academics is often vital for gaining post-doctoral grants, a lab to work in or a teaching position. Mentioning key figures can both gain the writer credit and help project a scholarly persona, as these students seemed to realise:

(4)

> Some of the comparative results are from other labs and I will put these people in the acknowledgements. Some of these are from important people in the field and it is a good idea to include them.
>
> (Bio PhD interview)

> The acknowledgement is an important section for creating good impression.
>
> (EE PhD interview)

Acknowledging senior professors, particularly in the sciences, can therefore help ease the examination process, but more importantly it brackets the student with particular well-known academics, projecting an identification with others which can contribute to readers' identification of the writer.

## Identity as boast

In acknowledging senior figures, students recognise that the effective construction of a credible disciplinary self depends on who you know; in acknowledging individuals and institutions who have provided resources during the study, they appear to be asserting an identity as competent researchers. While the research process often depends on access to data, administrative assistance, technical help and financial support, we can also see in these acknowledgements the textual production of an academic self. In the detailing of thanks for the markers of academic success, such as prizes, prestigious scholarships, company sponsorships or travel grants, for example, we see identity construction as a boast to impress examiners and other readers. The scientists and engineers, in particular, were keen to document grants from industrial and public bodies:

(5)

> The research for this thesis was financially supported by a postgraduate studentship from the University of Hong Kong, Towngas Postgraduate Scholarship, Epson Foundation Scholarship, two University of Hong Kong CRCG grants and an RCG grant.
>
> (CS PhD)

> This project was generously supported by funding from Polytechnic University's Scholarship scheme. Support from Cathay Pacific Airways in the form of complimentary air travel has allowed me to attend several international conferences to take the research to a wider audience.
>
> (Bio PhD)

While the writer may feel obliged to refer to his or her funding agency, an examiner is unlikely to remain unimpressed by the writer's obvious academic know-how and income-generating prowess.

Similar constructions of a disciplinary self are evident in acknowledging individuals for cooperating on publishing and presentation projects. Again, this is more a feature of the sciences; where work is more likely to offer greater opportunities for collaboration, such gratitude clearly serves to enhance the writer's professional credentials:

(6)

> A special acknowledgement is extended to Y.S. Lee at Stanford University for providing spreading resistance analysis and to Prof. William Wu for reviewing my IEDM paper.
>
> (EE PhD)

> Portions of this thesis represent joint work with Dr Parco Lam, which appear in the following papers: 'Linear-Time Algorithms for Unspecified Routing in Grids,' in the Proceedings of International Conference on Algorithms; ... and 'Efficient Algorithms for Finding Maximum Number of Disjoint Paths in Grids,' in *Journal of Algorithms*.
>
> (CS PhD)

We can see the textual construction of an academic self in these apparently innocent appreciations from a grateful graduate. They help mark the writer out as an individual whose academic talents have already been recognised and who may therefore be deserving further honours.

In the human sciences, on the other hand, students tended to promote an academic identity by positioning themselves in relation to their subjects:

(7)

> I would like to acknowledge the invaluable help rendered by my subjects, the elderly diabetic patients follow-up at the Ap Lei Chau and Tang Chi Ngong out-patient clinic, who spent time to participate in this study without immediate benefit to themselves.
>
> (PA PhD)

> Finally, I am most indebted to the 517 companies that were willing to return my questionnaire with their responses.
>
> (BS PhD)

While subjects themselves are unlikely to read the text, quite subtle rhetorical intimations of professional commitment and academic competence can be communicated to professional readers, hinting at the authority and involvement of the writer and of trials overcome. This is a very different kind of academic to those cataloguing grants and cooperative research in the experimental research fields. It is often an identity built upon an ethnographic competence and empathetic quality as a researcher. This example underlines the point:

(8)

> I hope this work has given justice to the voices from the margins. For reasons that

they would understand, they would remain anonymous in this work. However, if someday they get the chance to read this work, I have no doubt that they will readily recognize their voices that have enlivened the many Sunday afternoons shared together in the parks, under the bridges and under the trees; in the sun and rain; enduring the heat and cold of the changing seasons. I also include those whose search for life's better promises has led them to the classrooms of the YMCA where I have had the opportunities to share moments, outside and inside classroom sessions, that have been made unforgettable by their laughter and tears. And the many nameless others whom I have met in countless encounters whose lives have touched and enriched mine in ways that I would find hard to articulate.

(AL PhD)

Doubtless such expressions of gratitude are sincere, but detailing the rapport established between researcher and subjects simultaneously makes a claim for a disciplinary identity.

## Identity as initiation

While students are able to create a disciplinary identity through associations and boasts, the fact that almost 40% of the thanks in the acknowledgements were to friends and family suggests that the genre also offers students the chance to project a more human face and a social identity. This is an opportunity which is not available in the dissertation itself.

(9)

Gratitude expressed to all my research teammates including Miss Irene Wo, Miss Carol Lim and Mr. Z. Q. Lee. Their humour and spiritual support smoothened my research progress.

(Bio PhD)

My heartfelt gratitude especially to my two mentors, my mother, Mrs. Gita Bhatia and my father, Late, Dr. V. K. Bhatia who said that I could do whatever I set my mind to.

(AL PhD)

More significantly, though, references to close ones were almost always tied to the tensions and hardships of research. The writer is here able to provide a picture of an individual with a life dominated by a commitment to research which has had consequences for his or her private life and identity. Alluding to the struggle and ultimate triumph over the difficulties of graduate study is a way of signalling that the end of the PhD is the completion of a rite of passage:

a life-changing experience that represents a transition to a new identity. It is an appeal for the writer to be recognised as a full-fledged academic:

(10)

> Most importantly, I would like to thank my parents and my dearest wife, Rebecca. Without their support and great encouragement, I cannot concentrate on my work and overcome the difficulties.
>
> (CS PhD)

> Last, but definitely not the least, I am greatly indebted to my family. It was my parents' unconditional love, care, and tolerance which made the hardship of writing the thesis worthwhile.
>
> (PA PhD)

> I want to thank my girlfriend, Ms Grace Choi. Without her support, I do not think that I could overcome the difficulties during these years.
>
> (AL PhD)

So while writers become more human, and perhaps more sympathetic to readers, they do not lose sight of the need to project an academically relevant identity. The hardships endured and the eventual success in the acceptance of a thesis marks an entry into a discipline's research discourse. It is the completed performance of a community ritual which bestows a new identity on its writer.

Here then, in one of the most explicitly interpersonal genres of the academy, writers can present a self firmly aligned with a disciplinary community. While the communicative purpose of the genre virtually obliges writers to represent themselves more openly, it is clear that acknowledgements are not merely random lists of thanks. They seek to demonstrate the writer's competent participation in a ritual and to stake a claim to a carefully crafted academic identity.

## 4.2　Prize applications

While the alignment of the self with particular academics, competencies and the completion of a ritual helps promote a scholarly identity in acknowledgements, a more explicit identity claim is made when applying for prizes and awards. Here the 'boast' takes on a more overt character and trumpets the quality of the individual's research, rather than his or her relationships or achievements. It is a scholar's research, and particularly its publication, that counts most in academic life, so that any claim to an academic identity has to be validated through the recognition of the quality of one's learned output. Graduate students have generally not yet reached a stage where their work is recognised in this way as their dissertation is often the only textual artefact which supports their claim to an academic identity. They do, however, have to defend the excellence of their research in a dissertation defence or, on occasion, when applying for grants, jobs or prizes.

In this section I explore the ways that graduate students seek to construct a disciplinary identity through the promotion of their work in applying for an annual doctoral prize in Education awarded by a UK university. Through examining the students' supporting statements, it is possible to see the systematic rhetorical orientation to the value system of a discipline in the claims made for the value of the applicants' research.

## The prize application genre

The prize application is actually a set of genres which, in this case, comprise an abstract of the thesis, a recommendation from the supervisor, and a supporting statement from the applicant. Because the judges do not read the entire thesis, the supporting statement is the most important text in this set for the construction of identity, both to students and judges. This comprises the applicants' evaluations of their theses and requires writers to marshal, in a text of around 300 words, their rhetorical and linguistic resources to persuade reviewers of the value of the research. My corpus comprised all supporting statements submitted over three years for a doctoral prize in Education, 70 texts in total containing just over 23,000 words. Topics covered a range of areas from state education policies and curriculum reform to learning theory and classroom discourse. They were submitted by both UK and international students. While these texts originate from a single institution, there is no reason to believe that they are unusual in any way and are not potentially representative of wider practices in this genre.

Preparing these statements typically poses a serious challenge to applicants, partly because of their unfamiliarity with the conventions of the genre and the expectations of its audience, but also because of the self-aggrandising nature of the genre itself. This is both an occluded and an un-researched genre, and its format is largely unknown to both text users and analysts. Clearly the prize application is a persuasive genre, designed to convince judges of the significance of a thesis and the credentials of its author. As such, it bears some similarity to previously studied persuasive texts such as applications for jobs (e.g. Bhatia, 1993), for graduate school places (Ding, 2007) and for research grants (Connor and Upton, 2004; Koutsantoni, 2009). The different purposes of these genres, however, make them poor guides to writing a prize application, and the focus of the analyses on genre structure means they are not particularly helpful in revealing its particular features.

So, neither students nor judges have a developed sense of genre expertise in this kind of writing, although some guidance is provided in the official call for applications:

(11)

> The Doctoral Thesis Prize celebrates outstanding post-graduate work at this university. It is awarded to the author of the thesis who, in the opinion of the judges, best demonstrates originality, contributions to the field, clarity of argument and potential impact. A prize of £3000 will be awarded to the winner.

The rubric explicitly asks applicants to evaluate the academic merit of their work, the subtext being that applicants should both highlight the significance of their research and provide evidence of a disciplinary identity. An academic self is rhetorically constructed here through a strong claim for the importance and scholarliness of applicants' research and an alignment with a disciplinary value system.

## Identity, evaluation and disciplinary values

These writers took on the voice of competent academics by the skilful adoption of a disciplinary value system. Value systems essentially concern what a community regards as good or bad. Hunston (1993) suggests that 'what is good' and 'what is bad' can be defined in terms of goal achievement, either helping or hindering the achievement of a purpose. If the achievement of outstanding postgraduate research is a goal, then presumably *originality, contribution, clarity* and *potential impact* are features to be positively evaluated. Evaluation is central to understanding identity construction in this genre. Hunston and Thompson (2001: 5) define evaluation as 'the expression of the writer's or speaker's attitude or stance towards, viewpoint on, or feelings about the entities or propositions that he or she is talking about'. It is a concept which allows writers to convey both a position on something and proximity to the shared values and attitudes of others.

Like many types of text in the academy, prize applications contain very few obviously evaluative terms such as *beautiful, excellent* and *terrible*. This is, however, an evaluatively loaded genre. In Martin and White's (2005) terms, a great deal of evaluation is not explicitly *inscribed* in the text (as in 'a great thesis') but *evoked* through reference to what is conventionally prized by a community ('an original contribution'). In other words, evaluation is concerned with the construction of communities of shared values and normative assessments; it acts dialogistically to maintain relations with readers and project particular positions which are recognised as positive or negative. As Martin (2001: 161) says:

> Socialization into a discipline involves both an alignment with the institutional practices involved and an affinity with the attitudes one is expected to have towards those practices.

The importance of evaluation in constructing a credible disciplinary identity therefore lies in the fact that it signals the evaluator's desire to identify with the standards and values of a particular field, prioritising what it considers worth embracing by drawing on discipline-shared estimations of worth.

A great deal has been written about evaluation in recent years (e.g. Hunston and Thompson, 2001; Hyland and Diani, 2009; Martin and White, 2005), but space prevents elaboration here and I will focus on just two broad aspects in these texts: judgements of quality on a 'good–bad' scale, and how far writers subjectively commit themselves to the veracity of these judgements. Broadly, these are what Hunston (1993) refers to as *value* and *status* and what Martin and White (2005) call *appreciation* and *heteroglossic dialogue*.

Prize applications, as we might expect, overwhelmingly impart a status of certainty to their content and fend off any dialogic contradiction. This is a discourse of assurance which aims to leave readers in no doubt of the worth of the thesis and which offers little space for the epistemic discretions of research writing. Here, then, proximity to the community takes a back seat to the writer's positioning towards his or her work. Typically statements are made categorically without mitigation of any kind, and are often boosted in a number of ways to impart an overall assurance to the subject matter. In other words: these things are *known*.

(12)

> As such it offers a **sturdy** theoretical framework and a **clear** methodological path through **rich** data. The work culminates in a strong argument regarding …

> My work represents a **huge** contribution to scholarly work in education and has secured an **important** foothold in the research into gender.

This robust stance means that writers offer readers a confident positioning of themselves towards their work, generating an enthusiasm which hopefully the panel of readers finds infectious.

## The expression of value

The expression of value reflects the shared concerns of a discipline and the writer's allegiance to it, representing a clear signal of disciplinary identity. While science disciplines appear to value features such as *accuracy, consistency, verity, simplicity* and *usefulness* (Hunston, 1993), these education texts stressed novelty (13), contribution to the field (14) and clarity of argument (15), with the first two of these occurring in every text:

(13)

Part of its **originality** lies in the conceptualisation and organisation of a theoretical model that has **not been presented before**.

This thesis was **groundbreaking** in that it was the first study to look at the non-formal learning of novice teachers in medical settings.

In addition, the thesis develops 'achievement oriented' and 'relationship oriented' concepts of approaches to mothering, which bring **new elements** to already-formulated concepts in the literature.

(14)

I believe my research has **significant implications** for government policy on higher education and for the way that universities deliver teaching and supervision to their students.

My thesis will make **a major contribution** to global literature in the field of research methodology in general and Sri Lankan literature in particular.

Furthermore, publications arising from my thesis have **already received favourable comment**. I have no doubt that the publication of the thesis itself and the lecture series already begun will excite academic debates on research methodology.

(15)

It constructs, however, a **clear and continuous argument** through these multiple engagements.

Drawing from a complex and extensive data, the thesis builds up **a clear argument** that links the theoretical and the practical.

Disciplinary identity is therefore displayed through alignment to the values of the educational community. But while their graduate training and experience encouraged a scholarly perspective towards their writing, not all students found this an easy task. The prize application is a competitive genre which conflates a promotional and an academic genre, but this involves attempting to sell one's research after years of rhetorically machining arguments with appropriately tentative claims and author-evacuated arguments. This is a purpose like personal annual reviews and promotion applications which academics typically loathe, and the task is not made any easier by the fact that over 60% of the applicants for the prize were international students. As Swales and Feak (2000: 229) observe, audience expectations for personal statements are often 'more shaped by local cultural values and national academic traditions than is the case with more technical writing'.

Consequently, some arguments seemed a tad naïve, as when applicants simply referred to the criteria directly, apparently lifting the key words verbatim from the application rubric:

(16)
Prof Lewis and Dr. Yardley stated in my viva that my thesis is a contribution to knowledge and that they have learned a lot from my work.

All arguments in my thesis are clearly set out, informed by existing literature and supported by empirical evidence.

When you consider the contribution of my work to the field of education studies in Ireland and its ongoing impact, you will be quite impressed with my research work.

The adoption of an unfamiliar self-promotional stance perhaps accounts for the awkwardness of some formulations, but there is clearly an attempt to position work in the values and perspectives of the field and so establish proximity with the community.

## Displaying research expertise

In addition to explicitly addressing the criteria of the prize rubric, these doctoral graduates also displayed their claims to a competent academic identity by highlighting expertise in various areas of research. One indication of an academic identity, for instance, is to suggest know-how in the development of theory and innovative research methodologies, drawing on shared symbolic meanings to press a case for competence. The applicants managed this with some aplomb:

(17)

**My approach** is to examine the seldom-heard accounts of professionals working with these families using an innovative synthesis of theoretical ideas from discursive psychology, Foucauldian discourse analysis, critical disability and childhood studies.

**I employed** a modified version of the 'circuit of culture' – a theoretical model which holds that meanings are distributed across a series of key moments from product production through to consumption. This original descriptive-cum-analytical framework combines elements of content, discourse and social semiotic analysis.

**I try, in my own claims**, to dispense with all technical terminology that is coloured by conceptions of rationality borrowed from business, economic, or systems-organisation theories.

The use of the first person here is clearly not a casual or neutral choice. It functions to display a professional competence by suggesting that, in other hands, things could have been done differently.

Years of study in doctoral research have enculturated these students into the ways of their discipline and the ways of speaking of their discipline. As a result, we find them demonstrating disciplinary membership through the use of specialised terminology and mention of esoteric theories and celebrated theorists:

(18)

This thesis works within **Geographical and Environmental Education** and **Education for Sustainable Development and Global Citizenship (ESDGC)** to address matters pertinent to 'philosophy of education' (notably psychology, comparative philosophy and postmodern and critical theorising).

A major theme is the theoretical development of **Dowling's Social Activity Method**.

The study is a **multidimensional, multiscalar and holistic conceptual enquiry** into the nature of '**human-place' relations** with a view to suggesting crucial dimensions of a '*place-based education*'.

The control of these disciplinary resources and knowledge of in-group terms, concepts and celebrities not only represent specific understandings, but display considerable expertise. This grasp of membership mechanisms, allied to the expression of disciplinary values, is not merely 'doing academic writing well'; it is a means of constructing a competent academic self.

In sum, these postgraduate students, reflecting on their research in applying for a prestigious and financially rewarding prize, seek to represent themselves and their work within disciplinary frameworks of understanding. Displaying a carefully considered proximity to the discipline and taking a promotional position on their completed research, they seek to persuade the panel of judges of their own credibility as academics as much as of the particular value of their theses. Writing like a disciplinary expert is, therefore, more than mastery of particular disciplinary genres such as research articles or theses. It is a process of disciplinary acculturation that involves control of an entire semiotic system of rhetorical resources and values.

## 4.3   Academic homepages

The final genre in this chapter makes a particularly forthright and public statement of identity and provides academics with a platform for global visibility and standing. Unfortunately, however, it is a construction of identity which is often only partially, if at all, under the control of individual actors. While an increasing number of faculty members maintain a presence on the Web, identity has become a marketing tool for universities who frequently manage this genre in ways which promote the legitimacy of the institution at the expense of the individual, marginalising academics in the name of university branding. Here identity is constructed in a university-administered space and so reveals an individual supported by institutional infrastructures and linked into networks of colleagues, publications, interests, courses and students, all of which are carefully selected to assert both the professional credibility of the subject and the legitimacy of the employer.

This section therefore represents a significant departure from the self-aggrandising genres discussed earlier as the boasting is typically done by an employing institution. It reminds us, however, that identity is always constructed in particular institutional contexts and often involves the positioning of individuals by others. Here I explore how language interacts with other semiotic resources to construct identity in this context and in the space remaining to academics in institutional representations.

## Homepages, identity and institutional branding

The homepage owes its rapid rise, at least in part, to the fact that no other medium is better suited to fulfilling the present-day demands of identity work which seek to balance the differentiation of modern life with the construction of coherence and meaning. For Parks and Archley-Landas (2003), the homepage provides 'an incredibly flexible and unencumbered stage for the construction of identity'.

Creating this identity involves *bricolage* (Chandler and Roberts-Young, 1998), where the author doesn't so much *write* as *assemble* the culturally valued attributes of his or her trade: the set of symbolic resources from which identity is constructed for public approval. The inclusion, omission, adaptation and arrangement of elements and the indirect allusion to others all reflect certain assumptions and values (Chandler, 1998). It is also a genre which facilitates the joining of diverse aspects of the self together through links in its hypertext-structure (Chandler, 1998; Turkle, 1997). Representing one's 'patchwork identity' (Kraus, 2000) on a personal homepage can therefore help foster a sense of self-integration (Lillie, 1998), but more importantly, it can convey an impression of how one would like to be seen by others, and it is therefore especially well suited for strategic self-presentation (Chandler, 1998; Wynn and Katz, 1997).

As I have noted, however, this aspect of homepages has not been lost on universities who now find themselves operating in a competitive global environment driven by league table positions and a constant search for additional sources of funding. So while part of the allure of maintaining a homepage is to present oneself online, the fact that it is located on a university server and accesssed through a university website means that it can act as a means of institutional governance. The fact that institutions seek to legitimate their own credibility through the expertise of their staff means that individuals are often constructed as workers on these pages (e.g. Hess, 2002). As Thoms and Thelwell (2005) observe:

> The institution merely constructs these (academics) in the model that is ideologically suited in order to promote the institution. Academics are thus denied any autonomous subjectivity construction, and yield to the constructed display items in the university electronic window.

From a Foucauldian (1972) perspective, of course, this is not surprising as identities are regarded as the product of dominant discourses tied to social arrangements such as these. The institutional oversight of the homepage changes the subject's discursive position so that the university 'owns' the homepage and so also the identity that it constructs.

## Presentations of identity in university homepages

This section explores 100 academic homepages with 50 taken from each of philosophy and physics, representing practices in the humanities and hard sciences respectively (Hyland, 2011). I selected these pages from academics affiliated to universities in the top 25 of the *QS-Times Higher World University Rankings for 2009*[i] to ensure some consistency in institutional status. The QS-THS listings rank over 600 universities based on various criteria including the opinions of academics themselves. This selection was then stratified according to rank and gender, with 25 full professors and 25 assistant professors and 25 men and 25 women from each discipline. This was based on assumptions about the possible significance of these factors in mediating self-representation.

I then analysed the homepages, looking at their text, visual design and hyperlinks, all of which can contribute to the construction of identity. I used *NVivo 8*, a qualitative software program, to code the text by what was mentioned. The position, size and content of photographs were also recorded, and the hypertext links were followed and categorised. I also conducted email interviews with a random sample of a dozen homepage subjects to explore the reasons for selections and to better understand the extent of agency available to them. The content writers included was considered in terms of how it was structured as rhetorical units, each unit seen as a distinctive communicative act projecting a particular aspect of the self. This scheme embraced all the text data:

- Achievements and awards
- Community service
- Educational background
- Employment
- Personal details
- Publications and conferences
- Research interests
- Teaching
- Contact details

## Textual representations of identity

The interviews confirmed that options are often restricted by institutional design. While only one of my, admittedly small, sample of respondents mentioned having to 'write to a template', academics often felt constrained in creating their profiles by space or the attentions of department webmasters. Consequently, as can be seen in Table 4.3, homepage identities offer advertisements for what Miller (1995) refers to as a 'focal-self', emphasising an academic identity.

Employment was the highest frequency move, with subjects almost always stating their current and past positions. Together with a statement of research interests, this comprised a substantial portion of the text of the corpus. Employment histories and research concerns are available to every academic regardless of status and act to promote both the individual and the institution, linking the academic into a network of credible associations as well as advertising the university to potential graduate students and employees. References to the author's publications and teaching are less frequent, with just two-thirds mentioning publication output and just a third their teaching and supervision. Clearly academics are not simply following instructions to legitimate the authority of their employers. In interviews, respondents pointed out that some negotiation goes on here:

(19)

> I gave them some info for the webpage but didn't fill in all their boxes. I thought some information was more important about who I was and how I saw myself as an academic. It was more important to include it than some of the other things they wanted.

(Phy interview)

> I've published a lot in the last couple of years as we had a major project come to an end and I wanted to highlight that on my page. Nobody seemed to mind that I left out the courses I was teaching.

(Phy interview)

Gender differences appear minimal, although females were more likely to highlight publications and awards and men give more attention to their teaching. More substantial differences result from the status of the author, with assistant professors falling back on their qualifications and education in the absence of the publication and teaching records of their more senior colleagues. The biggest differences, however, are disciplinary, with philosophers making

**Table 4.3 Frequency of homepage themes by social characteristics (% of all academics)**

| Moves | Education | Employment | Personal | Research | Publications | Teaching | Award | Service |
|---|---|---|---|---|---|---|---|---|
| Overall | 62 | 96 | 16 | 91 | 68 | 34 | 14 | 12 |
| Male | 61 | 96 | 16 | 91 | 60 | 35 | 9 | 11 |
| Female | 60 | 97 | 11 | 91 | 76 | 31 | 16 | 13 |
| Professors | 52 | 96 | 19 | 92 | 80 | 39 | 17 | 20 |
| Assistant professors | 70 | 96 | 9 | 90 | 54 | 27 | 7 | 4 |
| Physicists | 57 | 92 | 12 | 90 | 57 | 26 | 21 | 10 |
| Philosophers | 69 | 100 | 19 | 93 | 79 | 43 | 6 | 14 |

greater use of most categories except awards. Physicists were far less likely to post details of their teaching and publication outputs, and often simply listed a few recent references or a hyperlink without comment. The philosophers, on the other hand, generally provided a commentary on the text and a sketch of its argument or impact:

(20)

'Structuring Ends' forthcoming in *Philosophia*. In this essay I defend an account of human well-being which seeks to capture the virtues of both aim-constituted and substantive good approaches. I explicate a kind of end that has received insufficient attention in the literature on practical reason and I show how to use this end to reconcile these two approaches to the theory of well-being.

Even where frequencies were relatively even, as with research interests, there are disciplinary differences, with physicists making far more use of the third person and using their lab membership as a way of presenting their interests and establishing their research credentials:

(21)

How did the Universe begin? Chao-Lin Huat's group seeks to answer this profound question by studying the most ancient light, the Cosmic Microwave Background (CMB) radiation, emitted when the universe was in its infancy.

While the physicists positioned themselves as players in a domain where results are the collective endeavours of a team, philosophers wrote more personally and tended to characterise themselves in terms of the more individualistic ethos of a discipline which sees interpretations and arguments as the creative insights of the author:

(22)

I am mainly interested in how scientific method could possibly lead us to true generalizations about Nature; generalizations that extend infinitely beyond our current, finite perspective.

Here knowledge is shared and part of a cooperative context rather than personally owned.

## Identity and branding in visual design

University governance is most striking in the visual design of academic homepages. The aesthetics of websites contributes not only to their attractiveness, but also to the way the subject is positioned. This is because online texts are never purely linguistic. For Kress (2010) and other theorists, the screen is organised by the logic of *image* which orders the various 'systems of meanings' that are found there. Page formatting and colour, however, are almost always determined by the employing institution. Design therefore serves the corporate interests of the university, but it also squeezes the space available for individual representation without requiring further work by the viewer to link to other screens. The example in Figure 4.2 is typical.

University and department names and logos dominate the page with banner text along the top, departmental links down the side and university 'meta' links along the bottom. These features repeated across the homepages of all the members of a department have been seen as symbols of ownership which help position the individual as an employee (Thoms and Thelwell, 2005). Information about the individual is not only compressed into a third of the available space but is depersonalised in a dot-point format labelled 'research', 'education' and 'recent publications'. For multi-modal semioticians, the position of elements is significant, so that placement of the department name is clearly given prominence at the top of the page and the text on the left is intended to be scanned first. The 'new' information is on the right, however, and the eye is drawn to the subjects' information and, in particular, the photograph. This is heavily cropped to passport dimensions, but it reveals something of the academic's personal self: a man who seems to be reading a paperback on a chilly beach.

This is more information than most photographs in the corpus, however, for although photographs allow viewers another way of understanding the subject, most gave little away. All but a dozen homepages contained a photo of the author, but these were generally tightly cropped portraits looking straight ahead with no articulated background and betraying little context. This absence of setting not only reduces personal information about the subject but disconnects him or her from time and place (Kress and van Leuwen, 1996). Where a background could be discerned, it was likely to be an office, although about a quarter of all authors were represented in a leisure context. Depicting individuals in this way offers nothing to contradict an exclusively professional persona and reduces our ability to see the individual as anything more than a generic academic filling a vacant place on the homepage.

Hypertext links similarly position the homepage subject in this corpus. Potentially, hyperlinks are key aspects of an online identity construction as they can be seen as flagging topics, stances and people which the author regards as

**Figure 4.2 A sample academic homepage**

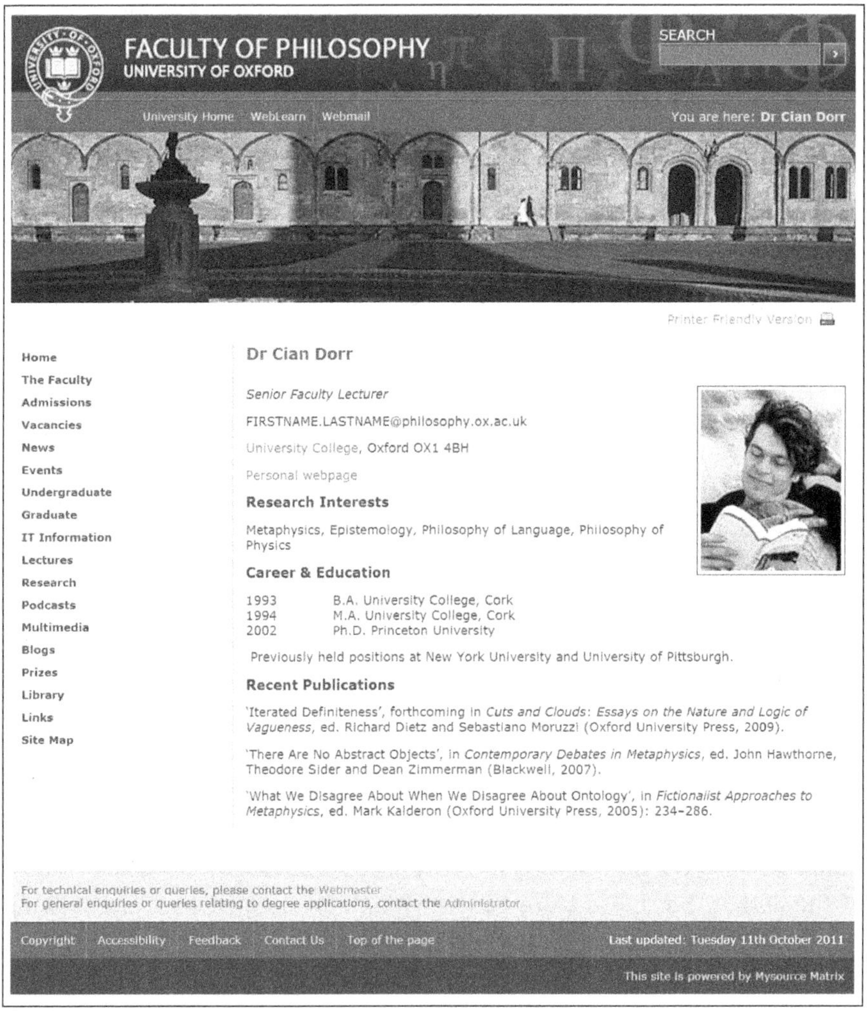

significant. Turkle (1997: 258) observes that 'one's identity emerges from whom one knows, one's associations and connections', while Miller (1995), puts this more directly: 'Show me what your links are, and I'll tell you what kind of person you are.' Through links to the pages of research groups, labs, friends or departments elsewhere, authors can construct a 'virtual community' (Rheingold, 1995), so individualising their homepages through networks of associations and claims to membership of particular groups. Perhaps unsurprisingly, however, links were overwhelmingly institutional, channelling visitors to pages of their choosing and revealing a subject enmeshed in institutional programmes, events, news and so on.

The 100 homepages in the corpus contained just under 1,400 links, ranging from a handful per page to over 40. The overwhelming majority of these were to the academic's department (38.2%), courses (18.3%) and publications (12.6%). Just 57 links (4%) are to non-academic sites, largely personal homepages. Once again, the page in Figure 4.2 is typical. Of 32 hyperlinks on this page, 5 are to the university, 21 to the department's activities, 1 to a print version of the page, another to the college, 2 for navigation, and 3 to site administrators. Just one link takes the reader to pages which might reveal more about the individual presented here. So by allowing university web design teams to construct their homepage, academics risk having their online identities hijacked by the institution and shaped by a template from a uniform assembly line to project a positive view of the university.

## The personal page: The independent self?

The tendency towards uniformity in university-administered personal websites helps explain why large numbers of academics create their own homepages and half of the 100 homepages are linked to a personal page. Stripped of university branding, logos, advertising and glossy homogeny, these 'home-made' pages tend to adopt a more personal way of addressing readers. They are altogether more idiosyncratic and distinctive, reflecting the decisions, and expertise, of their creators through the particularity of their design. But while reflecting greater authorial choice, they are often accessed from a university-sponsored page, and many simply mirror the references to teaching, research and publications which are already listed on academic sites. We do, however, often find pages which include more personal qualities, such as interests, hobbies, personal icons and families. Figure 4.3, for example, offers a more idiosyncratic self-representation.

Two clicks removed from a university-sponsored homepage, this page constructs a more multi-faceted identity for the author. There is greater biographical detail here, with hobbies, personal likes and humour contributing to the creation of a different self from the university-constructed academic on the institution-sponsored page.

The photograph of the languid chimp, the tongue-in-cheek mention of the author's home-town celebrities, and the self-deprecating list of 'dweeb

**Figure 4.3 'Personal page': A self-maintained academic homepage**

# Ian Howarth – Personal Page

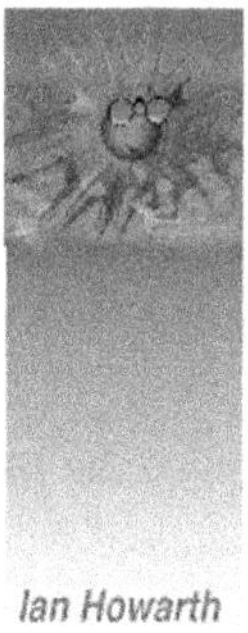

Ian Howarth

## *It's cool to be hot!*

You should probably be looking elsewhere...

I'm a Professor of Astronomy at UCL, and a member of the Stars & Galaxies subgroup.

I was born -- very recently -- in Portsmouth (aka `Sunny Southsea' in the brochures), and am thereby condemned to follow the very variable fortunes of its Football Team. I now live in Rickmansworth, Hertfordshire; the area's other famous residents include the glamorous and talented Cilla Black, and former England, Arsenal and Man City goalkeeper David Seaman.

My research interests span all the Hot-Star Group's projects, and I'm also interested in interstellar absorption-line spectroscopy and the applications of statistical techniques in astronomy. I was a `back-yard' astronomer before starting my professional career, and still follow amateur activities, especially variable-star work, with interest. I've been Senior Secretary to, and Vice-President of, the Royal Astronomical Society, and maintain a mirror of the Astronomy Picture of the Day.

Outside the Department, I enjoy the complete suite of dweeb pastimes: listening to Radio 4, birdwatching, politely refusing alcoholic beverages... Unfortunately, having been born too late for The Age of Steam, I never developed into train-spotting.

My favourite things include: hamsters , Rocky Mountain National Park, Here and There in The Observatory magazine.

pastimes', acknowledging a rather over-studious and perhaps socially inept individual, speak to a more complex and rounded character than the university poster boy. Despite this, however, he ensures that much of what is constructed here is his academic self and that key aspects of the homepage are related to his profession and discipline. The first link, for example, points the reader 'elsewhere' – to his professional homepage – and the following two links are to his research groups at his university.

While pages may show the author as a game-player, a devout Christian, or someone, like Howarth, with 'dweeb pastimes', most links served to support the projection of a professional self. Of the 800 links on personally constructed homepages, just 88 (10.8%) referred readers to non-work pages. About two-thirds of these took readers to personal interest and hobby sites, revealing something of a more personal self through photographs, favourite books, jogging maps, sports clubs and so on. Another third, however, simply load a curriculum vitae, filling out professional biographies which emphasised the writer's academic credentials, as in this example:

(23)

> Past President of the Australasian Association of Philosophy, Member of the editorial boards of *The Bulletin of Symbolic Logic*, and *The Australasian Journal of Philosophy*, Fellow of the Australian Academy of the Humanities, Chief Investigator in the Australian Centre of Excellence for Risk Analysis, Core Researcher in the Commonwealth Environment Research Facilities Research Hub: Applied Environmental Decision Analysis, Member of the Biotechnology, Ethics, Law and Society Network.

This emphasis is even apparent in those cases where authors have individualised their sites with a more human face which tempers a purely professional version of identity:

(24)

> If you've been following my twitter feed, you'd realise I'm still alive. You wouldn't think that from the activity – or lack thereof – here. (Though a few papers have appeared – or changed their publication status – on my writing page.) Tomorrow, I'm off on a short trip to Guangzhou, by way of St. Andrews and Bristol. It's the long way around, but somebody has got to do it. I'm busy clearing the decks here of as much as I can before the trip. One of the decks to be cleared is this blog, so a post is in order. Here's a link to something you might like if you're a logic person like me. Lately, I've enjoyed playing around with Wandering Mango's program *Deductions*. It's a very neat natural deduction educational tool:

it helps you produce valid Fitch-style natural deduction proofs, using the format of the major texts used in intro teaching.

The interpersonal tone of this extract helps shift the boundaries between professional and personal, yet the content and links remain predominantly academic. This is a relaxed and informal man, comfortable using contemporary communications media, who maintains a twitter feed and a blog and has a passion for formal logic. At the same time, we find an academic plugged into a network of colleagues and universities, with scholarly interests, and a bibliography of publications to share with others. The site projects a human face, but it is the face of an academic.

## 4.4　Conclusions

Every text projects an identity claim, but as this chapter has attempted to show, context plays a decisive role in how such projections are enacted. Any individual's presentation and interpretation of self will vary from one situation to another depending on the purpose of the encounter, the audience, the individual's relationship with that audience and the genre in which identity is constructed. To summarise the argument: we can see individuals negotiating their identities within interactional orders, mobilising rhetorical competencies within particular contexts, communities and genres. In this chapter I have focused on genres rather than disciplines in order to highlight issues of power and audience and to throw the importance of context into sharp relief.

I have also deliberately chosen to focus here on some relatively modest and unexplored sites of identity construction. But while they may be among the more peripheral discourses of the academy, they are also ones which involve a self-conscious and reflective representation of self. Here the art of impression management is revealed most clearly.

Acknowledgements and prize applications show students' emerging control of a disciplinary ethos and orientation to the community values that provide specialist frames of understanding within which they can construct, even boast, a disciplinary identity. Both are reflexive, self-promotional genres where identity construction is a primary purpose, revealing how the process of postgraduate research offers an induction into the ways of a discipline that can be used to situate one's self effectively in unfamiliar genres. The homepage is rather different in that it is a 'broadcast' genre designed to represent the self to a wide, and largely unknown, audience. Certainly these pages promote the individual academic and his or her accomplishments, but equally they discursively construct the individual as a member of an institution which profits from these accomplishments. Here I have stressed something of the tensions and compromises of the online construction of self in a corporate context. But while university-managed homepages often marginalise faculty members as simply institutional functionaries, self-made homepages also often construct the author in terms of a professional self.

In sum, these genres help reveal something of how a disciplinary identity is constructed through competent interactions with others. In the next chapter I look more closely at this idea in what is probably the most explicit announcement of self-representation in scholarly life: the academic bio.

## Notes

i The QS-THS listings rank over 600 universities based on the proportion of international students and staff, citations per faculty and staff–student ratios, but it is weighted heavily (40%) towards an opinion survey of 10,000 academics worldwide.

# 5 Self-representation in Academic Bios

While every social encounter entails projections and attributions of identity, the biographical statement which accompanies a research article is probably the most explicit public assertion of self-representation in scholarly life. It sits in stark contrast to the prescribed anonymity of the article itself, which has been stripped of identifying information for blind peer review, and generally approximates to conventions which discourage too much personal exposure. In this context, then, the bio provides writers with an opportunity to construct a disciplinary-aligned presence and shape a professionally credible self. Surprisingly, however, it is also a somewhat disregarded genre which has largely escaped the notice of discourse analysts. We know little, for example, of its typical structure or of the language writers use to present themselves in it. Do established celebrities construct the genre in the same way as novices? Is there a common pattern of self-representation across disciplines? Do male and female academics do things similarly?

In this chapter I seek to rectify this neglect and address these questions, offering an account of the biographical statement by drawing on 600 bios in three disciplines. It turns out that, despite its brevity, the bio is an important means of representing an academic self through the recognition of collective values and membership.

## 5.1   Bios and situated identity claims

Readers, apparently, are interested in knowing more about the person behind the words when they read a research article, and publishers are prepared to indulge them. In the academic bio we find a rhetorical space where, in 50 to 100 words, authors are able to reflexively craft a narrative of expertise for themselves, albeit within the tight constraints of a relatively unvarying genre. The bio, then, is a key opening for academics to make a claim for a particular identity by the careful recounting of achievement. It is also an authentic statement of identity whose linguistic choices are available for analysis.

## Authenticity and purpose

As I have noted (see 3.4), a great deal of identity research focuses on what people say about themselves in formal interviews (e.g. Block, 2006). But while autobiographical reconstruction offers subjects the opportunity to represent a coherently motivated picture of themselves, interviews lack the consequences of everyday interactions. It would seem preferable to capture the same kinds of deliberately constructed identity claims where the elicitation is not the motive for the telling. Although all communication performs identity work, indexing who we are, genres which require writers to reflect explicitly on their experiences and accomplishments in this way are few indeed. The short personal bio statements in research journals are therefore like the homepages and prize applications discussed in the previous chapter in this regard. In sum, the bio is an important but mundane way for academics to make autobiographical claims in support of a disciplinary identity.

Bios are authentically produced, naturally occurring texts constructed to achieve meaningful interactional goals: a site where academics stake a claim to a certain version of themselves for their peers and institutions. This is a genre which requires a self-conscious and public recounting of a professional persona that fits both who individual academics want to present themselves as being and the relatively constrained format that is available to them. Bios are not, then, influenced by an interviewer's agenda, institutional branding or any lack of engagement by the subject. Authenticity demands that the text is produced from the language that the genre and the discipline make available, using constructions and aspects of autobiography that are recognisably appropriate for the purpose at hand. Admittedly this is a fashioning of the self accomplished through relatively formulaic means, but it is produced for a genuine purpose to offer a conception of identity located in disciplinary realities.

Once again, the notion of 'identity claim' (e.g. Bechhofer et al., 1999; Kiely et al., 2001) is an important concept here as it leaves open the nature of the subjective experience. Nothing in the bio implies inner psychological states or unvarying personal commitment; it says little about whether the identity presented is deeply held or lightly worn. Instead, it simply tells us what individual academics explicitly say about themselves; connecting the ways they want to be seen with concrete instances of language. In other words, what writers choose to include in this genre and how they choose to express it offers insights into the dynamic between the personal (what I want to say) and the communal (what others will value). It throws light on what he or she holds to be important *in this context* and what is likely to be validated by disciplinary peers. The bio, in other words, allows us to explore personal identities and disciplinary values.

## Corpus, themes and processes

The corpus was compiled by Polly Tse and I and comprises 600 bios, with 200 taken from each of applied linguistics, electrical engineering and philosophy. Bios were selected from articles in six leading international journals in each of the three disciplines (as indicated by Thompson ISI rankings). In addition to selecting texts to represent a cross-section of academic practice, the selection also controlled for gender, with 100 bios written by males and 100 by females in each discipline, and status, with equal numbers of texts by writers in each of four categories (senior academic, junior academic, postgraduate and other <technician, manager, teacher, etc.>). The decision to stratify the sample in these ways was made to explore the impact of potentially important life experiences in mediating writers' self-representation. While discipline is assumed to be a key factor in identity performance, I sought to clarify the role of other possibly significant influences on actors' interpretations of proximity and decisions about positioning.

The qualitative analysis program WinMax Pro (Kuckartz, 1998) was used to code text passages according to content themes and process types. This methodology departs from that used in the previous chapter to some extent. While beginning with macro-level aspects such as moves and themes, as in acknowledgements, prize applications and homepages, I also focus here on how individuals represent themselves using options at clause level through verb choices. In this way it is possible to see both what they chose to mention and something of how they chose to express it. These decisions relate to the concepts of proximity and positioning introduced in Chapter 2 as both content and expression engage with a network of disciplinary-valued attributes and allow authors to exploit these to present themselves effectively. The content choices writers make are not arbitrary and individual but closely relate to an ideological system of meanings designed to persuade the reader that the author is someone worth listening to: that the research in the accompanying paper has been conducted to appropriate standards. By displaying a professional background and conforming to particular ways of representing these experiences, writers are able to demonstrate an alignment to disciplinary values and claim an insider identity.

First, we looked at the ways the texts were structured as a sequence of thematic units. Each theme is a distinctive step in how authors seek to project a particular aspect of themselves and, after several passes through the corpus, a coding scheme evolved which included all the data. Having coded these independently, Polly and I discussed and agreed uncertain cases (with 97% inter-rater agreement). We then entered the moves into WinMax Pro, with all accompanying examples, in order to cross-reference and retrieve cases. The themes are:

- Employment – past and current positions and places of work.
- Research interests – current and past projects and pursuits at graduate level and beyond.
- Education – places studied and qualifications gained.
- Publications – books, chapters, articles and other scholarly outputs.
- Achievements – prizes, awards, honours and other recognition gained by the writer.
- Community service – positions held as editor, committee and editorial board members.
- Personal profile – place and date of birth, family life, hobbies, etc.

Most themes were optional, but there were constraints on the sequence in which they occurred. Employment occurred in every text, for example, and if a theme occurred, it did so in the position set out above. More interestingly, as I discuss below, the frequencies of each theme differed by discipline and rank. It is clear from the headings listed here that writers, as in homepages, largely restricted disclosure of personal information to project a predominantly *academic* identity in this genre.

As mentioned above, I was also keen to see how writers chose to *express* these choices and here looked at the verbs they used to discuss themselves as the key aspect of the clause, classifying all the verbs in the corpus. I adopted the Systemic Functional Linguistic (SFL) perspective as this recognises that rhetorical choices are important in signalling a bidirectional connection between language and context (Ghadessy, 1999). This approach categorises verbs as process types and sees the clause as the linguistic expression of experience; it is where actors encode their understandings of their physical and imaginary worlds (Halliday, 1994). Verbs express different processes by recognising a systematic distinction in the grammar between *mental* and *material* processes, or those of *sensing* and *doing*. Verbs relating to perception, affection and cognition fall into the first group, and those concerned with action and activity in the world in the second. A third form of representation, what Halliday (1994: 119) calls *relational* processes, expresses *being* or the relationship between sensing and doing. In English this system has three main types:

1 Intensive: x is a something (*She is professor of linguistics*)
2 Circumstantial: x is at/in/on/for/with/about/etc. something (*He is interested in genes*)
3 Possessive: x has something (*She holds a PhD from Harvard*).

Other process types in Halliday's scheme, *verbal, behavioural and existential,* are related to these three main types and offer bridges between them.

Research into academic writing has shown the importance of such options. John (2009), for instance, notes the effect of process types on writer visibility with decreasing agency implied from clauses where a writer is an *actor* in a material process, a *sensor* in a mental process and a *behaver* in a behavioural process. Acting on the world in some way is seen to represent greater author visibility than subjectively interpreting it with mental processes or simply behaving. Interestingly, she found that students often delete the more agentive processes in their revisions to project less visible identities. Process types have also been found to differ considerably across disciplines and genres as writers choose to represent themselves and their work in different ways. For example, material processes, discussing what was *done*, dominate methods sections while relational clauses, discussing how things *are*, predominate in discussion sections of research articles (Martínez, 2001) and master's dissertations (John, 2009). Looking across disciplines, Babaii and Ansary (2005) noted the predominance of relational and existential types in physics book reviews but found material processes were more common in sociology and literature book reviews.

Such choices matter in identity performance. So for example, 'she is interested in … ' (a mental process) constructs the author as an active, thinking being exercising conscious choice in a research interest, whereas 'her research interests are … ' (a relational process) is more impersonal, downplaying the author's role to highlight something that belongs to her. While it may be disguised by passive constructions in the case of material processes and nominalisation in relational ones, we can usually recover human agency from a text, and in these bios we had little difficulty in identifying the animate sensor, doer, or 'be-er'. Other process types in Halliday's scheme – verbal, behavioural and existential – offer connections between these three types but are less important in the bios.

I turn now to the ways bio authors rhetorically negotiate the dynamics of gender, discipline and status in this genre, examining aspects of how they attempt to establish their own uniqueness in a context of sharing experiences and language as a member of an academic community. In this way I hope to reveal something of the ways that language choices reflect different presentations in constructing an academic identity in this context.

## 5.2   It's both what you say and the way that you say it

While bios do not occur in every journal, nor even with every paper in journals that typically carry them, they are nevertheless a ubiquitous part of academic publishing. Many journals insist on a bio of each author on the submission of an accepted paper, and some give guidelines as to length or, far less often, content. Instructions such as these are fairly common:

(1)

Each contributor should provide a brief biodata of about 90 words listing main interests, recent publications, and a contact address. Email address is optional.

(*Applied Linguistics*)

Curriculum Vitae. Include a short (maximum 50 words) biography of each author.

(*Assessing Writing*)

A biographical note of no more than 50 words should be included.

(*Journal of Moral Philosophy*)

Include in the manuscript a short (maximum 100 words) biography of each author, along with a passport-type photograph accompanying the other figures.

(*Computers and Electronic Engineering*)

House style therefore varies and offers authors some flexibility in representing themselves, although as we shall see, restrictions on word length and the weight of convention tend to circumscribe what people say about themselves.

Word length is, in fact, a distinguishing feature of bios across disciplines, with those in engineering about twice as long as those in applied linguistics. The gender of the writer also appeared to influence the length of texts, with males tending to occupy more space than women, although there was a more even distribution in applied linguistics where texts are shorter at under 60 words. Table 5.1 shows the word counts by gender for each disciplinary corpus of 200 bios.

**Table 5.1   Corpus length by discipline and gender**

| Themes | Philosophy | Applied linguistics | Electrical engineering | Total |
|--------|-----------|---------------------|------------------------|-------|
| Female | 6, 471 | 5, 849 | 10, 472 | 22, 792 |
| Male | 6, 828 | 5, 792 | 12, 185 | 24, 805 |
| **Total** | **13, 299** | **11, 641** | **22, 657** | **47, 597** |

**Table 5.2   Overall frequencies and percentages of themes and process types**

| Themes | Total items | % of all themes | % of texts with theme | Process types | Total items | % of all clause types |
|--------|-------------|-----------------|-----------------------|---------------|-------------|------------------------|
| Employment | 577 | 31.2 | 89.1 | Relational | 1330 | 52.2 |
| Research | 475 | 25.7 | 66.7 | Circumstantial | 132 | 9.9 |
| Education | 296 | 15.9 | 41.0 | Intensive | 841 | 63.3 |
| Publications | 283 | 15.3 | 42.7 | Possessive | 357 | 26.8 |
| Achievements | 88 | 4.7 | 11.8 | Material | 1103 | 43.3 |
| Community service | 84 | 4.5 | 11.8 | Mental | 58 | 2.3 |
| Personal profile | 50 | 2.7 | 7.0 | Verbal | 54 | 2.1 |
| | | | | Behavioural | 2 | 0.1 |
| | | | | Existential | 1 | 0.0 |
| **Total** | **1853** | **100%** | | | **2548** | **100%** |

Table 5.2 gives the frequencies for both themes and process types represented as raw figures and as percentages of total occurrences. The figures are presented in this way to offer an idea of the relative importance writers gave to different forms of representation.

As can be seen, authors overwhelmingly mentioned employment in their bios, almost always stating their current post, and together with research interests, this comprised over half of all themes in the corpus, appearing in the majority of bios. Employment histories and research interests are the staples of the curriculum vitae and are available to everyone from the Nobel professor to the lowly lab rat and so find their way into most constructions of the self. In terms of representing these experiences, writers used relational and material processes to discuss themselves in 95% of all clauses. The dominance of these process types stresses the importance of what the individuals claimed to *be* and what they *do*.

Relational process types largely clustered in what Halliday (1994: 119) calls *intensive* types, where a writer claims to *be* something, such as an assistant professor, a doctoral student or specialist in some field or other. These made up two-thirds of all relational processes, with possessives, where writers stated they *had* some form of experience or research interest, comprising another 27%. Circumstantial processes, where the process includes an attribute of some kind, such as what the writer is *interested in* or an institution he or she is *affiliated with*, were also present in these texts, but far less common. I now turn to look at moves and processes in the texts in more detail, picking out what appear to be the more interesting results.

## 5.3 'She was born in Coimbatore, India': Themes in bios

*Themes* focus on content and contain what writers assume will best represent them as credible academics and competent researchers, providing some detail on the anonymous writer behind the claims and arguments in the accompanying research paper. They comprise a collection of culturally valued attributes of the trade: the set of symbolic resources from which identity is constructed for public disciplinary approval. The selection and sequencing of content therefore presents an identity claim: projecting an individual buttressed by institutional associations, professional qualifications, publications and research interests.

### Status and themes

Themes varied considerably across status groups, with only research interests figuring highly across all of them. Table 5.3 shows the percentages of bios in each group which contained particular themes.

**Table 5.3    Percentage of texts with each theme by status**

| Themes | Senior academic | Junior academic | Teacher/ manager, etc. | Student/ post-doc |
|---|---|---|---|---|
| Employment | 100 | 100 | 96 | 56 |
| Research interests | 76 | 75 | 76 | 88 |
| Education | 32 | 39 | 68 | 93 |
| Publications | 66 | 42 | 20 | 14 |
| Achievements | 16 | 13 | 11 | 4 |
| Community service | 19 | 16 | 7 | 4 |
| Personal profile | 7 | 3 | 12 | 11 |

The table indicates that virtually everyone except students stated their current, and often past, positions in their bios. For many junior faculty with limited achievements and a thin publications list, this was often the only option available, as in these two samples, where this move comprises the entire bio:

(2)

John Berger is an assistant professor of Early Childhood Education at the University of Arkansas at Little Rock. Previous to his tenure at UALR, he was a reading specialist, a Kindergarten teacher, and a reading recovery teacher in the public schools for 20 years.

(AL)

Qadri Ahmadi teaches Postcolonial Studies at the University of Minnesota.

(Phil)

The fact that all senior figures also employed this move, however, underlines the importance of locating oneself firmly in the academic milieu through association with a particular institution:

(3)

Lindy Bradford is Interim Associate Dean and Chair of the Department of Special Education at the University of Colorado at Colorado Springs.

(AL)

Lu Wei Chen is a professor in the College of Computer Science, Zhejiang University, China. He was a visiting scholar in the Department of Computer

Science, State University of New York at Buffalo, USA from 1987 to 1988.

(EE)

Senior scholars, however, have a greater repertoire of experiences to draw on in constructing a biographical identity, and the data show an upward curve in publication, achievement and service themes in traversing across the status cline. Male senior scholars, in particular, were far more likely to discuss their publication outputs, and female professors their research interests:

(4)

Pål Arstan is PhD and professor in the sociology of religion at the University of Agder, Norway. He has written extensively on Norwegian religiosity and qualitative methods. His latest book in English is 'An Introduction to the Sociology of Religion: Classical and Contemporary Perspectives', Ashgate, Aldershot 2006.

(Male Phil)

Her research interests include embodiment, enculturation and identity; emotion and neurobiology; pain, suffering and religion; and death and dying.

(Female Phil)

Her research focuses on conceptual modeling, requirements engineering, software architecture, model-driven engineering and business process management.

(Female EE)

At the other end of the scale, setting out an educational background was important for research students. In the absence of attested and recognised academic credentials, they sought to manufacture a credible disciplinary identity through status claims which showed that they had taken a higher degree at a prestigious university. These credentials are also often supplemented, and mainly by females, by a specification of the writer's research interests, as here:

(5)

Chua Luan is currently a PhD student in School of Information, Renmin University of China. Her research interests include data warehousing, data mining, high performance databases and database architectures for new hardware.

(EE)

Charlotte Crawley is a doctoral candidate at Queensland University of Technology. Areas of research centre around young children's social interactions, with particular focus on their enactment of governance and the concept of children's places.

(AL)

Junior academics and teaching and technical staff also tended to fill in what they may have seen as gaps in their professional identity by communicating a more personal self. While the personal profile move is typically short and largely confined to junior academics and students, a surprisingly large number of senior academics also added a line or two of personal information. This helps reach behind the façade of a bland scholarly persona to present a different identity claim: one which seeks to reclaim parts of their identities that can be lost within such institutional representations:

(6)

    He lives in Jerusalem with his wife and three sons.

                                                                 (EE)

    Vijay Madhavan was born in Coimbatore, India, on October 21, 1985. He is a Baha'i.

                                                                  (EE)

    When not doing philosophy he writes poems and climbs mountains, sometimes simultaneously.

                                                              (Phil)

While the bios in this corpus largely functioned as a medium of professional self-presentation, a few scholars included a brief reference to another existence, opening a window to themselves as private individuals. It is a move which helps provide a more intimate revelation than the usual litany of professional accomplishments and, with the addition of an email address, adds a potentially interactive dimension to the bio.

## Gender and themes

Gender seemed to be less important than seniority in influencing how writers represented themselves in this genre. Table 5.4 suggests that what academics tended to say about themselves was broadly similar across genders, in terms of both the distribution of themes and the proportion of texts which included each of those themes.

**Table 5.4   Percentage of themes and bios including theme types by gender**

|  | Female % total themes | Male % total themes | Female % of bios with theme | Male % of bios with theme |
|---|---|---|---|---|
| Employment | 31.3 | 30.8 | 89.0 | 88.0 |
| Research interests | 27.5 | 23.9 | 70.3 | 60.5 |
| Education | 17.1 | 14.8 | 41.7 | 40.0 |
| Publications | 13.9 | 16.7 | 38.3 | 46.7 |
| Achievements | 4.0 | 5.6 | 11.3 | 12.5 |
| Community service | 3.7 | 5.3 | 10.3 | 14.0 |
| Personal profile | 2.5 | 2.9 | 6.0 | 7.0 |
| **Total** | **100%** | **100%** |  |  |

There were, however, some differences, with men giving greater emphasis to their publications, service and achievements, and women attending more to their research interests and education. There seems little obvious explanation for these differences, although if we take the figures for gender together with those for discipline, it is possible that seniority may play a role here. Philosophy and electronic engineering continue to be largely male-dominated fields where men are more likely to be heads of labs and assume posts of greater responsibility, such as holding chairs and editorships (Tse and Hyland, 2008). They therefore have a greater range of accomplishments to include in their representations. Many women simply offered a list of their educational experiences and professional qualifications:

(7)

> Feng Chau received the B.S. degree from Hefei University of Technology, Hefei, China, in 1986, the M.S. degree in electrical engineering from Institut National Polytechnique de Lorraine, Nancy, France, in 1991, and the PhD degree in computer science from the University of Metz, Metz, France, in 1995.
>
> (EE)

> She graduated with a BSc (Hons) in Speech and Language Therapy from the University of Ulster in 1993 and received a D.Phil from the same institution in 2000.
>
> (AL)

113

More usually, they also included their research interests without mention of publications:

(8)

> Her main research interests lie in the areas of Aesthetics, Ethics, and Philosophy of Mind, especially in the intersection between these areas.
>
> (Phil)

> Her current research is focused on investigating state-of-the-art CMOS devices, alternative high-mobility substrates, nanoscale magnetics, energy-harvesting devices, and power MOSFETs.
>
> (EE)

However, even senior females often sidestepped the 'institutional factfile' kind of identity claims and consciously avoided the badges of professional expertise. There are, for example, no cases of males offering such a bare-bones bio as these, which are complete texts:

(9)

> Ann Blake is Professor and Head of the School of Early Childhood at Queensland University of Technology.
>
> (AL)

> Lisbeth Leogaard is professor of the History of Religions at the University of Bergen, Norway.
>
> (Phil)

Males, on the other hand, tended to foreground what they had formally accomplished by way of publications (10), service to the academic community (11) and achievements (12):

(10)

> He is the coauthor of the book 'High-Fidelity Medical Imaging Displays' (SPIE Press, 2004).
>
> (EE)

> He is author of seven books and over 70 articles/essays on various topics in New Testament studies. His most recent books are …
>
> (Phil)

(11)

> He is a member of the editorial board of the *International Journal of Data*

*Warehousing and Mining* and has served on more than 40 program committees including ...

(EE)

He served as President of the Society of Asian and Comparative Philosophy (2001–2003) and is Series Editor of Lexington's Studies in Comparative Philosophy and Religion.

(Phil)

(12)

... and his 'Everyone Can Write: Essays Toward a Hopeful Theory of Writing and Teaching Writing' (2000) was given the James Britton Award by the Conference on English Education. NCTE recently gave him the James R. Squire Award 'for his transforming influence and lasting intellectual contribution'.

(AL)

Dr. Basturkmen was the recipient of the NSF Presidential Faculty Fellowship in 2005. He was elevated to the IEEE Fellow status for his contributions to Si and Si1 Gex epitaxy.

(EE)

From this data, academic identities are fashioned around professional discourses rather than displaying noticeably gender ones. While there are differences in some of the choices, both males and females seek to construct a credible disciplinary identity through the presentation of valued academic accomplishments in much the same way. It may be, however, that the females in this corpus are simply conforming to conventions which are themselves gendered and creating bios which construct them in terms of masculine ideologies. I take up this issue again in 8.2.

## Discipline and themes

While status and gender influenced the decisions authors made in assembling information for a bio, the decisive factor in these choices appears to be discipline. This largely results from the epistemological and social characteristics of the fields, and it would be surprising if the data had shown no differences in how authors represented themselves in this genre. Table 5.5, for example, shows that the gender distributions were relatively even by discipline compared with the differences across gender.

It is, perhaps, unexpected to find publications making such a relatively small overall contribution to disciplinary identity claims. After all, publication is 'the life blood of academia' (Becher and Trowler, 2001), facilitating both the promotion of knowledge and the establishment of reputation. No new discovery or insight has any significance until it is made available to others, and no individual receives credit for it until it has been published. But while books and articles are the currency of academic credibility, this badge of disciplinary membership occurs far fewer times as a theme in these bios. Employment background and research interests both exceed output in these texts, although disciplinary differences were most apparent in this category.

**Table 5.5   Percentage of themes by disciplines and gender**

|  | *Applied linguistics* | | *Electrical engineering* | | *Philosophy* | | *Totals* | |
|---|---|---|---|---|---|---|---|---|
|  | *F* | *M* | *F* | *M* | *F* | *M* | *F* | *M* |
| Employment | 36.9 | 37.4 | 24.8 | 23.9 | 34.6 | 35.7 | **32.3** | **32.9** |
| Research interests | 31.3 | 27.1 | 27.6 | 25.7 | 23.6 | 17.5 | **27.3** | **23.2** |
| Education | 12.4 | 10.7 | 25.9 | 21.9 | 10.2 | 8.5 | **15.3** | **13.0** |
| Publications | 12.4 | 17.8 | 6.0 | 6.3 | 25.2 | 31.4 | **16.0** | **19.1** |
| Achievements | 3.3 | 3.2 | 6.3 | 9.9 | 1.8 | 1.0 | **3.6** | **4.6** |
| Community service | 2.2 | 2.7 | 5.4 | 7.8 | 3.2 | 3.7 | **3.3** | **4.6** |
| Personal profile | 1.5 | 1.1 | 4.0 | 4.5 | 1.4 | 2.2 | **2.2** | **2.6** |
| **Totals** | **100** | **100** | **100** | **100** | **100** | **100** | **100** | **100** |

Philosophers were most likely to parade their publications. Publishing single-authored books is central to a philosopher's identity. Books in philosophy are explicitly interpretive and intensely personal products which address topics with long-range solutions, engage historically unresolved questions and involve complex discursive exposition. Research and publication times are slow and often the result of solitary efforts. Because of all this, publications take on a significance which is very different from the crowded fields of the hard sciences where a relatively small number of problems are pursued by a substantial number of scientists and publication is journal-based, frenetic and multi-authored. Books, then, are the gold standard of publications in philosophy, and books are perhaps easier to include in bios than a series of multi-authored papers.

Engineers, in fact, gave very little emphasis to publications in their bios, focusing instead on their research interests and education. In engineering, education was normally associated with the specific field of study, listing degrees as well as where these had been gained. This emphasis is particularly marked in this field and not only demonstrates an area of expertise but also promotes a scholarly insider-competence in esoteric skills and knowledge (13):

(13)

> Michael E. Smythe received the PhD degree in electrical engineering and plasma physics from Cornell University, Ithaca, NY, in 1975, with a graduate work on the generation and propagation of intense relativistic electron beams.
>
> (EE)

> She received the B.S. degree in automation from the Czech Technical University, Prague, in 2000, and the M.S. degree in automation with a focus on microsystem technology in 2003 from the Tampere University of Technology, Tampere, Finland, where she is currently pursuing the PhD degree in automation with a focus on microfluidics.
>
> (EE)

In many ways these results also reflect a more apprenticeship-based system of research training in the hard sciences, where inexperienced academics enjoy greater opportunities to play a fuller role in the research and publishing process as part of a lab-based team even while pursuing their studies. In engineering fields, for example, the focus of a PhD is liable to be part of a wider collaboratively conducted study and so more likely to warrant early publishing and count as an original contribution. Research is typically less individually conceived and independently conducted here than in the soft knowledge fields, and so for many engineers educational training is a major aspect of their career profile and therefore tends to be given more attention in their bios.

It is interesting that engineers also seem to attach some importance to establishing more of a personal profile than do those in other disciplines. Almost all bios mentioned the subject's birthplace, for example, and often the year of birth:

(14)

> Meiling Zhou was born in Changsha, China,

(EE)

> G. Quiroz was born in Villa de Guadalupe, San Luis Potosí, México, in 1979.

(EE)

> Sarah C. McQuaide was born in Ventura, CA, in 1976.

(EE)

In addition, engineering bios are often accompanied by a passport-style photograph, offering a *visual version* (Hess, 2002) of the author's identity. Essentially, these represented the individual in a professional rather than a social context, with simply a head-and-shoulders view and the subject centred in the frame. There is little here to present a more nuanced view of a private individual.

In contrast, applied linguists tended to attach some importance to their research interests, comprising about a third of all moves in this corpus:

(15)

> Jennifer Whistler's scholarship unpacks traditional and new media convergence within global markets. She is particularly interested in …

> His research interests include the (corpus-based) study of non-native writing, differences between spoken and written English, and the syntax of dialogue in fiction writing.

Here a claim is made for academic credibility through unpublished scholarly endeavours, both signalling an insider expertise in areas of current interest to the field and seeking recognition for membership of the disciplinary club. More than this, however, the research specialisms of applied linguistics provide insights into the tribal affiliations of the writer. Proximity here is a strategy to engineer alignment with a particular 'invisible college' of like-minded individuals.

## 5.4   'He works as a lecturer': Process types in bios

Identity is expressed in terms of not only *what* we talk about but *how* we talk about it. The ways that writers represent both outer and inner experience, the world of action and events and that of reflection and speech, are coded in SFL models as process choices. As I noted when discussing Table 5.2, the writers of these bios mainly used relational and material processes, either showing a *relationship* between something, usually the writer and an attribute of some kind, or reporting the writer *doing* something or having done something. Again, these choices represent resources of proximity which writers use to position themselves as members. As before, I will explore the use of processes in terms of writer characteristics, looking in turn at status, gender and discipline.

**Table 5.6    Process types by status: Frequencies and percentages**

|  | Senior | | Junior | | Students | | Admin/ Tech | | Unstated | | Totals | |
|---|---|---|---|---|---|---|---|---|---|---|---|---|
|  | Raw | % | Raw | % | Raw | % | Raw | % | Raw | % | Raw | % |
| Relational | 668 | 57.2 | 309 | 55.1 | 172 | 53.6 | 53 | 29.3 | 128 | 40.4 | **1330** | **52.2** |
| Material | 466 | 39.9 | 229 | 40.8 | 136 | 42.4 | 92 | 50.8 | 180 | 56.8 | **1103** | **43.3** |
| Mental | 20 | 1.7 | 17 | 3.0 | 10 | 3.1 | 6 | 3.3 | 5 | 1.6 | **58** | **2.3** |
| Verbal | 12 | 1.0 | 6 | 1.1 | 3 | 0.9 | 30 | 16.6 | 3 | 0.9 | **54** | **2.1** |
| Behavioural | 2 | 0.2 | 0 | 0.0 | 0 | 0.0 | 0 | 0.0 | 0 | 0.0 | **2** | **0.1** |
| Existential | 0 | 0.0 | 0 | 0.0 | 0 | 0.0 | 0 | 0.0 | 1 | 0.3 | **1** | **0.0** |
| **Total** | **1168** | **100** | **561** | **100** | **321** | **100** | **181** | **100** | **317** | **100** | **2548** | **100** |

## Status and processes

Beginning with the influence of status on identity construction, the analyses suggest that the proportion of relational forms increased and material forms decreased with rank (Table 5.6).

It is, perhaps, no surprise that relational processes dominate writers' choices among the academics and students in this genre, comprising about half of all expressions in these two sub-corpora. Bios are stretches of text which have something to say about the author, and what they mainly have to say is *who he or she is*, or rather, how he or she wants the reader to see who he or she is. In effect, Halliday's (1994) category of relational clauses generalises the traditional conceptions of 'copula' constructions and helps to construe 'being'. They imply no agency by the writer in the conventional sense of acting on the world and, as a consequence, John (2009: 278) suggests that they carry a relatively low *writer visibility*. Relational clauses, however, are a key way by which academics are able to convey an identity by expressing *who they are*. It is interesting, moreover, that visibility is increased by the preference for identifying over attributive choices, particularly among senior academics, where they are more than twice as frequent:

(16)

Beth Bellini is Professor of Anthropology at Hamish College, Clinton ...

(AL)

She is the author or co-author of over 40 technical papers and is the holder of two patents.

(EE)

Ms Morris has been the recipient of numerous grants ...

(Phil)

The examples show that these identifying choices impart a definiteness and uniqueness to the relationship expressed between the author and what is being claimed as part of the writer's identity. This relates to Thompson's (2004: 98) statement that these processes say something about 'the broader concerns and the values of the writer' as they signal that this is an important part of who they see themselves to be: they *identify* the writer. This is less obvious in the bios of students and non-professorial faculty where attributive options signal class membership rather than a unique identity:

(17)

She is an independent scholar.

(AL)

Ling Wu is a PhD student in Teaching English as a Second Language in the Department of Language and Literacy Education at UBC.

(AL)

Sangath is a member of the Institute of Industrial Engineers.

(EE)

Here writers make claims to be seen as one of many rather than as one alone; so their status is part of a wider group and not an exclusive position or distinctive aspect of their persona.

Finally here, I should mention the frequency of *verbal* processes among the bios of teachers and technical writers. While the raw differences are not huge, the fact that these authors used verbal clauses far more heavily than others is suggestive. These signal the presence of the writer in the text as an active *sayer*, a person who tells, informs, offers, commands or whatever, although in these texts the saying was principally concerned with lecturing and public speaking of various kinds:

(18)
He has presented at many conferences.

(EE)

He has spoken or run faculty-development sessions across the US and in 19 foreign countries. She now lectures in French at several schools in the Bay area.

(AL)

She reports the results of this work at international venues.

(AL)

**Table 5.7    Percentages of process types by gender**

|  |  | *Females* | *Males* | *Total* |
|---|---|---|---|---|
| Relational |  | 50.0 | 54.2 | **52.1** |
|  | Circumstantial | 12.1 | 9.2 | **10.0** |
|  | Attributive | 26.8 | 28.3 | **28.0** |
|  | Identifying | 32.4 | 37.9 | **35.1** |
|  | Possessive | 28.7 | 24.6 | **26.9** |
| Material |  | 43.7 | 42.9 | **43.6** |
| Mental |  | 3.1 | 1.8 | **2.2** |
| Verbal |  | 3.2 | 0.9 | **2.1** |
| Behavioural |  | 0.0 | 0.2 | **0.0** |
| Existential |  | 0.0 | 0.0 | **0.0** |
| **Total** |  | **100%** | **100%** | **100%** |

Like all bios in the corpus, writers refer to themselves in the third person, but in all cases of verbal processes we also find that the participant is always the source of the action, so imparting an active and *visible* presence in the text. Here are authors trying to establish a credible academic identity through choices which foreground discoursal activities valued by their communities.

## Gender and processes

As with themes, gender does not seem to greatly impact on how writers decide to represent themselves at clause level. Table 5.7 shows a broadly similar use of process types between males and females, with material processes being used equally and only a slight difference in the use of relational types.

Within the relational category, males used slightly more 'intensive' types (attributive and identifying) to express who they are through a relationship to a particular title or status:

(19)

John Burgess is an assistant professor of Early Childhood Education at the University of Arkansas.

(AL)

D. Lawrence is a senior librarian at the University of Madison's Main Library where he is responsible for the cataloguing of Eastern European publications.

(AL)

But it is also possible for relational clauses to involve additional meaning features in that they may be either possessive or circumstantial, conveying a relationship of ownership or custody (20) or one of time, place, manner, cause, etc. (Halliday, 1994: 130) (21). Females used slightly more of these forms:

(20)

Her research interests include second language acquisition, sociolinguistics and pragmatics.

(AL)

She has a PhD in musicology from the University of Michigan.

(Phil)

Her awards include the Significant Technical Achievement Award (2000).

(EE)

(21)

She is primarily interested in investigating involvement and meaning-making mechanisms of computer games.

(EE)

She is currently with Beijing University.

(AL)

She is currently on the editorial board of several international journals.

(Phil)

These claims to an academic identity are less forthright than those expressed through intensive process forms. Instead of saying that the writer has a status of x or is a member of a class of x, these insinuate more subtle appeals for a scholarly identity. There is an indirectness here which asks the reader to accept the writer's academic credibility in terms of an association with a particular research group, university or set of interests or hot topics. The frequency differences are small, but the fact that they exist may indicate something of gender-specific distinctiveness in the construction of scholarly identity.

It also appears that females used rather more verbal forms than males, presenting themselves as arguers and discussers:

(22)

She is now lecturing at Sanjesh College of Computing and Statistics, Tehran, Iran.

(EE)

She is known for her work in this area and is regularly asked to speak at international conferences on these issues.

(Phil)

She has presented numerous invited talks at national and international meetings ...

(AL)

Actual frequencies are too small to make generalisations about gender differences, but like mental processes, verbal choices highlight human agency, allowing the writer to project an energetic and active persona. The decision to present a self in this way brings the writer, lecturer or presenter to the forefront and so helps to construe her explicitly in a scholarly role. This is someone who has opinions and ideas and is recognised as someone able to communicate them to others.

Interestingly, female bios seemed to reflect a rather different approach to identity construction. While these texts also had their share of material processes projecting an active contributor to journals and universities, they also displayed the writer as a deserving beneficiary of disciplinary recognition. The verb *received* tends to be a very frequent form in the female texts together with other forms which emphasise the earning of honours and qualifications:

(23)

She **has made** great achievements on refractory metals and superconducting materials and **has received** many honours.

(EE)

Chrisoula Andreour **received** her PhD from the University of Pittsburgh ...

(Phil)

Sabina Morisso **earned** her PhD in linguistic and sociocultural anthropology at the University of Pennsylvania in December 2006.

(AL)

By stressing earned recognition and achievement, these authors underline their contribution both to valued academic goals and to the construction of a scholarly identity. The ways males and females express themselves in verb choices, however, do not vary enormously, and while these findings suggest some interesting avenues for future research, the more substantial differences lie elsewhere.

## Discipline and processes

Once again, discipline appeared to be a key determinant of linguistic choice. As with themes, decisions at clausal level reflect broad disciplinary preferences for self-representation. Table 5.8 shows that the engineers' texts contained more material and verbal processes, and that applied linguists employed more mental types and philosophers made greater use of identifying relative clauses.

While the figures are not high, the table shows that applied linguists made considerably greater use of mental types than writers in the other fields, representing research as an act of discovery and cognition rather than of work and writing. These examples are typical:

(24)

Her recent work **examines** the intersections of civic rhetoric and digital spaces.

He **investigates** writing skill in classroom and workplace settings …

His fascination with both historical and contemporary computers leads him to continually **wonder** why some technologies are taken up while others are abandoned.

**Table 5.8   Percentages of processes by disciplines**

|  |  | AL | EE | Phil | Total |
|---|---|---|---|---|---|
| Relational |  | 53.4 | 48.0 | 57.3 | **52.2** |
|  | Circumstantial | 7.1 | 14.3 | 7.4 | **9.7** |
|  | Attributive | 34.4 | 33.8 | 14.1 | **27.6** |
|  | Identifying | <sup>w</sup>29.9 | <sup>w</sup>21.5 | <sup>w</sup>51.3 | <sup>w</sup>**35.5** |
|  | Possessive | 28.6 | 30.4 | 21.2 | **27.2** |
| Material |  | 40.9 | 47.8 | 38.7 | **43.4** |
| Mental |  | 3.6 | 1.4 | 2.4 | **2.3** |
| Verbal |  | 1.9 | 2.8 | 1.2 | **2.1** |
| Behavioural |  | 0.2 | 0.0 | 0.2 | **0.0** |
| Existential |  | 0.0 | 0.0 | 0.2 | **0.0** |
| **Total** |  | **100%** | **100%** | **100%** | **100%** |

This choice adds a more reflective and studious shade to a bio than other options, representing the writer as a thinking academic rather than as an intellectual worker grinding out a quota of presentations and papers. Here is a depiction of academic work as intellectual quest and the individual academic as a thinker and explorer, projecting a distinctively intellectual identity to the writer. Once again, the frequencies are too small to draw meaningful conclusions, but an intimacy with the nuances of language may encourage these writers to reflect more on their choice of expression than those in other fields.

In contrast, engineers, and particularly male engineers, almost never exercised this option and rarely represented themselves as analysts. Instead, they characterised themselves using material clauses. These are processes of *action*, expressing the notion that some entity *does* something and so emphasises both the actor and the act itself. This category covers both concrete and abstract processes, and while *teaching* and *publishing* are common verb forms in these clauses, the mental activity of research and reflection is often transformed into the physical acts of writing and publishing, or even more corporal activities:

(25)

> She has published more than 90 refereed journal and conference papers and serves on the editorial board of several journals.

> (EE)

> ... where he works on designing, implementing, and deploying cutting edge RFID systems in environments ranging from distribution centers to pickup trucks. Most recently, he led the design and implementation of the Tool Link asset tracking system in collaboration with Ford Motor Company.

> (EE)

In engineering texts, then, experience is represented as work. The use of material processes conveys a sense of activity to the author, giving him or her greater visibility in the text and helping to project the sense of a dynamic identity. Here, we might suppose, is an academic taking on tasks to test accepted understandings and confront new problems. It therefore reflects the practice-oriented nature of the discipline and situates the author firmly within it. This is a field which prioritises epistemic values founded on empiricism and which celebrates research as academic *work* whose purpose is to transform the physical world.

The table shows, however, that the greatest disciplinary variations were in the ways writers employed relational processes, and in particular the use of identifying relational clauses. Explicitly naming oneself as something or other is a major aspect of identification, and philosophers did this twice as frequently as applied linguists and nearly four times more than engineers. Principally, this was to state their position in terms of status and institutional affiliation (26), although it also included publications (27) and detailing of service to the community through various activities (28):

(26)

> Jeanne Ravencroft is senior lecturer in Religious Studies at the University of Edinburgh.

> (Phil)

> Kathleen Swale is professor of philosophy.

> (Phil)

Isaac Neusner is distinguished service professor.

(Phil)

(27)
   She is the author of *Seeking Bauls of Bengal*.

(Phil)

   She is the co-editor of *Philosophy of Film and Motion Pictures* (Blackwell, 2005).

(Phil)

   He is the author of Warcraft and the Fragility of Virtue (1992).

(Phil)

(28)
   She is the co-editor of *Philosophy of film.*

(Phil)

   She is the organiser of the 2007 World Congress of Aesthetics in Ankara, Turkey.

(Phil)

   He has been President of the International Association for Aesthetics, Secretary Treasurer of the American Society for Aesthetics, and …

(Phil)

It is unclear why this pattern was so prevalent in philosophy, although there is a more individualistic ethos in this discipline which encourages writers to put their personal stamp on what they write. Research practices which stress interpretations and arguments as the creative insights of the author offer a way of positioning oneself in relation to colleagues, which is very different from the self-effacing ideology which sees results as the collective endeavours of a team simply reporting experimental outcomes. Here knowledge is personally constructed and owned and so contributes to an individual ethos rather than being shared and part of a cooperative context of labour.

# 5.5  Conclusions

In this chapter I have sought to uncover something of the systematic rhetorical choices which underlie identity production in research bios. On the face of it, this seems to be a relatively standardised genre whose tight word restrictions constrain individuals to a limited range of representational options. Perhaps because of this, the journal bio is a genre where writers choose to downplay, if not completely eliminate, any reference to their lives outside the academy. Families, religion, hobbies, personal experiences and social lives are airbrushed from the individual's identity representation and a self is constructed which projects proximity: a scholarly competence through engagement with valued disciplinary attributes and values.

We see in this corpus of 600 texts, however, that variations emerge in the ways these bios construct an academic identity for their writers, in terms of both what aspects of experience are selected for inclusion and how these experiences are expressed grammatically. We see, for example, that senior academics drew on a wider repertoire of experiences which includes references to employment, research, publication and achievement to suggest a fuller academic identity. It is also clear that they used far more relational processes, and particularly identifying clauses, to increase their rhetorical visibility and their unique status. Junior academics and students, on the other hand, presented themselves as members of groups using attributive clauses. Their identity claims were also more closely associated with their qualifications and institutional affiliations, and they tended to flesh this out with personal data such as birthdates and family information. Gender appears to make relatively little impact on the projection of an academic identity, although males highlighted their publications, service and achievements rather more and women focused on their research interests and education.

Most importantly, the analyses reveal the importance of discipline. Despite the conventions of anonymity in the sciences, for example, or perhaps to compensate for these, electrical engineers are generally asked to submit bios which are twice as long as the other fields and to include a passport portrait. More centrally, they also gave greater weight to education and personal details and used material processes more frequently. Such decisions reflect disciplinary-imbued self-representations related to socialisation practices which are often based around situated learning in particular research groups and which value an activity-focused approach to academic research.

Philosophers, in contrast, felt that research interests and publications should form a more central part of a scholarly identity and favoured identifying relational clauses. All these choices emphasise an identity which aligns with a discipline where individuality plays a prominent role. Visibility and credibility depend on unaided research and single-authored publications which offer novel angles on old problems. Creating a disciplinary identity thus emphasises individual contributions and achievements and the occupation of a unique position. Applied linguists sit between these extremes, highlighting their research interests and employment histories and representing their work through mental processes. Here we might see the influence of disciplinary ideologies which stress the importance of research and membership of particular intellectual factions, and where academic engagement is an act of discovery and cognition.

The question arises, perhaps, of why this should be of any interest. After all, a small piece of text tagged on to the bottom of a research article carrying no serious risks for a writer's h-index or article acceptance is not something that seems to be immediately remarkable. It does, however, have considerable significance as a self-representational genre. Most importantly for the study of identity, the bio reveals something of the interaction between self and collectivity, and between positioning and proximity. It points to hegemonic academic ideologies which position writers' representations of themselves while suggesting how these may be cross-cut by more personal experiences. In particular, the bio offers the opportunity, perhaps uniquely among academic genres, to study the influence of gender, status and discipline as mediating the performance of an academic identity. Each of these variables is potentially hugely important in understanding how individuals craft an explicitly scholarly version of themselves from a community repertoire, but research remains a work in progress. Some of these issues, however, are taken up in the next few chapters where I explore how reputation, gender and culture can influence the disciplinary construction of identity.

# 6 Culture: Authority and Visibility

I have argued that identity results from the command of an 'idiom', or mastery of a community repertoire, which we appropriate and shape to our own needs and personal proclivities. We locally construct an identity through relationships between the self and community, what I have called *proximity*, and through relationships between the self and the message, or *positioning*. The former ties us into the collective through the social and discursive practices of a discipline and the power relations these draw upon. The latter refers to the ways individuals employ these resources to express a distinctive point of view, a personal 'take' on what is being discussed. One emphasises conformity and the other difference, but both are essential to effective communication and to the individual's claim to be taken seriously as a credible member of a discipline.

Proximity and positioning generally work in tandem but not always in concord. This is because while we can successfully express our evaluations and stances towards topics only using the language our disciplines accept as logical and persuasive, we may not always feel comfortable in using those forms. The 'self' that is inscribed in academic discourse is unfamiliar and strange to community newcomers and novices who often feel a conflict in the identity they are portraying using these prescribed conventions. However, while all students have to adapt themselves to the requirements of academic ways of thinking and seeing, practices which require writers to adopt the role of an autonomous, rational mind resolving the inconsistencies of the world, this can appear particularly alien to those educated in other traditions of knowledge.

This chapter takes up this key identity issue by exploring how students in Hong Kong of China use and experience academic writing in English. Taking first-person mention as one way of expressing subjectivity in texts, and recognising the contested nature of 'culture', I examine how prior learning experience can influence constructions of identity. First, though, I will outline something of how students can experience academic conventions and the potential impact of their wider culture on this.

# 6.1　Student experiences of academic conventions

Student discourse, and particularly writing, is at the heart of teaching and learning in higher education. This is largely because knowledge is inseparable from discourse, so that the subject matter that students must acquire is accessible only through specialist forms of language and, in turn, it is this content which gives meaning to those forms. More directly, the spoken and written genres students are asked to produce at university serve the institutional purposes of demonstrating learning. They are used to assess the extent of students' understanding of subject content and control of disciplinary literacies; and this can mean success or failure for students. A student's mastery of genre is a complex process which involves learning both specialised knowledge frames and relevant discourse forms. At the same time, students are developing a disciplinary identity through the specialised content, practices and language choices of their fields.

However, this acquisition of disciplinary argument practices is by no means a smooth process. Writing conventions are typically taken for granted as unproblematic by tutors (e.g. Lea and Street, 2000) and viewed with suspicion by students. This is because academic discourses make communicative demands on students which are very different from those of the home or school and so seem inexplicable and cold to many learners, forcing them to adopt identities which are alien to those they want to project (Ivanič, 1998).

## Discourse, difference and habitus

It is worth repeating here that the writing practices of the academy, which are so familiar and unremarkable to many insiders, are actually disciplinary-peculiar ways of representing reality. Academic writing, in fact, differs massively from the ways we typically see the world, disrupting our everyday perceptions of how things are. In everyday uses of language, for example, we tend to represent things as we experience them so that events unfold linearly, one after another, and agents accomplish actions. Put simply, we call it as we see it. This 'natural' or congruent representation (Halliday, 1998) is turned on its head by academic writing, which treats events as existing in cause and effect networks, disguises the source of statements, foregrounds events rather than actors, and engages with meanings defined by the text rather than in the physical context. Wignell et al. (1993), for instance, characterise the sciences as representing experience by establishing a range of technical terms which are organised to explain how things happen or exist. This technicality is then used to create further technicality through defining, classifying and explaining. Humanities disciplines, like history and philosophy, on the other hand, employ abstraction rather than technicality, moving from instances to conceptual representations.

These discourses are acquired slowly over time as newcomers are exposed to new ways of thinking, about both themselves and the world, as they write themselves into their disciplines. This is what Bartholomae (1986: 4) had in mind when he wrote:

> Every time a student sits down to write for us, he has to invent the university for the occasion – invent the university, that is – or a branch of it, like History or Anthropology or Economics or English. He has to learn to speak our language, to speak as we do, to try on the peculiar ways of knowing, selecting, evaluating, reporting, concluding, and arguing that define the discourse of our community.

A growing awareness of the conventions of disciplinary discourses helps socialise students into academic practices and valued ways of thinking and expressing. The notion of *practices* is important here as it not only emphasises the connection between language and what people do in the social world, their academic lives, but also draws attention to the fact that what people do with language is repeated and slowly routinised. Ways of using language are *practised* and gradually become part of our implicit life behaviours.

In Bourdieu's (1990) terms, these routinised discourses are an individual's *habitus*, and one's social, and so disciplinary, identity emerges because the social structures that characterise a particular social situation have been quietly embodied within it. An individual's habitus unconsciously incorporates the patterns, norms and regularities that structure a social setting: the behavioural codes, habits, bodily attitudes and ways of speaking of that setting. As habitus embodies these normalised structures over time, individuals begin to adopt them into their repertoires and to perform them through their behaviours. Concrete instances of language use, such as specific essays, dissertations and presentations, involve drawing on these existing practices, and the performance of such repeated patterns works to anchor us as increasingly belonging to particular communities. Habitus thus provides a socially structured explanation for the formation of a disciplinary identity. As Dressen-Hammouda (2008: 235) puts it: 'One's disciplinary identity is an ensemble of socio-historical regularities and norms that practitioners embody as a result of specializing within their disciplines.'

## Identity, mystery and alienation

Students have not yet imbued these specialised communicative conventions into their habitus, however, and several studies have documented the struggles students often experience in navigating higher education. The incongruence, abstraction and technicality of what Scollon and Scollon (1981) call the 'essayist literacy' practices of the academy are a mystery, and they do not feel at home with the writing expected of them. The forms of discourse that have grown up around the disciplines are founded on participants suppressing their personal interests and distinctive social and cultural identities to foreground disciplinary arguments and subject matter. Students are asked to employ a style of writing at university which involves anonymising themselves and adopting the guise of a rational, disinterested, asocial seeker of truth. This is not easy for them.

For Halliday and Martin (1993), the acquisition of an academic variety of language involves both significant losses and gains. By stepping into an essayist literacy, writers sacrifice concreteness, empathy with discussed entities and ways of representing change as a dynamic process. On the other hand, they gain the ability to discuss abstract things and relations, and to categorise, quantify and evaluate according to the understandings of their discipline. Such gains, of course, are only perceived as such if students value what this literacy allows them to do, and the kinds of people it allows them to be. These particular ways of understanding and discussing the world therefore mean that the acquisition of an essayist literacy not only provides access to new communities and experiences, but is also closely linked to issues of identity. Students bring a range of social and cultural experiences to their classes and texts, and are not always willing to drop their everyday lives to take up this new identity.

The fact that specific forms and wordings are marked as more or less appropriate, or more or less prescribed, can create conflicts with the experiences students bring from their home community and the habits of meaning they have learnt there. The discourses and practices of their disciplines support identities very different from those they bring with them (Barton and Hamilton, 1998) so that authoring becomes a complex negotiation of one's sense of self and the institutional regulation of meaning-making. The studies by Ivanič (1998) and Lillis (2001) into the experiences of 'non-traditional' students in British higher education show how such regulation can be seen as confining and perhaps even threatening. A Creole/English-speaking student, for example, gave this response to Lillis' questions about the non-acceptability of contracted forms:

> It makes me sick ... I don't think it's important at all [laughs]. But you have to do it? It's like I'm imprisoned, honest to God [laughs] ... Everybody knows what 'I'm not' means. It's like trying to segregate, you know, you've got like a boundary that sets, you know, you apart from other people. Why? What difference does it make as long as you get your message across ...?
>
> (Lillis, 2001: 85)

Adopting these grammatical and lexical choices therefore positions writers as sharing the interests, beliefs and practices of an academic community, and clearly this is not to everyone's liking.

This feeling of opposition between the new identity they are being asked to assume and those they are already comfortable with can provoke resistance. Both Lin (2000) and Canagarajah (1999) show how students passively resist the assumptions and values which they are assumed to share by using the language. Ivanič (1998), discussing mature L1 students, argues that adults often find the literacy demands of the academy alienating and their practical knowledge undervalued:

> Their identities are threatened and they respond either by attempting to accommodate to the established values and practices of the context they are entering, or – more radically – by questioning and challenging the dominant values and practices, and recognising the possibility of change.
>
> (Ivanič, 1998: 9)

In other words, the identity which manifests itself in discourse is often one which is painfully constructed for writers and which can involve contesting the discourses of their fields.

## 6.2 Self-mention, culture and identity

The view expressed by many of the students in the above studies was that they wanted to feel personally connected to their texts but the conventions of academic discourse prevented them from doing this. Essentially, it was the *impersonality* of academic writing which frustrated the expression of personal views and left no space for a sense of self in their writing. Located in a more informal and everyday habitus, they found it difficult to communicate appropriate integrity and commitments and so sought to reject the discourses they encountered. A recurrent issue in these narratives is the feeling of relinquishing their personal authority by anonymising their writing. They sacrificed what they feel to be their 'authentic' identity to talk like a book.

## Authorial identity and self-mention

I have suggested in earlier chapters that there *is* room for negotiation of identity within academic writing and that personal positioning is accomplished through a range of rhetorical and linguistic resources. Perhaps the most visible manifestation of an authorial identity, however, is the use of first person (Hyland, 2001b; Kuo, 1999; Tang and John, 1999). In student and professional academic writing, these are overwhelmingly subject pronouns (Hyland, 2001b, 2002c), which announce the writer in the text and typically occur in first position. While the focus of academic writing tends to be the events or concepts discussed later in the clause, the choice of first position is very significant. The way a writer begins a clause not only foregrounds important information, firmly identifying the writer as the source of the associated statement, but also helps the writer control the social interaction in the text (e.g. Gosden, 1993). Consider the impact of such choices in these examples from single authors in my research article corpus described in Chapter 3:

(1)

    *I* agree with that, although *I* differ in the details as to the analysis of ...

        (AL)

    *I* will show that a convincing reply is available to the minimalist.

        (Phil)

    *We* shall prove, however, that this is not the case.

        (Phy)

But while it clearly signals where a writer stands on an issue, his or her *positioning*, it can also be a source of confusion and anxiety as I will discuss further below. It is plain that the conventions of personality are rhetorically constrained in academic writing, but these constraints are uncertain, and the extent to which one can reasonably explicitly intrude into one's discourse, or assert one's personal involvement, remains a dilemma for novices and experienced writers alike.

    On one hand, impersonality is seen as a defining feature of expository writing as it embodies the positivist assumption that academic research is purely empirical and objective. Geertz (1988) calls this 'author-evacuated' prose, and many textbooks and style guides advise students to avoid personal intervention:

> To the scientist it is unimportant who observed the chemical reaction: only the observation itself is vital. Thus the active voice sentence is inappropriate. In this situation, passive voice and the omission of the agent of action are justified.
>
> (Gong and Dragga, 1995: 55)

> Write your paper with a third person voice that avoids 'I believe' or 'It is my opinion'.
>
> (Lester, 2005: 144)

On the other hand, some commentators regard the first person as an important means of unequivocally getting behind one's views to assert a confident and authoritative stance. Other textbooks therefore encourage writers to make their own voice clear through the first person:

> I herewith ask all young scientists to renounce the false modesty of previous generations of scientists. Do not be afraid to name the agent of the action in a sentence, even when it is 'I' or 'we'.
>
> (Day, 2006: 166)

> Most of our recommendations are designed to help you maintain a scholarly and objective tone in your writing. This does not mean (and we have not said) that you should never use I or we in your writing. The use of I or we does not make a piece of writing informal.
>
> (Swales and Feak, 2004a: 20)

For these authors, the use of first person allows writers to emphasise, and to seek agreement for, their own contributions, speaking with authority and leaving readers in no doubt where they stand. In reality, things are a little more complicated, with over 60% more cases in humanities and social science papers (Hyland, 2002c) where authors are more concerned to link themselves with their ideas more explicitly rather than subsume their voice to that of nature.

## Academic discourses and cultural differences

In contrast to Ivanič's and Lillis' students, who all felt institutional disapproval of their personal involvement and pressure to remove the first person from their texts, many students from non-Western backgrounds feel uncomfortable using the construction precisely *because* of its connotations of personal authority. This represents a conflict between the disciplinary discourses they encounter at university and the autobiographical identities which have been shaped by very different traditions of literacy. In a real sense, it encapsulates a clash of cultures.

Seen ethnolinguistically and institutionally, culture implies a historically transmitted and systematic network of meanings which allow us to develop and communicate our knowledge and beliefs about the world (Lantolf, 1999; Street, 1995). Language and learning are therefore closely bound up with culture and our lived experiences. This is partly because our cultural values are carried through language, but also because cultures make available certain taken-for-granted ways of organising our understandings, including those we have of ourselves. The identities inscribed in academic conventions can therefore pose a serious challenge for second language students whose identities as learners and writers are often embedded in very different epistemologies. Educational processes in Western contexts reinforce an analytical, questioning and evaluative stance to knowledge, for example, encouraging students to criticise and recombine existing sources to dispute traditional wisdom and form their own points of view. Many Asian cultures, however, favour conserving and reproducing existing knowledge, establishing reverence for what is known through strategies such as memorisation and imitation. While such strategies demonstrate respect for knowledge, they may look to Western teachers like reproducing others' ideas.

Most centrally, observers such as the linguistic anthropologist Shirley Brice Heath (1991) have argued that there is an individualistic view of the self implicit in the educational practices of Western cultures, while students from many Eastern societies are socialised into very different values and beliefs. This quote from a study of classrooms in the People's Republic of China highlights such contrasts:

> Seeing such classes, with communicative approaches in mind and an uncomfortable feeling that memorising is rote learning, Western teachers might deplore the lack of interaction and individualisation, the absence of creativity and self-expression, or dearth of personal interpretation and experiential learning. Chinese counterparts ... could point out that every Chinese child is an individual with different abilities and needs, but that in Chinese society – and in the classroom – the priorities are that each person must be part of a group or community;

> learning interdependency, co-operation and social awareness; becoming oneself in relation to significant others; expressing that which is socially shared rather than individually felt; creating on the basis of mastery rather than discovery.
>
> (Cortazzi and Jin, 1996: 177–178)

Obviously not everyone's experience will be the same and it is not easy to generalise, but students who have grown up in an educational environment such as this are likely to develop very different expectations about learning, different conventions of expression and different conceptions of the self. When one day they find themselves in a lecture theatre of a Western university, or having to write an assignment using Western academic discourse conventions, then they are at a serious disadvantage.

## Independent vs. interdependent selves

Conceptual systems which tend to assert individual responsibility versus those which lean towards the nurturing responsibilities of the collective have been identified across a range of cultures and are seen to have discourse implications (e.g. Lakoff, 2002). Markus and Kitayama (1991) distinguish cultural views which they term 'independent' and 'interdependent' construals of self, for instance, and various studies have shown how children are socialised into such differing versions of selfhood (e.g. Clancy, 1986).

The academy's emphasis on analysis and interpretation means that students must position themselves in relation to the material they discuss, finding a way to express their own ideas and arguments (Cadman, 1997). Writers are required to establish a stance towards their propositions, to get behind their words and stake out a position. Yet such behaviours represent a highly individualistic identity which can be problematic for students from cultures where the self is more collectively constructed, representing a potentially serious barrier to acquiring an appropriate academic identity. Ramanathan and Atkinson (1999), for instance, point to the importance given to the metaphorical notion of *voice* in writing in Western educational settings, which foregrounds and valorises the individual. This concept is central to what I have referred to as *positioning* in disciplinary identity and

> is seen to represent linguistic behavior which is clear, *overt, expressive,* and even *assertive* and *demonstrative.* However, a broad range of the world's peoples conventionally adopt models and norms of communication that are almost diametrically opposed to the one just described, in that they foreground the *subtle,*

*interpretive, interdependent, non-assertive,* and even *nonverbal* character of communicative interaction.

(Ramanathan and Atkinson, 1999: 48)

A concept of written voice that centrally assumes the expression of a 'unique inner self' may therefore be problematic for some second language student writers.

Chinese students appear to be among these writers. Scollon (1991), for example, found his university students from China's Taiwan Province had considerable difficulties with presenting a clear stance in their writing because this kind of self-expression is 'squarely based on the Western, individualist sense of self' (p. 4). Instead, they were not writing primarily to express themselves but to become integrated into a particular kind of scholarly community. Following the Chinese tradition, they were seeking to pass on what they had received rather than learning to take on a scholarly voice in critiquing others. In the Chinese writing tradition, it is assumed that what is presented as fact is inseparable from who said it (Matalene, 1985), and this contrasts markedly with the Western conception that to be associated with what they have written, authors must indicate it is their own view. Thus, the statement 'Shakespeare is an excellent writer' can be presented without a source in the Chinese tradition, for example, but needs to be modified by 'In my opinion' in Western practice. This means that Western demands for rhetorical objectivity are sometimes seen as artificial, cumbersome and unnecessary (Scollon, 1994).

Clearly we need to be cautious here and recognise that students have identities beyond the language and culture they were born into. Spack (1997), for instance, argues that invoking culture to explain writing differences prompts a normative, essentialising stance which leads to lumping students together on the basis of their first language. However, while students are not merely cultural types, it is helpful to recognise that student difficulties in writing or speaking as an academic insider may be due to the disjunction of the writer's and reader's view of what is needed in a text and that different writing styles can be the result of culturally learnt conceptions of the self.

## 6.3 Self-mention and identity in Hong Kong undergraduate reports

To summarise the key point of the chapter so far, the conventions of Anglo-American composition require an authorial self with 'characteristics of individuality, rationality and autonomy' (Scollon, 1994: 36) which are likely to conflict with the culturally constructed selves of Asian writers. I have also stressed that an important aspect of this 'interdependent self' is suspicion of self-mention in writing compared with that of native English speakers (Ohta, 1991; Scollon, 1991). In this section I want to explore how this conflict plays out in the writing of L2 undergraduates at a university in Hong Kong of China, exploring the frequency and role of self-mention in 64 final-year undergraduate reports.

## Participants and procedures

The final-year report is the product of a research project typically spanning an entire year with credit for two courses. Students are assisted by a supervisor who, through regular individual consultations, approves their proposal, guides their research and monitors their progress. The purposes of the projects are to enable students to apply theories and methods learned in their courses and demonstrate ability to effectively review literature, conduct research, analyse results and present findings. Reports are typically between 8,000 and 13,000 words long and follow guidelines which reflect the research article formats of the particular discipline. They are assessed by two examiners in terms of how well students meet the objectives of the project and on the quality of the written work. This, then, is a high-stakes genre for students and is by far the most substantial and sustained piece of writing that they will do in their undergraduate careers.

This study was based on reports collected from biology (Bio), mechanical engineering (ME), information systems (IS), business studies (Bus), TESOL, economics (Econ), public administration (PA) and social sciences (SS), producing a corpus of 630,000 words. The texts were searched for the words *I, me, my, we, us* and *our*, checked to ensure they were exclusive first-person uses, and examined for their pragmatic function. A sample analysed by a colleague achieved an inter-rater agreement of 91%. The next step was to compare the results with a large corpus of 240 published research articles (RA) in similar fields. The professional corpus comprised articles from ten leading journals in each of eight related disciplines, totalling 1.4 million words (Hyland, 2001b). The corpus was twice as large as the student database, to strengthen observations about mainstream academic conventions which could be compared with the student uses. Clearly, there are difficulties in making broad comparisons between expert and novice practices which need to be acknowledged. However, the purpose was not to evaluate learner performance or to suggest a deficit in students' uses, but to learn something of what the two groups actually *do*: what any differences tell us of writers' linguistic schemata and sense of authorial identity.

These text analyses were supplemented by semi-structured interviews with one supervisor from each field (all native English speakers) and focus groups of student writers (all Chinese speakers). Participants were asked to provide information about their own writing and their impressions of disciplinary practices. These sought to elicit participants' understandings of the meanings and effectiveness of first-person use, and to uncover their own discoursal practices.

## Disciplinary and genre preferences for self-mention

Self-referential pronouns and determiners occurred about ten times in every 10,000 words in the student reports, roughly ten in every text. Table 6.1 shows that *I* was the most common form used and first-person singular pronouns comprised 60% of the total. A surprisingly large proportion of forms, however, were plural self-reference, even in individually written reports, and this was not entirely explained by the collaborative research on which these reports were often based.

**Table 6.1 Frequency of author pronouns and determiners in student reports (per 10,000 words)**

| Discipline | Author | All writer pronouns | Singular (I, me, my) | Plural (we, us, our) |
|---|---|---|---|---|
| Business studies | Multiple | 12.2 | 0.4 | 11.8 |
| Information systems | Individual | 15.6 | 9.1 | 6.5 |
| Economics | Individual | 12.9 | 7.8 | 5.1 |
| Public administration | Individual | 10.9 | 10.5 | 0.4 |
| Social sciences | Individual | 8.9 | 5.7 | 3.2 |
| TESOL | Individual | 8.3 | 7.3 | 1.0 |
| Mechanical engineering | Individual | 8.6 | 4.5 | 4.1 |
| Biology | Individual | 5.3 | 1.9 | 3.4 |
| Overall | | 10.1 | 6.1 | 4.0 |

These disciplinary variations only broadly correspond to expert practices, and differences are not marked in the student reports. In international journal articles we find the writer's presence, often signalled by a personal pronoun, to be an important rhetorical resource for gaining approval for his or her work, particularly in humanities and social science disciplines (Hyland, 2001b). In these fields the criteria for judging what is a valid analysis of data is less clear-cut, so the writer's personal intrusion can help establish the author's credibility and authority to persuade readers of an interpretation. It is an index of positioning.

What is most striking when we compare the student and published texts is that the professional writers were *four times* more likely to explicitly position themselves using the first person. This is despite the fact that active, agent-fronted sentences are structurally simpler and likely to be easier to construct for L2 writers. Table 6.2 groups cognate disciplines from the two genres to show something of the considerable differences in the use of author pronouns.

**Table 6.2 Personal reference in research articles and student reports (per 10,000 words)**

| Field | Totals | | Singular reference | | Plural reference | |
|---|---|---|---|---|---|---|
| | Articles | Reports | Articles | Reports | Articles | Reports |
| Science and engineering | 32.7 | 9.4 | 0.1 | 4.9 | 30.6 | 4.5 |
| Business and professional | 46.9 | 10.5 | 22.2 | 6.7 | 24.7 | 3.8 |
| Overall | 41.2 | 10.1 | 14.4 | 6.1 | 26.8 | 4.1 |

Clearly, the different purposes and writer–reader relationships of these genres will influence the ways authors represent themselves in their texts. So, while the articles are designed to construct knowledge through negotiation with peers, the reports are written to display knowledge to a more powerful assessor. While the research writer studiously cultivates the illusion that social distinctions of power, status and standing do not exist, or at least are unimportant to how a research paper will be received, the problem for students is to demonstrate an appropriate degree of intellectual autonomy while recognising readers' greater experience and knowledge of the field. Such differences, however, do not fully explain the undergraduates' rhetorical choices, and any tendency of students to acknowledge the authority of their readers is exacerbated in a culture which places a certain emphasis on respect for authority and the importance of face. So, while writers can always resist the relationships implied in a genre, awareness of audience in this context is typically manifested in rhetorical choices which recognise the reader's authority.

## 6.4 Discourse functions of authorial reference

While the frequency of self-mention can indicate something of the ways these students chose to represent themselves in their academic writing, what writers actually *do* with it reveals a lot more about authorial identity. The points at which writers choose to make themselves visible in their texts suggest the kinds of commitments they are willing to make and the information they are prepared to give about themselves: it indexes the identity they seek to construct.

### Identity and authorial roles

Refining a more general typology of pronoun use developed by Tang and John (1999), I explored the authorial roles implied in the use of first person from a study of the surrounding co-text. I examined each case of first person to categorise its function, and as can be seen from Table 6.3, students mainly used self-mention to state a discoursal goal and to explain a methodological approach. These are both functions which present a low-profile representation of self, carrying no implications of commitment to the argument presented in the text and asserting what is, essentially, a learner identity. More argumentative functions, such as presenting and justifying claims, were more commonly expressed without reference to the author. This reluctance to offer a clear stance towards what they had discovered in the research and their interpretations of what these meant also signals a clear authorial identity: one which takes no personal or rhetorical risks. Here, then, is an identity constructed as a reporting observer, a non-assertive and uninvolved writer.

These findings contrast markedly with the ways the 'expert writers' chose to project themselves into their research articles. In those texts almost half the occurrences of self-mention were used to present arguments or claims, compared with only a quarter in the student texts, while the least frequent use in the research articles, stating a purpose, was the most common in the project reports. As I have noted, these decisions impact powerfully on identity construction, with students adopting extremely cautious, low-visibility and risk-averse positions. I discuss the student responses further below.

**Table 6.3  Discourse functions of self-mention in student reports (%)**

| Function | Total | Bio | ME | IS | Econ | BS | TESOL | SS | PA | % |
|---|---|---|---|---|---|---|---|---|---|---|
| Stating a goal/ purpose | 228 | 36 | 21 | 36 | 32 | 43 | 37 | 38 | 35 | 36 |
| Explaining a procedure | 199 | 31 | 32 | 29 | 37 | 31 | 27 | 34 | 32 | 31 |
| Stating results/ claims | 103 | 16 | 29 | 19 | 9 | 26 | 13 | 14 | 13 | 18 |
| Expressing self-benefits | 58 | 9 | 11 | 8 | 18 | 0 | 11 | 3 | 11 | 8 |
| Elaborating an argument | 49 | 8 | 7 | 8 | 4 | 0 | 12 | 11 | 9 | 7 |
| **Totals** | **637** | **100** | **100** | **100** | **100** | **100** | **100** | **100** | **100** | **100** |

## Expressing self-benefits

A number of writers included comments on what they had personally gained from the project, a function which several departments included in the report rubric to add a reflective dimension to the learning experience. This use of self-mention performs a very low-key function which does not expose the writer to any threat of contradiction or move him or her beyond a familiar low-key student identity. These examples are typical of this kind of use:

(2)

> After finishing the project, I found that information system (IS) techniques can be applied to the real world. This helps me to be an IS professional in the future career.

(IS)

> This is a worth experience to me especially in the last year of my tertiary study. I hope the success of the fatigue test program will become an educational tool for the student to know more about fatigue in the Mechanical laboratory.

(ME)

The student here is not the originator of ideas or interpreter of results, but the presenter of the bland and commonplace: avoiding an individual stance towards the research undertaken to simply offer a comment on the experience. The usage suggests a subordinate identity and positions the individual firmly as a learner.

## Stating a goal/purpose

In a third of all cases, students used authorial pronouns to state their discoursal purposes, either signalling their intentions or providing an overt structure for their texts. Framing of this kind helps clarify both the direction of the research and the schematic structure of the argument, but it also foregrounds a fairly low-risk writer role, simply signposting readers through the text:

(3)

In this section, *I* am going to describe the findings from *my* interviews with the students based on their experience of the lesson in which *I* used task-based grammar teaching approach.

(TESOL)

*We* are interested in the strategy of Coca-Cola when it started to open the China market.

(BS)

In this research, *we* look at the elements in the demand for private cars.

(Econ)

Although there is an explicit intervention of an individual writer in these examples, the intervention is metadiscoursal, relating to facets of the text and not the research. It is therefore a function which, again, carries little threat of criticism or rejection, being essentially either text-internal, working to organise the discourse for readers, or related to a research purpose formulated in consultation with a supervisor. Explicit author presence here is therefore relatively innocuous, commits the writer to little and rarely shades into explicit claim-making. A number of students recognised this.

(4)

'I' is suitable for organising the report, we are just saying about the research not about the ideas. It is only about the intention of the research and this is OK. The supervisor already approved this.

(Econ student interview)

We are planning the essay here. This is not an important part so 'I' is OK to use.

(PA student interview)

The writers here present an identity which recognises the importance of proximity to discipline by taking responsibility for structuring and organising material for readers, acting as a text guide.

## Explaining a procedure

This is the second most frequent use of authorial reference in the reports and represents a similar metatextual dimension to describing the research procedures. It also reflects a similarly low degree of personal exposure. All the course guidelines stressed the importance of students clearly presenting their methodological approach, and this was also a feature of supervisors' comments. The ability to plan and carry out a viable and appropriate research methodology, demonstrating an ability to integrate and apply professional skills, surmount difficulties and set out procedures, was seen as a crucial element of the report. Students recognised the importance of accomplishing this purpose and many were willing to detail their approach as a first-person account, pairing *I* with material process verbs such as *interview, work, read, test* and so on:

(5)

*I* have interviewed 10 teachers, there were 10 teachers from different primary and secondary schools in Hong Kong of China.

(TESOL)

In this study, *we* use the zebrafish, Danio rerio, as an indicator for this aquatic toxicity test because it is very sensitive to pollutants especially in the early life stage.

(Bio)

In this project, *we* make use of the Hounsfield tensile testing machine to perform the test.

(ME)

Taking responsibility for their methodological choices using the first person seemed to hold few terrors for these students, despite the admonishments of some textbooks concerning the anonymity of experimental replicability. This may be because they were comfortable with the conventions of a narrative schema which they largely adopted for accomplishing this purpose:

(6)

> The method is very important. We have to be clear to describe it and show we can follow it from the beginning to the end. It is like a story, isn't it.
>
> (Bio student interview)

> This is the correct way to write the method section, step by step.
>
> (TESOL student interview)

> My supervisor wants to see that I can use a suitable method and overcome the problems. I use 'I' when I describe this because I am just telling what I did. This is not a difficult part to write.
>
> (IS student interview)

Human agents are integral to the meaning of research practices, and students were confident enough to align themselves explicitly with the procedures they had performed. However, they seemed unaware that author prominence here might make a claim for disciplinary competence and emphasise the writer's unique role in making fine qualitative judgements. In expert genres, self-mention here can remind readers that personal choices have been made and that, in other hands, things could have been done differently.

## Elaborating an argument

Setting out a line of reasoning would seem to be a key feature of academic writing, but it is one that students would prefer not to take explicit responsibility for. While there were considerable disciplinary differences, the writers of research articles were far more likely to see this as an expression of an individual contribution, choosing to stake their commitments to their arguments with the use of first person, as in these examples:

(7)

> *I* think it works something like this: suppose we start with a new, just-assembled ship.
>
> (Phil RA)

> During our experiments, *we* detected even-order diffractions, which should have been missing in the binary grating configurations. *We* believe that it is connected with the high nonlinearity of the spatially dependent refractive index distribution.
>
> (Phy RA)

Most students, on the other hand, sought to disguise their responsibility when elaborating arguments and giving opinions. Very few students were prepared to use first-person pronouns for this function, and even fewer to link this pronoun with mental process types, such as *think, believe* or *assume.* Moreover, they preferred not to express agreement, disagreement or interest in a position but rather to dip into the range of grammatical options which allowed them to avoid the potentially problematic role of writer-as-thinker, a role which carries accountability for the propositions expressed. Thus, we find considerable use of dummy-*it* subjects, passives and the attribution of agency to inanimate things:

(8)

Therefore, it is believed that motivating oneself is a way to get good school academic results.

(TESOL)

Gender differences are shown to exist with males using more avoiding style and females using more accommodating styles in managing conflicts.

(SS)

The table demonstrates that the pupils chose the most appropriate menu options …

(IS)

This does not suggest that the students did not have arguments or ideas, but only that they sought to create a distance from them, often failing to personally engage with their beliefs and their audience. If these writers knew there was some elbow room to negotiate their identity in this context, then they gave little indication of it in their language choices.

## Stating results/claims

This is the most self-assertive, and consequently potentially the most face-threatening, use of self-reference. Not surprisingly, then, only eight students were prepared to align themselves firmly with their claims in this way, in contrast to the research papers where this function comprised a quarter of all first-person uses. Because the knowledge claim is the heart of an academic argument, the individual contribution of the author is most clearly displayed when writers choose to attach an *I* pronoun to it. This explicitly foregrounds his or her distinctive involvement in the paper and commitment to a position: it is the most explicit feature of positioning and the adoption of a confident, assertive identity. In the published papers, writers in all disciplines used the first person to represent their unique role in constructing a plausible interpretation for a phenomenon, thereby establishing a personal authority based on confidence and command of their arguments. These examples from the articles illustrate how, by strongly linking themselves to their claims, writers can solicit recognition for both:

(9)

We attribute the variability to the long half-life of the GUS enzyme.

(Bio RA)

Likewise, *I have offered evidence that* some critical thinking practices may marginalize subcultural groups, such as women, within US society itself.

(AL RA)

Pledging a personal conviction to a conclusion in this way is obviously a risky strategy, and often one that novice writers lacked the will to take. Rather than demarcating their own work from that originating elsewhere, these undergraduates preferred to downplay their personal role in interpreting results by removing themselves from their claims altogether:

(10)

The experiment shows that the relationships between wear hardness and thickness can be found. From the result, the wear is directly proportional to the load and inversely proportional to the hardness; also, the hardness is inversely proportional to the thickness.

(ME)

Overall, there are several interesting findings in this research. First, it has been found that the abnormal return of the Hang Seng Index Component Stocks tends to be negative during the pre-event period but positive in the post-event time.

(Econ)

To summarise, then, these L2 writers chose not only to avoid self-mention but to avoid it at exactly those points where it involved making a commitment to an interpretation or claim. They generally sought to downplay their authorial identity by restricting their visibility to more innocuous functions, such as guiding readers through the discourse.

## 6.5 Authority, subjectivity and cultural identity

There are several possible reasons why these students might choose to avoid self-mention in their reports. It may have something to do with the recommendations of style manuals and textbooks advocating anonymity, or their own uncertainties about disciplinary conventions. Equally, however, culturally shaped epistemologies and views of authority, conflicting teacher advice and the preferences of individual students are also potential candidates. Evidence from my student interviews, however, suggests that underlying these is an awareness of the kinds of identity claims made by a reference to the subjective opinion of the writer. This section elaborates this view.

## Conventions and preferences

Some students saw the use of the first person as closely linked to a subjectivity which they considered inappropriate for academic discourse. Conventional wisdom promotes objectivity in academic writing and, in the absence of a strong English language culture outside classrooms, these novice L2 writers are largely dependent on their teachers and textbooks for advice. But while supervisors were divided concerning students' use of the first person, most encouraged students to stand behind their arguments:

(11)

> The project is not just about demonstrating research and presenting it in a scholarly way. It is a chance for them, maybe the only time they will get to do this, for them to explore something in real detail. We want them to really get involved and show us what they think. It is their project, a year's work, and it is important they leave no doubt about their own views.
>
> (Econ supervisor)

> I get a bit frustrated with this actually. Perhaps it's something cultural? We try and get the students to tell us what **they** did and what **they** think about what they find, to make a commitment to their research and their ideas. Often they don't do this though. I get an impression of the writer when I read these reports, and often my impression is that they are trying to hide themselves. Maybe they don't know it is OK to use these.
>
> (Management supervisor)

> Yes, I like to see students use the first person. Their own interpretations are important but often it is difficult to see what is theirs and what is lifted from sources. Maybe this is something to do with how they are taught to write essays at school. They hide themselves.
>
> (TESOL supervisor)

Students themselves showed that they were responsive to the academic conventions of objectivity, but they were also aware of the interpersonal consequences of projecting a prominent individual identity:

(12)

> We have to be objective in reporting our results. I don't like to be definite because my idea may be wrong and not what my supervisor believes. He might have a different idea. I think it is better to be quiet and not use 'I' but just tell what the experiment shows.
>
> (IS student)

> I don't want to make myself important. Of course it is my project and my result, but I am just ordinary student, not an academic scholar with lots of knowledge and confident for myself.
>
> (TESOL student)

Attempts to avoid the personal responsibility that subjectivity entails may help account for the sporadic use of inclusive *we* in almost half of the single-authored student reports. The reasons for this use are complex. Several students mentioned the collaboratively conducted research which contributed to the individual reports, but underlying many responses was a clear desire to reduce attributions to self:

(13)

> I use 'we' as I worked with my classmate on this project. Anyway, it is easier to say 'we' than 'I'. I just feel easier to use 'we'. The work is shared so I call it 'we'.
>
> (PA student)

> This is a correct use, I think. I have seen it in books. I want to say what I did but I am not so confident to use 'I' all the time. 'We' is not so strong, isn't it?
>
> (BS student)

Many of these students seem uncomfortable with the subjectivity and assertiveness of the singular form and seek the rhetorical distance that the plural meaning allows, reducing their personal intrusion while not completely eliminating their presence from the text.

This reluctance to get behind their interpretations obviously does not obscure the ideational meanings the students are seeking to convey; most of these writers display the kind of competence in formal written English that would be expected of graduating students in similar contexts around the world. What is at issue here are differences in realisations of interpersonal meanings and expressions of self that can be traced to cultural and rhetorical variations between learners in Hong Kong of China and target academic practices.

## Identity and authority

Most important, however, is the notion of authority. As I have mentioned, academic literacy is a 'foreign culture' to students of all backgrounds, where they find their previous understandings of the world challenged, their old confidences questioned and their ways of talking undermined. For students struggling to gain control of their discipline and master its content, this can lead to a sense of powerlessness and uncertainty. In such circumstances it may be difficult for students to project an authoritative self. Respondents frequently said they wanted to dissociate themselves from the connotations of personal authority they believed the first-person use carried:

(14)

> I try to not use it. It is too strong. Too powerful. It means I am firm about my belief but often I am not sure. It is better to use passive sentence.
>
> (Bio student)

> I have seen 'we' and 'I' in academic papers but it is a good writer, isn't it? They have confidence to give their ideas clearly, their own ideas.
>
> (SS Student)

These students therefore tended to see self-reference as a marker of self-assurance and individuality which they did not feel when composing, preferring to take refuge in the anonymity of passive forms.

Part of their reluctance to stake out a firm authorial identity stemmed from the inequalities of power in the writer–reader relationship. Genres signify certain roles and relationships as a result of their institutionally defined purposes, and these relationships are conspicuously unequal in the final-year project report. This is a significant undergraduate genre and the judgements of reader-examiners can have a major impact on students' grades and futures. This, then, is not the best forum to declare an authoritatively independent self. But while this kind of institutional positioning influences students' choices, it does not fully explain their obvious reluctance to take 'ownership' of their work. The learners in Hong Kong of China felt ambivalent about the discoursal identity implied in authorial commitment and rejected the authority associated with first-person choices:

(15)

> This is OK for scholars, but not our project. I think no one will use 'I' in his project.
>
> (Bio student)

> There is a conflict. My supervisor told me to give my interpretation, but I can't do this. I feel embarrassed to do it.
>
> (SS student)

> In Chinese we don't write like that. If I use 'I' it is not really me who thinks something. When I read it back I feel a different person wrote it.
>
> (BS student)

Taking a stance and demonstrating confidence clearly implies that the writer is a distinctive, individual creator with a firm position and rights to ownership of his or her perspectives and text, but this kind of identity is not shared by all cultures. Scollon (1994: 34) suggests that academic writing 'is as much the construction of an authorial self as the presentation of fact', and that this notion of a rational, uniquely individual writer is a product of a culturally specific ideology. Authorship in academic writing in English both carries a culturally constructed individualistic ideology and places the burden of responsibility for the truth of an assertion heavily on the shoulders of the writer. Such an identity both exposes the writer and reduces group solidarity, and as a result L2 students often view the use of *I* with misgivings.

## 6.6 Conclusions

Self-mention constitutes a central pragmatic feature of academic discourse since it contributes not only to the writer's construction of a text, but also to the writer's construction of a rhetorical self. The authorial pronoun is a significant means of promoting a competent scholarly identity and gaining acceptance for one's ideas, and while these students were sensitive to its rhetorical effects, they were reluctant to accept its clear connotations of authority and personal commitment. As a result they significantly underused authorial pronouns and determiners, downplayed their personal role in the research and adopted a less clearly independent stance compared with expert writers. Simply, they position themselves differently from academic insiders.

The ways that writers choose to report their research and express their ideas obviously result from a variety of social and psychological factors which can vary from one person to another. It might also be prudent to be wary of explanations which draw on the idea of homogeneous cultures. Social groups are infiltrated by outside forces, and considerable effort has gone into exploring the overlaps and interpenetrations of cultural groups in recent years (e.g. Appadurai, 1996; Gupta and Ferguson, 1997). But while individuals frequently act in ways that modify, resist or ignore culture norms, corpus techniques help reveal repeated patterns of language use which suggest particular practices and meanings of social groups. In this case, these rhetorical preferences strongly indicate an avoidance of authorial pronouns and show that these choices differ markedly from Western academic practices. So, while Anglo-American academic conventions encourage a conscious exploitation of identity to manage the reader's awareness of the author's role and viewpoint, these writers seem reluctant to promote an individual self.

To speak with authority in academic contexts, students feel that they must use another's voice and another's code, weakening their affiliations to their home culture and discourses to adopt the values and language of their disciplinary ones (Johns, 1997). Both Ohta (1991) and Scollon (1994) suggest that the use of first-person pronouns is largely unacceptable in the traditions of Asian cultures because of its association with individual rather than collective identity. As Hinkel (1999, 104) observes: 'Using *I* to stand for the individual would undesirably increase the individual's responsibility for the truth value of the proposition and diminish solidarity and group belonging.' Culture, therefore, intrudes into our communicative practices in significant ways, and undergraduates familiar with different writing traditions and conceptions of teacher status have little incentive to challenge the authority of reader-examiners.

There is also a message here for teachers, who might benefit from an awareness of how academic conventions position students as well as a sensitivity to the struggles of novice writers seeking to reconcile the discursive identities of their home and disciplinary cultures. The focus-group interviews confirm what has become a widely held view of Asian writers: that this tentativeness and reluctance to display an authoritative persona may, in part, be a product of a culturally and socially constructed view of self which makes assertion difficult. The corpus studies have demonstrated the effect of this on the discourse produced by the students in this genre. Teachers have an important consciousness-raising task here to ensure students understand the rhetorical options available to them and the effects of manipulating these options for interactional purposes. With this rhetorical understanding, learners will be better able to gain control over their writing and meet the challenges of participating in academic genres in a second language.

# 7 Reputation: Individuality and Conformity

In this chapter I return to the issue of positioning and proximity, agency and conformity, in academic writing and the ways that consistent patterns of language choices work to realise a coherent and consistent individual identity. I have argued that identity is, above everything, social, and that identity can be seen as a framework through which we seek to unify our processes of creating meaning while participating in social communities. The idea of positioning is key here as it seeks to emphasise the importance of the discoursal repertoires that writers bring to an act of writing and which shape their understanding of proximity. These repertoires are influenced by their prior interactional experiences with texts in a range of contexts. Every word we write, therefore, represents a meeting of our subjective sense of a solid and continuing self and the many roles we play as part of our various memberships. Our writing is an encounter, possibly a struggle, between our multiple past experiences and the demands of the current context.

The production of texts is always the production of self, but negotiating a representation of self from the standardising conventions of disciplinary discourses is clearly a skilled accomplishment, involving both recognising and exploiting community constraints. This is the tension between positioning and proximity. While individual agency is not eliminated by the cultural authority of convention and the editing of disciplinary gatekeepers, it may be established figures in the disciplines, rather than novices, students or journeymen, who have the confidence and expertise to find ways to express a distinctive identity. In this chapter I move away from my focus on proximity in previous chapters to look at positioning and to explore how disciplinary experts exploit rhetorical options. I do this by interrogating the published work of two leading figures in applied linguists, Deborah Cameron and John Swales, and comparing these texts with mainstream work in the field. The research suggests how personal proclivities can contribute to an independent creativity shaped by shared practices.

# 7.1  Identity, community and individuality

Writing captures the dynamic of who we are. This is because it expresses our awareness of our individuality within the possibilities for constructing an identity made available by the discoursal conventions and meanings of a social community. Acts of writing represent the negotiation of what has been with interpretations of the here and now, combining our interpersonal experience and organised performance legitimated through authorised discourses. Such discourses are powerful constraints on the kind of person we can be in any context but do not determine what we are: the experience of a unique selfhood overflows the semiotic categories which these discourses offer us. As I discussed in Chapter 2, we do not simply inhabit predefined roles or accept the package that is offered. Positioning is the space we make for ourselves within the context of accepted disciplinary conventions. We are often able to code-shift our identity performance because of our competence in more than one domain of identity repertoire and our confidence to employ this in another.

## Idiolect and priming

The concept of *idiolect* is a useful way of beginning to understand how writers position themselves rhetorically to shape a distinctive identity. Idiolect refers to the fact that speakers and writers have their own distinct and individual version of the language they speak, and that this manifests itself through idiosyncratic grammatical, lexical, phrasal and rhetorical choices (Halliday et al., 1964: 75; Coulthard, 2008). What this means is that every speaker not only has a vocabulary, built up over many years, which differs from that of others, but also a distinctive preference for routinely selecting some items over others. So while any writer can use any word or pattern at any time, we tend to make typical selections of preferred words and patterns, which helps distinguish us from others.

As I discussed in Chapter 3, every word we use and everything we know about each one is a result of our encounters with it, so when we formulate what we want to say, the wordings we choose are shaped by the way we regularly meet them in similar texts. This accumulation of experiences contributes to what Hoey (2005: 8) calls *priming*:

> As a word is acquired through encounters with it in speech and writing, it becomes cumulatively loaded with the contexts and co-texts in which it is encountered, and our knowledge of it includes the fact that it co-occurs with certain other words and in certain kinds of context.

Every time we use a word or encounter it once more, the experience either reinforces or weakens the priming, so that we build up an understanding of contexts and institutions. At the same time, the repeated use of collocational groupings is creating a grammar for each individual, while our use of words in moment-by-moment interaction contributes to the reproduction of social structure. This does, of course, produce a certain amount of conformity and reinforces proximity, but it also helps provide the basis for individuality.

As individuals we have a set of unique, personal, unrepeatable experiences which include experiences with language, as words come at us from a huge variety of sources. Certain primings are likely to be shared by large numbers of people and particularly those who routinely use the language of a particular social group, such as an academic discipline. But the kinds of data that we are exposed to in our communities are never going to be the same as everyone else's. Every person's experience with language, as with anything else, is different and so their primings are different, and this will contribute to them making different language choices. This is because writers are oriented to more than an immediate encounter with their text when composing; they also draw on their own backgrounds and conjure up institutional patterns which naturally and ideologically reflect and maintain such patterns. These can only be seen by viewing activity as socially and culturally constituted modes of praxis rather than distinct acts of individuals.

While the means of indentifying idiolects is still emerging (Coulthard and Johnson, 2007), corpora allow us to see what is distinctive about an individual's way of writing. The main investigative technique is comparison. Comparing the features of target writers' texts with a much larger corpus of work in the same discipline can help to determine what is general in the norms of a community and what represents more personal choices to distinguish proximity and positioning more clearly.

## Corpora and analyses

My analysis here is based on two corpora representing a considerable proportion of the two writers' single-authored output over their careers. My corpus of Cameron's published writing consists of 21 single-authored papers made available by the author. It represents some 20 years of publishing and comprises 125,000 words. The corpus of Swales' work was compiled at the Michigan ELI. It consists of 14 single-authored papers together with the bulk of his three monographs, representing 18 years of output and comprising 342,000 words.

To get a clearer idea of the features found more generally in applied linguistics texts, I also compiled a reference corpus of published work in the same genres as the target texts. It comprises 75 research articles taken at random from 20 leading international journals and 25 chapters from 12 books all published in the last ten years and totalling 750,000 words.

Again, I took a corpus-driven approach so that the corpora themselves provided the data for evidence of similarity and difference in the linguistic choices made by my target authors compared to the conventions represented by those evidenced in the monitor corpus. As discussed in Chapter 3, this provides an empirical basis to extract data and detect linguistic patterns without prior assumptions and expectations (Tognini-Bonelli, 2001). I used two methods of word selection: raw frequencies and relative frequencies using 'keywords'. Neither involves specifying which items to search for, but one is based on what is most common in a corpus and the other on what is most common compared with another corpus. By focusing on the first we get an idea of an author's preferred choices, and by focusing on the second we can identify which features conform to and which diverge from community discourse norms. These approaches throw into sharp relief what is distinctive and what conventional in the work of individual writers through how they choose to consistently position themselves in relation to their colleagues and their material.

Using WordSmith Tools 4 (Scott, 2007), I first generated word lists of the most frequent single words and four-word strings for the two authors and the reference corpus. These strings, which Biber et al. (1999) call *lexical bundles* and Scott (2007) *clusters*, were mentioned in Chapter 3. They are simply words which follow each other more frequently than expected by chance, and so contribute to our sense of distinctiveness in a register. I then compared each list in the author corpora with those from the larger applied linguistics reference corpus using the Keywords tool. As noted in Chapter 3, this program identifies words and phrases that occur significantly more frequently in the smaller corpus than the larger using a log likelihood statistical procedure.

This approach provides a better characterisation of the target corpus than a simple frequency comparison as it identifies items which are 'key' differentiators across many files, rather than simply being the most used. It identifies which words best distinguish the texts of these authors from those in applied linguistics more generally. After reviewing the keyword lists and identifying individual words and multi-word clusters, I concordanced the more frequent items and then grouped common devices into broad pragmatic categories which seemed to capture central aspects of their writing.

Uncovering the regularities in frequency and collocations of words, senses and phraseology can help identify authorial preferences and how writers seek to position themselves with their readers and to project a consistent authorial identity. It has to be admitted, however, that I am an interested member of this community and know the central characters in this drama quite well. While I have not consulted sources outside those discussed in writing this chapter, I am nevertheless familiar with their work and personalities, and it is entirely possible that this has influenced my reading of these texts. I reiterate, however, that no analysis is ever entirely free of researcher interpretation. While the generation of frequency counts, word lists and concordances are automatic processes, the categorisation of items and the explanation of their occurrence is always subjective. All I can do is acknowledge this and hope that my analyses relate as closely as possible to what I have found on the pages of these writers' texts.

## The protagonists

Deborah Cameron and John Swales were selected as case studies for this chapter largely because of their disciplinary celebrity and their contrasting personal and professional backgrounds. Both are perhaps the foremost researchers in their respective fields, holding professorships at leading research universities on either side of the Atlantic with substantial research and writing careers. On the other hand, they also represent opposites in terms of personality and philosophy. Cameron is a committed left-winger and active feminist from a working-class background. Swales had a middle-class upbringing and his career follows that of the typical peripatetic English teacher wandering through Europe and Africa before settling in the United States. An important reason for recruiting applied linguists into this chapter, however, was their reflective attitude to language. As Cameron points out in an email commentary on this chapter:

> I would say I am a pretty deliberate and self-aware writer of prose, I think about what I'm doing and am conscious of at least some of the recurrent features that make my style what it is. Many choices are conscious considerations. You could call some of them 'aesthetic' (i.e. I like language to look a certain way on the page and read a certain way to the internal ear) while others are to do with a commitment to clarity and accessibility.

It is worth setting out a brief biography of these central characters.

Deborah Cameron is Rupert Murdoch Professor of Language and Communication at the University of Oxford. A sociolinguist known most widely for her work on gender, globalisation and language, and discourse in the workplace, Cameron is also a high-profile commentator in both print and broadcast media in the UK. She grew up in the north of England and left school at 17 doing low-paid, drudge jobs before going to university. She began her academic career in 1983 as a lecturer at Roehampton University in England, and then taught at the College of William and Mary in Virginia, USA, Strathclyde University, Scotland, and the Institute of Education in London. Her books include *Verbal Hygiene* (1995b) and *Good To Talk?* (2000), both dealing in different ways with contemporary normative practices of regulating communication, a collection of articles called *On Language and Sexual Politics* (2006) and *The Myth of Mars and Venus* (2007), a best-selling book debunking the popular idea that men and women metaphorically 'speak different languages'.

John Swales, until recently Professor of Linguistics and long-time director, teacher and creative force at the English Language Institute at the University of Michigan, is the doyen of the ESP movement. Chalk to Cameron's cheese, Swales' career has taken him from an 'Assistente' post at Bari in Italy in 1960, through Lektor and lectureships in Sweden, Libya, Leeds and Sudan to a senior lectureship at Aston in Birmingham, England, and so to Michigan. Swales is perhaps the single most influential champion of *genre* as a force in English language teaching and research, and his contributions to areas such as *textography*, *community* and *academic discourse* have helped define the field. His main work consists of three monographs: *Genre Analysis* (1990), *Other Floors, Other Voices* (1998) and *Research Genres* (2004), as well as two research-based textbooks (with Chris Feak) that many regard as the best ever written for advanced EAP learners.

It is the rhetorical awareness, and confidence to deploy it, which this seniority and experience bring that interests me here. So while the analysis may not throw any light on what we already know of their work, the important question for me in this chapter is how far does this authorise the employment of discursive constructions which stray from disciplinary norms and allow the local management of a discoursal accomplishment of identity?

## 7.2  Personal interests and professional niches

Academics construct whatever status they manage to achieve by advancing knowledge, and in a field marked by considerable competition for space, this is an imperative which requires precise contributions. As a result, and over time, academics carve a niche of expertise from the mass of disciplinary subject matter, creating a specialisation which forms the basis of their career and reputation. Exploring the content items and keywords most frequently used by these authors therefore seemed a good place to start as these are likely to reflect the key themes of their work and serve as motifs for their contribution to the field.

### Content words and clusters

Looking first at raw frequencies, the most common content words in Cameron's writing are *women, language, gender, men, social, linguistic, talk, people, discourse* and *work,* all of which occur more than 200 times and in 19 or more papers in her corpus. These items clearly identify the terrain marked out and occupied by Cameron as her own, indicating her concern with the ways language functions to structure social relations in diverse settings, particularly in work contexts, and in the ways gender-linked patterns of language use are made significant in social relations. Her studies of gender are acknowledged as pivotal in helping to undermine a binary model of gender to take account of intra-gender diversity, revealing both the ways gender is enacted locally and the institutional factors that operate to construct inequality. These observations are supported in her preferred multi-word clusters which are *men and women* (76 times), *language and gender* (74), *women and men* (56).

The top eight content items from the larger Swales corpus are: *research, genre(s), English, discourse, language, academic, writing* and *students.* All these items occur over 500 times and, like *texts, community* and *rhetorical* which appear a little further down the list with over 300 occurrences, appear in 90% or more of the articles and chapters that make up the Swales corpus. The most common multi-word clusters are *spoken and written* (104), *in the corpus* (103), *English for Specific Purposes* (45) and *non-native speakers of English* (34). Again, these are some of the areas by which Swales is identified as an individual academic, encompassing his work on discourse analysis and international students using English to study in higher education.

## Authors' keywords

More importantly than raw frequencies when characterising the work of individual authors is that of *keywords*, those which are most unusually frequent compared to a larger reference corpus. Keywords give a reasonably good idea about what a writer's work is about and the ideas which best distinguish it within the discourses of the community. Table 7.1 summarises the words and phrases which are far more typical of each writers' work than those in the 725,000-word applied linguistics corpus (at p < 0.1 significance).

**Table 7.1  Keywords in the Swales and Cameron corpora**

| Cameron corpus | | Swales corpus | | |
|---|---|---|---|---|
| *Singles* | *3-grams* | *Singles* | *3-grams* | *4-grams* |
| women | language and gender | genre(s) | would seem to | the University of Michigan |
| gender | men and women | dissertation | in terms of | English for Specific Purposes |
| men | women and men | herbarium | various kinds of | as might be expected |
| female | top down talk | I | the research world | as far as I |
| is | the female voice | Michigan | the English language | I have tried to |
| male | in public contexts | have | the fact that | the North University Building |
| call | the gender genie | species | at this juncture | a genre-based approach |
| it | female verbal superiority | my | in the herbarium | turns out to be |
| genie | male female misunderstanding | specimens | The Testing Division | over the last decade |
| public | the call centre | ELI | the research article | have been able to |

Not surprisingly, the Keywords tool returns the nouns and noun phrases which characterise the research interests of these two academics. Some odd forms in the Swales' list like *herbarium, species, specimen* and *the North University Building* are attributable to his research into the lives and texts of those inhabiting a university building published as *Other Floors, Other Voices.* There are also some unexpected items in Cameron's list. *The gender genie*, a website which supposedly predicts the gender of an author of a supplied text, for instance, is critiqued in several papers. *The call centre* also appears in several papers as an example of the technicisation of communication; how the commonplace social activity of talk has been transformed into a technical skill and what this means in the production-line contexts of service calls. Her 4-grams merely extend the 3-grams (e.g. *between women and men, of language and gender, female voice in public*).

Beyond these items, non-content words and phrases emerge from the keywords lists as consistent patterns of individual choices. Rhetorical conventions obviously reflect the epistemological assumptions of a discipline, and applied linguistics tends to be seen as a 'soft-applied' field: functional, oriented to the improvement of practice, and employing explicitly interpretive, data-informed methods (Hyland, 2004a). But within these broad institutional practices, individuals have recourse to different 'interpretive repertoires' or positioning: ways of constructing their versions of events. In the next sections I show how grammatical keywords and functions are central to this construction of positioning. The corpus shows that 13 of the top 50 keywords in Cameron's writing and 19 in Swales' top 50 are grammatical items. I single out *is, that, not, but, though* and *arguably* for discussion in Cameron's writing and *I,* together with mental process types, hedges and attitude words in Swales' work, to see how these features help characterise the discursive identities of our two linguists.

## 7.3   Deborah Cameron: The radical linguist

Deborah Cameron has created, through her writing, a reputation as a radical linguist, challenging orthodox conceptions of workplace and gender discourse. Part of this impact is due to what is the most striking feature of her discourse: her willingness to engage in head-on debate with alternative positions, thus projecting a confident, combative identity while at the same time aligning herself with her disciplinary colleagues. This is a highly politicised rhetorical style which projects an identity as well as an ideology. Here I look at the rhetorical means by which she constructs this identity. Starting in each case with the grammatical keywords, I look at the concordance lines for each, and then find frequent phraseologies and interpret these in terms of identity.

## Establishing truths

Classification and identification are commonplace in academic discourse, but in Cameron's writing they take on an assertive and confident quality. WordSmith identified *is* as the fifth most common keyword in the Cameron corpus, representing a significantly above average use. This is, of course, one of the most common words in English (Sinclair, 1999: 176), and in academic prose it usually specifies a logical relationship between referents, typically occurring with full noun phrase subjects (Biber et al., 1999: 448–450). In Cameron's work these are *gender* (62 times) and *language* (53), which are variously defined, described and commented on, as here:

(1)

> The term gender is used in this chapter primarily to refer to the social condition of being a man or a woman.
> ... gender is regulated and policed by rather rigid social norms.
> ... language is actually the symbolic arena in which some other ideological contest is being fought out.

More often, however, we find other collocational patterns with *is* in her writing. *It is* co-occurs most frequently (370 times), with a particularly high use of *it is* + ADJ + *to* infinitive (161 times):

(2)

> **It is reasonable to** suppose that a diner wouldn't enquire about the existence of a particular foodstuff out of idle curiosity...
> **It is important to** distinguish between the ideological representations of gender found in texts like conduct books and the actual practice of real historical gendered subjects.
> **It is difficult to** think of any human occupation whose performance does not depend on some kind of knowledge.

The fact that this structure occurs just 222 times in the 750,000-word monitor corpus illustrates that Cameron uses the pattern some four times more frequently in her style of argument than in applied linguistics more generally.

Thematic *it* introducing an embedded clause as subject helps to shift new or complex information towards the end of a sentence, to the rheme, where it is easier for readers to process. It also, however, functions to assert the writer's opinion and recruit the reader into it. This is a strategy which explicitly attempts to take control of readers' thinking, allowing them nowhere to go except along with the writer, and as a result it carries a high risk of rejection. To pull it off, Cameron has to recognise a potential diversity of viewpoints and be prepared to engage with these. She therefore creates a sense of solidarity by writing the reader into the text while underlining the strength of conviction she has in her views, encouraging the addressee to share this conviction with her. She is willing to take them on and win them over to her position through the confident, unambiguous expression of her commitments.

The preference for *is* over hedging and passive constructions gives an assertiveness and a strong authorial positioning to Cameron's writing, which is also realised through other uses of the verb *is*. For instance, it also occurs frequently in the company of *that* (230 times), which is itself among the most highly listed keywords in Cameron's writing (ranked 53). A common use of this collocation in the corpus is to express what Hyland and Tse (2005) have called '*evaluative that*', a grammatical structure in which a complement clause is embedded in a superordinate clause to project the writer's attitudes or ideas. These examples are typical:

(3)

**It is my own view that** generalization remains a legitimate goal for social science
...
**What has not changed is my conviction that** theoretical arguments about meaning are not just a side-issue in debates on sexism in language.
In this context **it is problematic that** unmarked or generic occupational terms are also often masculine.

A *that*-clause governed by a noun or adjective is a powerful construction for expressing evaluative meanings in academic discourse as it allows the writer to thematise the evaluation, making the attitudinal meaning the starting point of the message and the perspective from which the content of the *that*-clause is interpreted. While rarely employing a first-person subject, Cameron nevertheless leaves us in no doubt of her attitude in these examples, fronting her statements with a strong personal evaluation.

## Challenging contrary positions

Another way in which Cameron deploys the linguistic resources of the discipline to construct a distinctive identity as a political linguist is through the use of rebuttal and counter-argument, with *not* (904 times), *but* (572) and *though* (144), all in the top 20 keywords. Once again this is a forceful and dialogistic means of engaging with others' views, but instead of proclaiming a position, it disputes alternatives.

Cameron employs negation far more than is common in applied linguistics, responding to possible viewpoints through direct challenge. This is a typical example:

(4)

> The idea that access to higher education should be widened, that degree courses should be for the many and not just the few, has attained the status of received wisdom, and it is hard to dispute it without appearing snobbish, reactionary or simply out of date. What lies behind it is not, however, a desire to democratise the 'life of the mind', but a set of ideas about the changing nature of work.

Negation is thus a resource for introducing an alternative position into the dialogue in order to reject it. Here Cameron appears to concur with the apparently reasonable policies promoting wider university access for non-traditional groups, agreeing with the construed reader that such policies are positive and democratic. She then steps back to question the assumptions which underpin it, presenting her own position that 'knowledge work' is better characterised as a skill acquired for the benefit of employers. The reader is not bludgeoned by her argument but construed as potentially vulnerable to a pervasive ideology, which she then disputes. So once again, Cameron shows she is sensitive to the addressee's beliefs and seeks to adjust these with her own decisive views, a radical rhetoric which constructs a self as much as an argument.

This is also evident in cases where she counters a contrary position rather than negates it, mainly using the conjunctions *but, though* and *however*. Like denials, these are dialogistic in that they acknowledge other voices only to dispute them. Often this is to contest a claim in the prior literature, as in this example where she discusses views on non-sexist language and then offers a restrictive modification of this work:

(5)

> Apart from their criticisms of it, Shortland and Fauvel seem curiously undecided as to whether non-sexist language makes any political difference. But once again, this

entire discussion is locked into a framework dictated by false premises, for within the authors' problematic the reformist's rationale can only be determinism (change language and you change the world) or less accurately (change language and you reflect reality better).

Alternatively, the view which is countered does not originate in the disciplinary literature but is regarded as more widespread among an educated audience and projected onto readers themselves. In (6), for example, Cameron raises the widely held view that norms of verbal effectiveness are now seen to be increasingly influenced by female values and practices. This concession is followed by the countering conjunction *but*, where she observes that 'communication skills' is a cultural construct, not a natural phenomenon and that it is unwise to routinely attribute certain verbal skills to women while denying them to men:

(6)

Another argument that has sometimes been made is that the triumph of a 'caring and sharing' interactional ethos reflects the growing feminization of British society. Certainly, new-style experts on communication tend to extol the virtues of women, while reserving their sternest warnings for stiff upper-lipped British men. But we should not be misled by the fact that therapeutic norms for interaction somewhat resemble the popular 'Mars and Venus' stereotype of the way women interact.

Similarly, in (7) when commenting on an NHS advertisement for hospital cleaners, she first voices the 'accepted view' only to dispute it, overturning what she projects as common beliefs:

(7)

The specification just quoted attracted criticism in the mid-1990s as an instance of the 'politically correct' impulse to dignify even the most menial positions by describing them in absurdly elevated terms. In my view, however, what it really illustrates is a more general discursive and rhetorical shift in the way experts think and talk about all kinds of work.

This is a highly productive move in persuasive discourse (e.g. Azar, 1997), but while often labelled 'adversarial', it is both reader-sensitive and highly dialogistic, in that it invokes a contrary position. Cameron recognises that persuasion requires the involvement of her readers and so seeks to align herself with their value positions before leading them to her own. Interestingly, by marking the counter explicitly with 'in my view' in (7), for example,

Cameron both states her view unequivocally and presents it as just one possible opinion among others; the reader is invited to follow her critique and not reject it outright. I discuss this further below.

## Establishing solidarity

By presenting her own position in the context of another, Cameron is not only able to situate her arguments to better demonstrate their distinctiveness and supremacy, but also to claim solidarity with her readers.

Claiming temporary agreement with a thesis before following up with a counter-claim is common in the Cameron texts, a sensitivity to addressees' understandings which not only helps circumvent any rejection of her argument, but represents a radical rhetoric. She first implies that it is not unreasonable to hold the countered position – after all, anyone might be deceived into doing so – and then adjusts their knowledge to her own. This generally involves correcting rather than confronting readers' expectations and is typically prefaced with a stance adverbial, often *arguably* (which occurs six times more frequently in Cameron's texts than in the five times larger applied linguistics corpus):

(8)

It is true that both are most entrenched in the US, and are therefore easily seen as emanating from it. But arguably the diffusion of new norms is less a consequence of American cultural influence per se than a consequence of the spread of the same social conditions which have enabled certain practices to flourish in the US.

In most cases the styles of speech women are urged to adopt are presented as gender neutral; they are simply the most effective ways of using language in a particular domain, regardless of the speaker's sex. Arguably however, this is only a subtler form of androcentrism.

Undoubtedly, the call centre industry is a hi-tech service industry which deals in symbols (words and bits); but as I will shortly seek to demonstrate by describing their work regime, the suggestion that operators have to deploy high levels of knowledge or skill in order to perform their functions is extremely misleading.

In other words, while she addresses issues head-on, she takes the trouble to avoid doing the same with her audience.

Forging an alignment with readers is also accomplished in Cameron's writing by making space for them using conditional arguments which occur significantly more frequently in Cameron's writing (239 times and 66th keyword). While often considered a hedging device by making one circumstance dependent on another, thereby raising the uncertainty of outcomes, conditional sentences also tend to bring the writer and reader closer to agreement. In specifying an 'open condition', she makes her argument epistemically accessible, but explicitly dependent on the reader's agreement, as in the following examples:

(9)

> If we accept that women and men are internally diverse groups, the fact that some women do one thing while others do the opposite need not be considered a paradox at all.
>
> If the hallmark of a mature academic field is its ability to set its own agenda for research and debate, should we not be addressing the questions we consider interesting rather than spending time debating other people's unquestioned assumptions?

So once again, she acknowledges the heteroglossic context of her argument but addresses voices assumed to be shared by both the writer and the addressee.

The way Cameron aligns herself with her readers against an alternative viewpoint is nicely illustrated in the following extract. Here she employs a series of *if*-clauses to patiently set out the arguments which support the ideological basis of education for the 'knowledge society'. Sensitively construing the reader as perhaps sharing this apparently reasonable paradigm, she then, using the stance marker *arguably* and the contrasting conjunction *though*, expresses her own view. The final conditional, combined with the writer–reader inclusive *we*, suggests that all readers need to do is consider the nature of 'knowledge work' to arrive at the same conclusions she does:

(10)

> There is a sense in which the trend to upskilling actually makes this assertion true. If even quite low-level employees are thought to require formal instruction in such matters as how to talk to customers/clients/patients, if this is considered to be a highly skilled form of behaviour which needs to be supported by a body of codified knowledge, and if acquiring the knowledge and skills through training becomes an obligation imposed on the workers by their employer, then these employees do, in a sense, become 'knowledge workers'. Arguably, though, the sense in which they become knowledge workers is a very trivial and superficial one. And if we actually look at what is involved in many kinds of contemporary service work, we will soon have cause to ask whether the rhetorical upskilling of these jobs masks a real deskilling of the workers who do them.

In Cameron's discourse, then, we see a range of rhetorical features used to confidently and forcefully advocate particular realities that often contradict those of others. Her preferred argument strategies actively construct a heteroglossic backdrop for the text by explicitly grounding propositions in her individual subjectivity, recognising that her view is one among others and then taking on these alternatives through a combative and confident dialogue. A key consequence of this is the projection of a distinctive and highly politicised identity. Identity and ideology are constructed in accord. The self-representation as a radical linguist is projected through radical discourse choices. It is difficult to see a more conservative linguist using exactly this kind of rhetoric, both challenging and engaging, confronting orthodoxies while drawing the reader into the argument.

# 7.4   John Swales: The inquiring colleague

John Swales, while enjoying similar academic celebrity, projects a very different identity to Deborah Cameron. Here is an altogether more self-effacing and reflective writer, projecting the identity of a cautious and inquiring colleague who explores the mysteries of the ways people use language with the same curiosity and eye for classroom practice that his readers might do. He does this through rhetorical choices which impart a clear personal attitude and a strong interpersonal connection to his readers.

## Self-mention and reflection

Frequent use of the first person is perhaps the most striking feature of Swales' discourse, with both *I* and *my* occurring in the top ten keywords. Self-referential *I, me* and *my*, in fact, occur 9.1 times per 1,000 words in the Swales corpus compared with 5.2 in the applied linguistics reference corpus, conveying a clear authorial presence and a strong sense of personal investment to his writing. As these examples suggest, the reader finds a thoughtful and well-informed colleague in these texts: an impression of a real person thinking through issues:

(11)

> But before I attempt to develop my main argument, it may first be helpful to place this aspect of applied linguistic research in a wider context lest I am thought to be even more obsessive-compulsive about the importance of genre analysis than is actually the case.
>
> I have on occasion proposed that students utilize models in their writing. I have

done so only in those situations where I feel that research into the genre has reached a level of credibility to permit some generalization.

Here is a writer making decisions, weighing evidence and drawing conclusions, engaging the reader in the discussion and investing his argument with personal experience. This reflexivity is apparent in this extract, where he comments on his changing teaching practices:

(12)

> My students come from every conceivable department, but I try to make them a socio-rhetorical community, a support group for each other. I do a lot of rhetorical consciousness raising and audience analysis ... I take them behind the scenes into the hidden world of recommendations, applications and evaluations ... In actual fact, I am much less sure than I used to be that I am a language teacher. I have come to believe that my classes are, in the end, exercises in academic socialization.

This kind of writing conveys an openness and honesty which reaches out to readers as someone on the same wavelength and familiar with their own contexts and workplace challenges. At the same time, it is equally interesting to consider what is omitted, for Swales rarely risks his relationship with readers by directly challenging others' views.

An interesting aspect of the Swalesian identity is the extent self-mention is used in a self-deprecatory way. Swales does not duck the fact that research involves uncertainties and failures, perhaps encouraging novice researchers by admitting that even the field's most illustrious figures have their setbacks:

(13)

> The account presented there was incomplete and somewhat misleading. It failed to do justice to the major struggles most people experience in shifting material from one genre to another. Another failure was to focus exclusively on public genres.
>
> But I am very unsure whether I will ever use these particular materials again. As matters stand at the moment, these materials have been, I believe, an educational failure.
>
> Indeed, despite some trying, I have so far been unable to repeat my earlier success. Perhaps in the same way that composers only seem able to write one violin concerto, discourse analysts can produce only one successful model.

More generally, a concordance of the first person in Swales' writing shows how far agency is explicitly associated with modality, or at least a deliberative attitude. The most frequent main verbs related to *I* are *think* (86), *believe* (71), *suspect* (35), *hope* (33), *tried* (31) and *guess* (29), all of which point to some degree of tentativeness and care in handling claims and readers.

While *I* also appears frequently in Cameron's writing (keyword 42), this appears mainly with relational verbs such as *have*, *will* and *am*, indicating that its significance for Swales is not just about frequency. It is also worth noting that, as I discussed in the last chapter, even experienced writers are equivocal about the use of the first person, suggesting that these two celebrated authors, and particularly Swales, may be less constrained by wider academic practices. It is, in fact, the *extent* and the *use* of self-mention in Swales writing which helps set him apart and distinguishes his individual authorial identity.

## Conveying hedging and attitude

A significant aspect of Swales' personal involvement in his writing is the extent to which he annotates his texts with commentary on the accuracy of claims and his stance towards them.

The use of language to express caution and commitment is a key feature of academic writing as it not only conveys the writers' assessments of reliability but also recognises the heteroglossic character of statements (Hyland, 2004a; Martin and White, 2005). Swales employs hedges throughout his work, opening a discursive space which invites readers into a dialogue where they can consider and perhaps dispute his interpretations. This is, of course, if they are not beguiled by his candour. As these examples suggest, his arguments often accommodate any expectations that his readers have that their views will be acknowledged in the discourse:

(14)

> The upshot of all these figures would seem to suggest that the anglophone grip on published research communications is both strong and tightening.
>
> I was, I suspect, rather too easily seduced by the concept of discourse community. Perhaps all too willingly I made common cause with all those who have their own agendas for viewing discourse communities as real, stable groups of consensus holders.
>
> I would suggest, therefore, that we need more HRD-type training for ESP instructors and practitioners, as an addition to advanced training in Applied Language Studies.

By marking statements as provisional in this way, Swales is able to both express his views and involve readers in their ratification, conveying respect for colleagues and their positions. This is because hedges help present statements as contingent and subjective, a product of the writer's reasoning and therefore open to challenge. However, while offering space for dialogic alternatives suggests doubt and expands possibilities for debate, it is also disarming. Swales' experience and confidence is evident here as he takes on views which are potentially in tension with his own. So in making room for alternatives, he presents an identity as a reasonable and open-minded seeker of truth, more interested in reaching a plausible interpretation for events than pushing his own.

The intent behind this readiness to concede and negotiate is perhaps demonstrated by a willingness to present claims with unambiguous robustness where necessary. The restrictive adverbs *indeed, doubtless, certainly* and *especially*, for example, all occur three or four times as frequently in Swales writing than in the much larger applied linguistics reference corpus. Expressions which boost his claims and restrict alternatives are evident at key points of his arguments:

(15)

> However, in other ways it is definitely non-standard.
>
> Such pressures have undoubtedly contributed to the exponential growth of research journals and articles in the last few decades.
>
> The key point I want to make here is that when matters do not go smoothly, we can find opportunities within encounters for conversation management.

But Swales never *demonstrates, proves or establishes*, and only rarely *finds* or *shows*. Instead, his categorical assertions are more usually accompanied by an evaluative comment of some kind.

The expression of affect is relatively uncommon in academic articles and attitude usually concerns estimations of probability and value rather than ethical evaluations or emotions. Swales' writing, in contrast, is peppered with attitudinal lexis of various kinds, with *scholarly, important, best*, and *interesting* among the top 30 keywords. These are almost always positive attributes which he largely employs to generously evaluate the research of others or underline strongly felt commitments to a particular viewpoint:

(16)

> Certainly, I find it remarkable that even as proficient a non-native user as Yao should have introduced such an unexpected, subtle and self-evaluative question about her writing into the discussion.
>
> However, the most interesting feature of the above extract is the way in which the method is described.
>
> Some shift in the reading research area towards a genre perspective would seem highly desirable.

Through these acts of personal involvement and professional investment, we are invited to share his understandings and subscribe to his take on the ways that both people and language behave. By scattering expressions of attitude and mitigation through his texts, Swales creates for himself a distinctive discoursal style which allows him to convey ideas in a very personal way, engaging readers as a collegial guide, sharing their interests and creating a sense of participating in an unfolding exploration of issues.

## Engaging with readers

In addition to this extremely personal authorial stance, Swales constructs a collegial identity by taking the trouble to recognise and respond to the potential objections, misunderstandings and processing difficulties of his readers. As well as softening his arguments to accommodate readers, he also draws them into a collusive web of agreement by assembling a professional context in which they are construed as intelligent colleagues sensible enough to follow what he has to say.

One aspect of this, and extremely unusual in current practice, is a quaint and rather dated reference to '*the reader*'. There are 16 mentions of *the reader* in the Swales data compared with just one in the reference corpus, and Swales uses it much like the eighteenth-century novelists to explicitly bring readers into the discourse at certain points, reminding them that they are linked by a common curiosity and engaged in the same fascinating endeavour. These cases are typical:

(17)

> By now the reader may have recognised that all our encounters so far lack what Professor Erickson calls 'leakage' – the leaking into the functional frame of social and interpersonal elements.
>
> Now, I can hear the reader thinking 'Surely we can solve this problem by having the same teacher teach two matched groups of learners using two different methods?'

This projects a sympathetic and almost avuncular tone to the discourse while, at the same time, leading readers to the writer's view by putting thoughts, and even words, into their minds.

A more conventional way of engaging readers is the use of inclusive *we*. While binding the writer to the reader in this way is common in persuasive prose (Hyland, 2005b), it is particularly salient in the Swales' corpus where it is among the top 50 keywords. Unsurprisingly, most of these collocate with primary auxiliaries and modals, but we also see the considerable interactivity of this pronoun in Swales' writing by noting the most frequent main verbs it combines with. Table 7.2 lists these together with their frequencies for up to three words to the right of *we*.

**Table 7.2 Main verbs (lemmas) collocated with *we* in the Swales corpus (Hyland, 2008)**

| see | 201 | expect | 24 | go | 14 |
|---|---|---|---|---|---|
| need | 61 | note | 22 | want | 12 |
| find | 60 | use | 22 | seem | 12 |
| know | 54 | take | 16 | examine | 10 |
| recognise | 25 | look | 15 | learn | 10 |

The fact that mental processes (*see, find, know, etc.*) head the list suggests something of how Swales uses inclusive *we* to recruit the reader into the interpretation process by assigning them a researcher role, guiding them towards a preferred reading of the evidence. Examples, however, show how this shades into explicit positioning of the reader:

(18)

In retrospect, we can see that the great attractiveness of this approach lay in the fact that it seemed eminently manageable to early LSP practitioners.

I think we know in our hearts that the real issues are about how ESP operations are perceived in the wider administrative and operational environment.

Don't we all find that our scholarly drafting is slower than we had hoped, and don't we often feel that other scholars of comparable interests and experience must surely be writing faster than we do?

There is an attempt to build a relationship through an implicit claiming of solidarity with readers here, soliciting agreement by dialogue with equals. As he points out in his memoir:

Tim Johns used to say in our Birmingham days in the 1980s: 'A good writer is one who makes a friend of his or her reader' and that, as much as anything, is what I am still trying to do.

(Swales, 2009: 206)

## Claiming solidarity

The use of inclusive pronouns not only functions to 'make friends with readers' but is a strategy in a rhetorical armoury. This is because Swales frequently uses *we* with obligation modals to position readers and lead them along with the argument. In this way, he is able both to claim solidarity with readers and to adopt a more assertive stance by focusing readers' attention and navigating them through his exposition to a particular understanding:

(19)

> We can salvage something of our hopes. First, we need to go back and review what we mean by discoursal competence. Here we need to recognise both the difference between and the relationship between conversation management and oral genre skills.
>
> I now believe that we should see our attempts to characterize genres as being essentially a metaphorical endeavor.

More usually, however, he dilutes the imperative force of such *directives* (Hyland, 2002a) by framing them with a modal to mitigate the imposition and transform an instruction into an invitation:

(20)

> We might conclude, then, that the role of the subject specialist informant in RA genre analysis remains, given the current levels of evaluated experience, somewhat controversial.
>
> However, it could be noted that in the research world there may be more occasions when we have (at least ostensibly) 'a distinct communicative situation'.

Once again, these linguistic resources allow him to present his arguments with consideration for the reader, while not compromising the strength of his convictions.

Finally, in addition to the devices Swales uses to impart a particular interpersonal tenor, he engages readers through an array of *interactive* metadiscourse options: resources which set out an argument for readers (Hyland, 2005b). There are numerous words and expressions among the keywords which indicate the attention Swales gives to monitoring his evolving text to make it coherent for readers, and particularly assessing what needs to be made explicit by frequently comparing and summarising material as he goes along. An interesting, and quirky, variation on this regular gisting of material is his use of introductory prefaces like *it turns out that* (14 occurrences) and *as it happens* (21), which cataphorically alert the reader to findings which might be considered somehow unexpected or counter-intuitive:

(21)

Thus it turns out that certain legal, academic and literary texts all point to another kind of contract that can exist between writer and reader.

As it happens, one of the major roles of the Herbarium is to loan out specimens on request to botanists working in other institutions.

These expressions help readers to navigate the discussion, but they do so by lending a strong interpersonal element to it, injecting an attitude of conviviality as Swales shares a certain surprise with readers at the unfailingly interesting nature of rhetorical and human behaviour.

# 7.5   Conclusions: Patterns of positioning

In this chapter I have shown how individuals are able to construct fairly consistent authorial orientations by using the disciplinary resources available to them. While normative and constraining, the rhetorical conventions of our communities are also the raw materials from which we fashion our professional selves, creating, through recurring selection of a rhetorical repertoire, the people we want to be. From the limits of proximity, we are able to create individual positions towards our colleagues and arguments. The analyses suggest that these two experienced writers project *who they are* to readers in very different ways through the rhetorical choices they make in arguing for their ideas and engaging with their readers.

A caveat here must be my interpretation of these patterns and the motives I attribute to the two writers in selecting them. While these repeated rhetorical choices represent both writers' more or less conscious choices to project themselves and their work in their own particular ways, my take on them is, of course, subjective. Not only do I have some insider access to these texts and authors, but both writers are themselves professional discourse analysts and are more aware of the effects of their choices than the average academic. Cameron, for example, cited the importance she attaches to the 'aesthetics' of language and to making her ideas as accessible as possible so that her avoidance of hedging has more to do with 'an aesthetic desire to avoid verbal clutter' than to present a committed persona:

We all know how ubiquitous hedging is in academic prose, and no competent academic writer can avoid it completely, but I do try to minimize the kind which

I think of as just clutter. I am not sure it directly, or only, reflects my construction of myself as someone who is not much troubled by uncertainty: it's also to do with the fact that I'd rather come across as crude or even arrogant than leave the reader struggling to parse my sentences, or wondering at the end of them 'what the hell is she actually saying?'

(personal email communication)

It also has to be said that these orientations are by no means unique and draw on recognisable cultural traditions. Cameron's energetically and intelligently combative style, which explicitly pits her ideas against others, seems to be informed by British traditions of public debate. The fact that she positions herself as a very public intellectual, at home in the media and in popular genres and with a variety of high-profile issues, brings a wider significance to her writing. Swales' style, on the other hand, seems to represent a different kind of intellectual in public discourse, quieter, more donnish and gently self-deprecating. This is not to say of course that they have not given these styles an individual stamp influenced by their own backgrounds and experiences, but simply that the identity options provided by academic disciplines do not exist in isolation from wider social and cultural practices.

Overall the data point to consistent patterns of distinct rhetorical choices within broad disciplinary borders. It also suggests that the performance of an identity is always shaped by our goals and by the demands of the context. Making authorial choices involves walking a tightrope between projecting an individual persona and taking on social roles and qualities valued by community readers. It is a matter of orienting to position and proximity. This is because language choices are always made from culturally available resources and involve interactions between the conventions of the literacy event, the ways that communities maintain their interests, and the values and prior cultural experiences of the participants. Academic communities are sites where differences in worldview or language usage intersect as a result of the myriad backgrounds and overlapping memberships of participants.

In summary, this chapter has sought to reveal something of how authorial positioning is consistently accomplished through repeated rhetorical acts. Beyond this, of course, there are other questions. Not least it makes sense to address the wider political operation of discourse communities and to ask, with Bizzell (1989: 225), 'who gets to learn and use complex kinds of writing' and who has rights to manipulate or resist the conventions of a discipline rather than merely accommodate to them?

# 8 Gender: Disciplinarity and Positioning

While current conceptions of identity stress the fluidity, complexity and context-sensitivity of identities, there are consistent patterns of experience in our biographies which influence how we interpret the here and now and so impact on the ways we perform identity work. As I have argued, building a sense of self means drawing on linguistic resources and discursive strategies to construct social categories about one's self and others, categorisations that involve ideas of both similarity and difference. Perhaps one of the more obvious aspects of similarity and difference between people is the fact that they have bodies. We see the world from an embodied point of view, so our awareness of our sex is one of our earliest experiences and provides an important element of our sense of continuity. Part of this awareness is how we actually *practise* being men or women. Because the self is an enactment and not merely an embodiment, gender is likely to be one of the most salient aspects of personal experience that a writer brings to a text.

Like identity itself, gender is a verb rather than a noun (Butler, 1990), and we might expect this enactment to influence how individuals engage with community conventions to construct an authorial identity. Surprisingly, however, this has been relatively little studied in published academic writing. In this chapter I address this gap by examining how male and female reviewers perform a disciplinarily appropriate identity in academic book reviews. This genre offers an excellent site for the study of gender in academic writing as it virtually obliges authors to stake out positions: to take a stance towards ideas and readers. Here then, is an explicitly personal and public engagement with another's work in a tightly argued space. Focusing on two diverse fields and considering both inter-gender and intra-gender language choices in the management of interactions, I explore what these stances reveal about identity construction.

## 8.1    Gender, identity and interaction

In an important sense, gender might be understood as a *primary identity* (Jenkins, 2008), which through socialisation in the family during infancy and beyond helps to organise our experiences and becomes integrated into our conceptions of selfhood (Berger and Luckman, 1967). Because it is established so early in childhood, and acquired with, and not only through, language, it is experienced as something core and authoritative. But while this is an important, and relatively robust, aspect of self-conception, it is one which is enacted through discourse on each interactional occasion. It plays out in a range of contexts against a canvas of different experiences. It needs to be emphasised, therefore, that while such identifications may be more resistant to change than ones we develop later in our lives, they are not etched in stone and they require constant work. The process of learning how we want to be male or female continues throughout our lives as we adapt and learn new behaviours, meet new people and have new experiences. Gendered behaviour, however, is obviously reinforced by the fact that the world is massively organised in gender terms and that it is a category which has consequences.

### Binary conceptions of gender

It is perhaps worth remembering that identification is neither entirely permanent nor completely malleable, and so identities should be seen as contingent: always open to change and possibility. I have stressed throughout that identity is a *discursive* practice and, as Butler (1990) has argued, the gendered subject is situated in, and endlessly produced through, discourse. But while Butler rejects the model of a fixed, essential gender in the constant flux of the performance, she also recognises that subjects are unable to transcend the gendered discourses in which they are situated. The construction of masculinity or femininity therefore involves individuals routinely orienting towards particular hegemonic discourses which surround their identity construction. Like Holland and Skinner (1987), we can see these discourses as shared cultural models that underlie and provide the context for locally performed identities, assisting the interpretation of roles while at the same time contributing to their endurance.

Such preferred cultural scenarios seem to be in the minds of those whose research paradigm equates the study of gender with the discovery of male–female discoursal differences. As Cameron (2006) argues, if we see gender as a binary opposition, rather than as a continuum, like age, or as a multi-valued variable like ethnicity, then studying gender means studying the *differences* between men and women. Most of this gender difference research has focused on oral communication, typically examining conversational dominance and largely concluding that men and women make different use of the linguistic resources available to them, with men preferring a more instrumental, factual, agonistic, competitive style of discourse than women (e.g. Holmes, 1995; Lakoff, 1975). Differences are often attributed to the fact that we belong to one or other sociolinguistic subculture and are said to both reflect and construct gender inequalities. It is a position popularised in airport best-sellers such as those by John Gray (1993) and Deborah Tannen (1994) on male and female 'interaction styles', one characterised by dominance, display and competition, and the other by connection, feeling and facilitation. These binary categories are generally presented as fixed and often create stereotypes which reduce women to victims and men to bullies.

When generalised, such bipolar contrast between a pair of universal categories (masculine vs. feminine) presents a monolithic conception of patriarchy which exaggerates inter-group differences and intra-group similarities to create a fixed and static notion of gender roles. In particular, it ignores the context of local meanings and the ways that gender is shaped by language use, rather than the other way around. In reality most of us experience masculinity and femininity as fuzzy categories to occupy, with membership-by-degree, but these research perspectives help solidify them by drawing on cultural stereotypes where an ideal of masculinity equals working-class masculinity and femininity is middle-class femininity. This strongly dichotomised view of language use has, however, fortunately been softened by more contextually sensitive studies which show the cross-cutting effects of participants' relative power and status in any given interaction (Cameron, 1992; Coates, 1989).

## Gender as contextual performance

In academic contexts, evidence for gender-preferential discourses has been mixed. Support for different interactional styles, for example, comes from work by Flynn (1988) and Rubin and Greene (1992) who found that female undergraduates tended to employ a more facilitative and less objectifying style of argument than men, while Crismore et al. (1993) observed that male undergraduates employed more certainty markers and a more confident style. In student peer reviews, Johnson and Roen (1992) found that not only did females use more positive evaluative items than males, but these compliments were more personalised, contained more intensifiers and attended far more to the gender of the addressee. While such results may support a view of different verbal cultures, Lynch and Strauss-Noll (1987), Francis et al. (2001) and Rubin and Greene (1992) found little difference in the use of assertion in the written argument patterns of male and female students. Schleef (2008), in fact, discovered that communicative role, speech mode and discipline were more influential than gender in how academics and students used a range of spoken interactional markers in lectures at a US university. Similarly, the research reported in Chapter 5 revealed that gender had little influence on how academics constructed their article bios.

In fact, of course, people are never *just* men or women, they are men and women of particular ages, classes, ethnicity, geographical origins, occupational categories, social statuses, religious beliefs, sexual orientations and political views. Forms and norms of masculinity and femininity therefore vary considerably and systematically by membership of social categories and, as we shall see, by disciplinary membership. It is in these varied contexts and spans of time that the repeated performance of gender identity offers possibilities for change as borrowings, reflexivity and reinterpretation provide actors with modes of agency.

Seeing gender as the repeated performance of particular norms of language conventions rather than essentialised categories of masculinity and femininity accommodates a more shifting, negotiated notion of gender which allows writers more choice in the resources they employ in acts of self-representation. This underlines Cameron's (1995a: 43) argument that 'each individual subject must constantly negotiate the norms, behaviours and discourses that define masculinity and femininity for a particular community at a particular point in history'. This chapter explores this kind of negotiation in a genre of academic critique: the book review.

## 8.2   Academic discourse and gender

I have stressed throughout that writers do not construct self-representations from an infinite range of possibilities. Because we live our lives through discourses, language choices in any situation are always made from culturally available resources. Identities therefore involve interactions between the conventional practices of the literacy event, the ways that communities structure and maintain their interests, and the values, beliefs and prior cultural experiences of the participants in the event. Enactments of gender are made across a range of different contexts and communities as 'individuals construct or produce themselves as women or men by habitually engaging in social practices that are associated with culturally- and community-defined notions of masculinity and femininity' (Ehrlich, 1997: 436). In this section, I attempt to elaborate this statement by reference to disciplinary contexts and a brief review of the literature regarding the interaction of academic discourses and gender.

## The feminist critique of science

For some feminist writers, the conventions of academic communication are themselves gendered, representing a male-dominated academic culture. If this is the case, then participation in academic communities through their authorised discourses is likely to advantage men and exclude women, less masculinised males and identifiable gay males. Much of this feminist criticism is directed at the hard end of the knowledge-construction spectrum and focuses on an objection to the removal of authorship and social context in academic texts, as Lutz (1995: 259) observes:

> Theory has traditionally allowed for the erasure of the subject who writes and the human subjects who are written about. It allows the theorist to avoid the roots of statements in real-world encounters, to speak for or appear to speak for the whole, and to speak from a transcendental vantage point.

This is not merely a critique of objectivity, however, but an assessment of academic discourse as a monopoly of the production of meaning. Academic discourse is seen to encode masculine values of competition, rationality and conflictual expressions of argument and so works to exclude female academics and their preferred forms of interaction (Kirsch, 1993; Robson et al., 2002).

For Lemke (1994), academic practices reflect 'masculine traits' such as autonomy, self-reliance, moderated aggressivity, dominant posturing, abstraction, objectification and theoretical-formal rationality. This is partly because academics are primarily heterosexual, middle-class, middle-aged males, but more generally because of the way that science has positioned itself more widely:

> Science has masculinised itself largely by association with military occupations (chemistry and munitions, physics and nuclear weapons) and to the degree that it

has become Big Science, i.e. big business, with a managerial elite (lab directors). The most masculinised roles in science, and among the sciences, are those associated with the greatest degree of power and control over other people and over resources.

(Lemke, 1994: 22)

This 'masculinist epistemology' (Luke and Gore, 1992: 205) therefore privileges competition, agnosticism and rationality and enables only a limited range of subject positions. It forces both male and female academics to adopt a particular style of writing which presents versions of themselves corresponding to imposed gender identities (Bergvall, 1999). Academic success, in this view, involves taking on assertive, competitive behaviour to perform a gender identity characterised as masculine, and excludes both certain types of people and less structured, dichotomising, non-universalising and abstract discourses.

## Social context and academic discourse

In some ways this is a persuasive view. It would be naïve to accept science's own ideology that it is a hermetically sealed system functioning independently of the larger community which sustains it. What science finds worthy of investigation, how it formulates hypotheses and models, its criteria of valid argumentation and evidence, its modes of discourse, its genres, and every detail of its practices are integrally related to wider social practices (e.g. Hyland, 2004a). In pursuing their professional goals and constructing knowledge, academics engage with others, and because of this, discourses carry assumptions about knowledge, relationships and how these should be structured and negotiated. As a result, disciplines are also sites of power and authority which influence differential access to resources for creating knowledge and which define discipline-approved realities. Social context therefore always impinges on the discourses of the academy and, by extension, this also implies that there will be political and cultural influences on the practices and discourses of scientific communities. This does not, however, mean that there is a gender preference in discourse practices.

The view that academic interaction is gendered offers a suggestive metaphor, but leans heavily towards the polemical rather than the analytical, drawing on unexamined stereotypes of binary discourses. Most contributions to this argument have been speculative and rhetorical, with findings for gender-preferential language use mixed where actual texts have been examined.

We need to keep in mind that academic discourse is not homogeneous and monolithic any more than gender behaviours are, and in fact, the humanities are often seen as mildly effete. Nor is it easy to substantiate the view that the use of conventional academic interaction patterns necessarily involves a conscious and unwelcome adoption of gender-specific cultural values and practices. Clearly some writers will be discomfited by employing adversarial rhetorical practices, while others may, presumably, feel liberated from the need to behave in stereotypical 'feminine' ways.

More centrally, there is a preoccupation with bipolar conceptions of academic writing which tends towards the reification of gender difference, so that individual acts of self-representation can only be interpreted as either socially determined or aberrant. The argument draws on what amount to essentialising discourses which polarise gender categories, attribute certain characteristics to them, and then interpret academic practices according to a few stereotypical behaviours. Indeed, the proposition that academic discourse is gendered veers dangerously close to Cameron's *The Myth of Mars and Venus*, which says that women have a particular gift for cooperative, rapport-seeking, empathetic communication whereas men are inarticulate, emotionally stunted, insensitive and aggressive. Academic discourses cannot be lumped together and crudely characterised as masculine, as analyses show us that they contain caution and plurality alongside certainty and dialogue, with cooperation and reflection as much as criticism and competitiveness.

## 8.3   Book reviews and interaction

This chapter now turns to look at the ways that male and female actors construct their identities as professional academics by evaluating the work of others in book reviews, reporting a study conducted by Polly Tse and myself (Tse and Hyland, 2008). In such review genres, the control of evaluative resources is central to both effective writing and authorial identity. The ways that writers judge others' work and express these judgements in their texts signal not only what they think, but also who they are, displaying both their status as disciplinary insiders and their individuality. While I will have little to say about the feminist debates on the gendered construction of identity, I will show something of the similarities and differences in the interactive rhetorical practices of men and women and how gender and discipline identities cross-cut each other in significant ways. First, I describe the corpus and methodology of this study.

## The book review genre

The book review is one of the most interpersonally loaded genres of the academy and an excellent site to investigate identity construction. Its important evaluative role as 'the public evaluations of research' (Lindholm-Romantschuk, 1998) means that it provides a platform for community members to engage with each other's ideas and research in a public forum (Hyland, 2004a). Reviews are highly visible and carefully thought about, providing both junior and established academics with an opportunity to announce their allegiance to a particular orientation and proclaim a position without detailed argument or a protracted review process (Hyland and Diani, 2009). Two female academics stressed this importance:

(1)

It is a bit of an honour to be asked by the editor of the journal to write a book review. You also feel you're helping your colleagues, because they don't want to buy a book and find it terrible.

(Female Bio interview)

In philosophy a book review can go down as a serious contribution to research in the field and it will be cited because in that review it may be the first time a person has articulated an argument which other people have found persuasive. Philosophers really take book reviews seriously. They try very hard to say something very smart. It's also contributing to the knowledge in the field.

(Female Phil interview)

Reviews function as 'a change agent, creating a critical climate of opinion' (Orteza y Miranda, 1996: 191) and are considered to be 'a crucial site of disciplinary engagement' (Hyland, 2004a: 41). Unlike research articles, book reviews do not simply respond to a general body of impersonal literature but offer a direct, public and often critical encounter with a particular text and its author. Interactions are, in fact, a key element of the discourse, balancing critique and collegiality to signal how the writer wishes to position himself or herself in relation to his or her readers. In this genre, then, we see the workings of the peer group in perhaps its most nakedly normative role, where it publicly sets out to establish standards, assess merit and, indirectly, to evaluate reputations. Book reviews thus provide an ideal place for the examination of disciplinary identities and how features of proximity and positioning interact.

187

## The book review corpus

Corpus approaches are ideally positioned to critique both lazy binary perspectives and gendered views of academic discourse because they are based on attention to detail and an awareness of the larger disciplinary contexts in which words appear. This study explores 56 reviews of single-authored academic books and interviews with reviewers and editors. The reviews were taken from leading journals in the contrasting disciplines of philosophy (Phil) and biology (Bio), corresponding to the humanities and natural sciences respectively. The corpus was created with an eye to the genders of both the reviewer and the book author, with fourteen reviews by males in each discipline (seven of books with male authors and seven with female authors) and fourteen reviews by females in each discipline (again, seven of books with male authors and seven with female authors). These texts produce a corpus of 61,000 words as shown in Table 8.1.

**Table 8.1    Number of words in book review corpus by gender and discipline**

| Gender combination | Discipline | | Total combined gender |
|---|---|---|---|
| | Philosophy | Biology | |
| Female reviewing female | 11,432 | 4,469 | 15,901 |
| Female reviewing male | 9,419 | 3,690 | 13,109 |
| Male reviewing female | 10,657 | 4,455 | 15,112 |
| Male reviewing male | 12,733 | 4,089 | 16,822 |
| **Total by discipline** | *44,241* | *16,703* | 60,944 |

We can see that the more discursive philosophy reviews were two and a half times longer than the more focused and formulaic biology reviews. It is also interesting that the male corpus was about 10% longer than the female, although one would hesitate to interpret this as endorsing those findings which suggest that men give more opinions, occupy more interactional space and contribute more in public discourses (e.g. Herring et al.,1995; Tannen, 1994).

## Metadiscourse and rhetorical presence

In focusing on interaction in these texts, I was looking for linguistic choices which have obvious consequences for writers' identities, that is, choices which position them as members of social groups or as particular types of people. Once again, I draw here on Halliday's (1994) account, which sees the construction of identity as an aspect of the interpersonal function of language. This involves interactions between interlocutors, focusing on how writers convey messages about their sense of their own authority and certainty, and about their relationship with their readers (see Chapter 3). These interpersonal features can be systematically explored by examining features of metadiscourse (Hyland, 2005b; Hyland and Tse, 2004a).

Essentially, the concept of metadiscourse is based on the idea that while the total meaning of a text is a result of the interplay of its component parts, we can analytically distinguish its ideational content from material which organises this content and conveys the writer's beliefs and attitudes towards it. This allows us to see how writers use language to acknowledge, construct and negotiate social relations to best represent themselves, their views and their audience. This is because academics do not just discuss ideas but simultaneously seek to claim solidarity with readers, evaluate material and acknowledge alternative views in various ways, and they use the resources of metadiscourse to do this. The writer's adoption of a particular position is motivated by an awareness of self and the reader and so provides a way of understanding how writers see each of these (Hyland, 2005a).

Borrowing Thompson's (2001) terms, it is possible to distinguish between *interactive* and *interactional* resources in characterising these metadiscourse options:

*Interactive resources* allow the writer to manage the information flow to explicitly establish his or her preferred interpretations. They are concerned with ways of organising discourse to anticipate readers' knowledge and so reflect the writer's assessment of the reader's processing abilities, background resources and intertextual experiences in order to decide what needs to be made explicit to constrain and guide readers' interpretations. These resources include:

- *Transition markers*, mainly conjunctions, which are used to mark additive, contrastive and consequential steps in the discourse, as opposed to events in the external world.
- *Frame markers*, which are references to text boundaries or elements of schematic text structure, including items used to sequence, label stages, announce discourse goals and indicate topic shifts.
- *Endophoric markers*, which make additional material salient and available to the reader in recovering the writer's intentions by referring to other parts of the text.

- *Evidentials*, which indicate the source of textual information that originates outside the current text.
- *Code glosses*, which signal the restatement of ideational information.

**Interactional resources** focus on the participants of the interaction and seek to display an interpersonal tenor consistent with the disciplinary identity the writer wishes to project. Metadiscourse here concerns the writer's efforts to control the level of personality in a text and establish a suitable relationship to his or her data, arguments and audience, marking the degree of intimacy, the expression of attitude, the communication of commitments and the extent of reader involvement. They comprise:

- *Hedges*, which signal the writer's reluctance to present propositional information categorically.
- *Boosters*, which express certainty and emphasise the force of propositions.
- *Attitude markers*, which express the writer's appraisal of propositional information, and convey surprise, obligation, agreement, importance and so on.
- *Engagement markers*, which explicitly address readers, either by selectively focusing their attention or by including them as participants in the text through second-person pronouns, imperatives, question forms and asides (Hyland, 2001a).
- *Self-mentions*, which suggest the extent of author presence in first person pronouns and possessives.

Metadiscourse therefore subsumes many of the features I have discussed when trying to unravel identity construction in earlier chapters of this book, such as in many of the process-type choices in Chapter 5, self-mention in Chapter 6 and in the interactional signals employed by Cameron and Swales discussed in Chapter 7. Because it is a key means of supporting a writer's position and building a relationship with an audience, it also has the potential to reveal similarities and differences in the communicative practices of male and female writers in different disciplines.

# 8.4   Genre and gender: Patterns of interaction

A computer search was made of the four different corpora for some 500 potential metadiscourse items derived from prior studies (e.g. Hyland, 2004b and 2005a) and a close reading of the texts themselves. Every instance was studied in its sentential context to ensure it was performing a metadiscoursal rather than an ideational role, contributing to a relationship rather than the expression of an idea. A random 7% sample was analysed by a colleague to guarantee consistent coding and this produced an inter-rater reliability of over 90%. These analyses were supplemented by interviews with three reviewers and one editor from each discipline following a semi-structured format focusing on the writers' language choices, their understandings of the constraints of the genre, and their views on identity, argument and gender in their discipline.

The analysis confirms the extent of interactions in this genre with some 4,000 examples of metadiscourse overall, over 70 per review. Table 8.2 shows that reviewers used twice as many interactional features as interactive ones, so that an explicit stance towards the text and reader accounted for two-thirds of all metadiscourse in the corpus. Clearly positioning oneself in relation to others' ideas is particularly important to constructing a credible identity in this genre.

**Table 8.2    Metadiscourse in academic book reviews (per 1,000 words)**

| Category | Female corpus | Male corpus | Category | Female corpus | Male corpus |
|---|---|---|---|---|---|
| Transition markers | 14.4 | 13.8 | Engagement markers | 13.2 | 15.2 |
| Evidentials | 3.6 | 3.1 | Hedges | 9.8 | 11.0 |
| Code glosses | 2.8 | 2.8 | Attitude markers | 9.1 | 8.5 |
| Frame markers | 1.4 | 1.6 | Boosters | 7.0 | 9.0 |
| Endophoric markers | 0.2 | 0.3 | Self-mentions | 3.0 | 3.8 |
| *Total interactive* | 22.4 | 21.8 | *Total interactional* | 42.1 | 47.5 |
| Overall | 44.2 | (33%) | | 89.6 | (67%) |

## Interactive vs. interactional features

This predominance of *interactional features* highlights how the visible presence of writer and reader plays a key role in this discourse. In contrast to distributions in research articles (e.g. Hyland, 1998b), textbooks (e.g. Hyland, 2004a) and postgraduate dissertations (e.g. Hyland, 2004b; Hyland and Tse, 2004b), patterns in reviews emphasise how explicitly interpersonal and evaluative this genre is. The fact that this is a direct encounter with a specific text means that interactions can carry significant interpersonal implications for the reviewer, with both male and female writers making use of these resources to a broadly similar extent.

The high use of engagement markers and hedges by both men and women, for example, demonstrates the importance of creating a shared evaluative context. *Engagement markers* such as inclusive pronouns and questions, for instance, help underline an appeal to scholarly solidarity and group understandings (2); while *hedges* tone down the author's judgemental authority (3):

(2)

> None the less Feagin's book gives **us** an interesting, original and substantive account of how and why **we** appreciate fiction, in a way which relates to central philosophical issues concerning the philosophy of mind, the emotions and evaluative judgements.
>
> (Male Phil)

> What counts as 'making sense', or as an explanation or answer to questions that biologists take as central? What is the 'making sense' process, and in particular what role do models, mathematics, mechanics, and metaphors play? How do **we** know when biologists have succeeded – at what? Keller organizes her book around the thesis that there is no simple answer to these questions.
>
> (Female Bio)

(3)

> Indeed, **he seems to** ascribe **some kind of** genuine representational mentality (though apparently no actual minds) to animals as Descartes conceives of them. But **it does not seem to me that he clearly explains or successfully defends** an alternative to the more traditional interpretation.
>
> (Female Phil)

> **I sometimes felt like** important research and references from other desert biologists were glossed over or conspicuously missing from the text and literature citations.
>
> (Male Bio)

The fact that the review is a typically short genre helps to account for the less frequent use of text-structuring *interactive metadiscourse*. But while there is less need to frame arguments or constantly refer back and forth, writers need to aid readers towards an unambiguous recovery of their argument with transitions. These forms do more than simply link pieces of text together, however, as they help encode evaluations as an outcome of logical reasoning rather than as unsubstantiated personal reaction:

(4)

> **Although** the author introduces new terms and concepts without assuming that they are familiar to readers, the text requires a reasonable familiarity with ecology, geology and their associated jargons. **Consequently**, the book will be useful for an upper-division undergraduate or graduate class in desert ecology, **but** will generally be beyond the interests of beginning students.
>
> (Male Bio)

> All this makes it easy and enjoyable to read. **On the other hand**, **whilst** the overall structure is made fairly clear, details of argument or developments of particular lines of thought are often missing.
>
> (Female Phil)

Generally then, both male and female writers conduct their interactions with readers in similar ways, following the well-rehearsed generic practices of a book review discourse. Discursively constructing an appropriate authorial persona in this genre appears to involve an explicitly interpersonal stance and substantial writer intrusion expressed through relatively high frequencies of attitudinal lexis, hedged evaluation and explicit rhetorical connectivity.

## Conviction and personalisation

While there are considerable similarities in the interpersonal uses of language in this genre, it is also true that males used more metadiscourse overall and some 13% more interactional features. They were particularly heavy users of hedges, boosters and engagement markers, all of which are indicative of a more personalised and engaging style often associated with female discourse (e.g. Holmes, 1988).

The case of boosters, used to reinforce arguments and express firm convictions, is particularly interesting, both because it represents the widest difference in gender use in the corpus and because its use by men and women has been described in different ways in the literature. Crismore et al. (1993) and Francis et al. (2001), for instance, observed that men used more boosters than women, while Johnson and Roen (1992) and Herbert (1990) found females using boosters to strengthen praise. The review data supports both these results. Female reviewers mainly used boosters to intensify praise, fully committing themselves to their positive evaluations of a book:

(5)

> With **considerable** scholarship and eloquence, the author, a communications professor at the University of California San Diego, traces the insidious link between the commercialization of nature and the manipulation of human nature.
>
> (Female Bio)

> This book is a **highly** readable and informative resource that ...
>
> (Female Phil)

> Wedin's interpretations are **extremely** detailed and dense, and they contain **many** subtle points, which are worthy of admiration and thought.
>
> (Female Phil)

Males, in contrast, were more likely to use boosters to underpin their confidence in their judgements and to effectively close down any opposition to their position, often framing these evaluations with a first-person pronoun. As discussed in Chapter 7, self-mention is an explicit intrusion into the text to stamp a personal authority onto one's views, and this was a strategy employed far more by male reviewers, imparting a strong opinion to the evaluation:

(6)

> **I strongly** recommend these sections of the book to anyone who has been frustrated by the distressing trend in some philosophical circles to ...
>
> (Male Phil)

> **I have absolutely no doubt** that Whitford's understanding of these seemingly simple, but (in reality) amazingly complex systems is **among the most** comprehensive in the world community of desert ecologists.
>
> (Male Bio)

> Despite the fact that **I reject the book's central idea root and branch, I found it a fascinating read**, and so will anyone who is interested in the metaphysics of material objects.
>
> (Male Phil)

The frequency and use of boosters represents an important caveat to the claim that gender plays a relatively unimportant role in the construction of a disciplinary identity. Females in this corpus appeared to use them to seek agreement and support the reviewed author, while males used them to seek confirmation of their arguments and support themselves. Thus, females negotiated an identity which looked for common ground and convergence, while males tended to exploit difference and promoted a more challenging stance.

## Seniority vs. masculinity

The male writers' greater willingness to get behind bold statements, boost their arguments and generally take a more confident and uncompromising line might, however, be a result of the liberty afforded to them by seniority. After all, fewer women hold chairs in these fields, oversee research labs or sit on important committees, as several informants noted:

(7)

> Yes scientists are mainly male … the imbalance is even greater when you go up the ladder … It's hard because part of being confident depends on how you're perceived. You know, many people think women are not as good in writing that kind of 'factual' report. I know this perception is wrong but it affects how you see and present yourself.

(Female Bio interview)

> Unfortunately there is a huge gender imbalance in professional philosophy. The observation that men use more 'I' and are more assertive may be due to the hierarchical thing that the women feel that they have to be more careful or less assertive and this has to do with masculine aggressivity.

(Male Phil interview)

It seems that men's greater use of boosters, self-mention and engagement markers, or perhaps more precisely, women's comparative reluctance to employ them, may, at least in part, be a consequence of seniority and the presence of men in higher career positions rather than the effect of a male-dominant culture in the academy. But not all informants concurred in this view. Many failed to pick up on the topic when it was mentioned in the interviews, while some male respondents denied that gender was an issue in how people approached their academic writing. This biologist is an example:

(8)

> Status makes a difference, gender doesn't. They're all scientists, they are not men and women. But yes this field is so male-dominated that some women might try twice as hard as men to project a style of a so-called professional poker face scientist because they feel they need to somehow.

(Male Bio interview)

Overall, this book review data tends to support Francis et al.'s (2001) contention that the academic writing of men and women exhibits far more similarities than differences. The power of the genre to constrain behaviour and influence practice, however, may be underpinned by, and itself support, more gendered social structures. While women are beginning to make their presence felt in increasing numbers in these fields, both philosophy and biology are traditionally masculine domains where those holding the most senior and prestigious positions tend to be men. The predominant discourse patterns and modes of argument which define these disciplines are therefore shaped by largely male communities which encourage and support the performance of particular professional identities. In sum, identity practices seem to be fashioned by disciplinary expectations of rhetorical interaction, although these are cross-cut by gender relationships. I turn to this issue below.

## 8.5 Gender or discipline?

Table 8.3 compares male and female use of interpersonal features by discipline, with differences in each feature in the final column of each discipline. The most immediate impression we get from this table is that biologists and philosophers write differently irrespective of gender: interpersonal language uses show greater similarity *within* each discipline, with more variations *between* the disciplines than between genders. I will briefly explore the main variations in the next subsections.

**Table 8.3 Use of metadiscourse by gender and disciplines (per 1,000 words)**

|  | Philosophy | | | Biology | | |
|---|---|---|---|---|---|---|
|  | *Female* | *Male* | *F–M* | *Female* | *Male* | *F–M* |
| Transition markers | 18.0 | 15.3 | 2.7 | 5.1 | 9.5 | −4.4 |
| Evidentials | 4.4 | 4.0 | 0.4 | 1.6 | 0.6 | 1.0 |
| Code glosses | 2.9 | 2.5 | 0.4 | 2.6 | 3.9 | −1.3 |
| Frame markers | 1.9 | 1.9 | 0.0 | 0.2 | 1.1 | −0.9 |
| Endophoric markers | 0.2 | 0.5 | −0.3 | 0.0 | 0.0 | 0.0 |
| *Interactive* | *27.4* | *24.2* | *3.2* | *9.5* | *15.1* | *−5.6* |

*(to be continued)*

|                    | Philosophy | | | Biology | | |
|--------------------|--------|-------|-------|--------|-------|-------|
|                    | *Female* | *Male* | *F–M* | *Female* | *Male* | *F–M* |
| Engagement markers | 14.7   | 17.2  | −2.5  | 9.3    | 10.1  | −0.8  |
| Hedges             | 11.0   | 11.4  | −0.4  | 6.9    | 9.8   | −2.9  |
| Attitude markers   | 8.8    | 8.3   | 0.5   | 9.8    | 9.1   | 0.7   |
| Boosters           | 7.3    | 9.6   | −2.3  | 6.1    | 7.4   | −1.3  |
| Self–mentions      | 2.7    | 4.1   | −1.4  | 3.7    | 2.9   | 0.8   |
| *Interactional*    | *44.5* | *50.6* | *−6.1* | *35.8* | *39.3* | *−3.5* |
| **Overall**        | **71.9** | **74.8** | **−2.9** | **45.3** | **54.4** | **−9.1** |

## Variation across disciplines

The greater discursiveness of philosophy helps account for the higher frequencies of features as both male and female writers sought to create more explicitly involved and personal positions than their colleagues in biology. The distinctive processes of knowledge creation employed by these fields often mean that reviewers approached their tasks differently, with the philosophers far more likely to argue for or against a position. This may be because the biologists are more familiar arguing from empirical evidence rather than personal reflection, but largely, I think, because of the different kinds of books reviewed in the two disciplines.

Academic books are actually more characteristic of what Becher and Trowler (2001) call 'rural research areas', where topics are less narrowly focused, slower moving and less competitively researched. Knowledge is constructed more discursively and unhurriedly in the pages of books. Because of this, book reviews continue to play a significant role in the scholarship of the soft disciplines, often consuming a considerable amount of journal space. In fast-moving 'urban' sciences, on the other hand, the concern with innovation and speed of dissemination means that books are no longer a major vehicle for scholarship and often assemble already codified knowledge rather than disseminate new work (Myers, 1992). Consequently, many of the reviewed books in biology were intended for students, and reviews addressed issues of concern to that readership, often focusing on features such as cost, durability, the clarity of diagrams and the quality of exposition.

Philosophers were therefore more likely to go beyond the obvious observable aspects of the book to vigorously engage with the perspectives presented in it, as this philosopher observed:

(9)

> Writing a book review in philosophy always involves talking about its author, its background, its relation to the field, your own observations. Writing a book review is very much like doing a meta-analysis of the field and involves bringing in different perspectives.
>
> (Female Phil interview)

Writers spell out their arguments in more discursive detail, work harder to establish their credibility and take greater care to create an understanding with readers, and this helps account for much metadiscourse. Intertextuality, for example, plays a greater role in the philosophy reviews and helps to explain why they contained higher uses of evidentials, bringing in other voices to support or critique a position in the review. One informant explained that book reviews in philosophy can provide an important mechanism for presenting new arguments:

(10)

> A book review can turn out to be like a discussion paper ... when you discuss the issues represented in the book, you must relate it to other perspectives ... discussions are very similar to those in a research paper.
>
> (Male Phil interview)

Elaborating an argument of this kind also entails a greater need to make logical reasoning and discourse relations explicit, a fact which helps to account for the greater use of transition markers in philosophy. Engagement markers were the most commonly used feature, however, although philosophers, both male and female, made far more use of inclusive *we* and questions to discursively construct writer–reader relations. The use of direct questions is overwhelmingly a feature of the philosophy reviews and is particularly interesting as it corresponds to the tradition of scepticism in that field:

(11)

> I was taught every belief is in principle problematic, you can't question everything all at once, but everything is in principle questionable ... it is a kind of philosophical spirit in questioning what you believe in and how you justify what you believe, and can you give good and sufficient reasons, and if you can't, why do you believe it?
>
> (Male Phil interview)

Finally, a word about hedges and self-mention, both of which occurred more in the philosophy papers and which were linked quite explicitly by informants to aspects of their disciplinary values and practices rather than gendered identities. The frequent use of hedges, for instance, seems to be a consequence of the fact that philosophical discourse does not seek to accomplish 'closure' by reaching consensus on a particular issue but is more like a continuing conversation (Hyland, 2002a):

(12)

> Our philosophical training forbids us to be too extreme or certain about our views. I mean you can have a strong belief in something, but you can't prove other people are wrong. The whole thing about philosophy is to constantly question ourselves. So it may not be about acknowledging other people's perspectives, but that we can't be certain about our own.

(Female Phil interview)

The desire of philosophers to widen an argumentative space through hedges, then, helps to explain a certain tentativeness in book reviews and reflects disciplinary traditions of open debate.

This self-conscious appreciation of the role of language in constructing a distinctive disciplinary identity for philosophy was also expressed by another respondent when discussing self-mention:

(13)

> This is different from social or natural sciences where they emphasize the notion of an 'ideal observer' who is disinterested and only focused on observable facts, but this idea of 'ideal observer' is exactly what humanities set out to challenge … we encourage these kinds of personal values and beliefs … so the use of 'I' highlights individual personality and perspectives, as well as creativity, in philosophical writing.

(Male Phil interview)

Through both their texts and their comments, these writers, both male and female, displayed a clear and consistent disciplinary orientation to their academic communities. The fact that disciplinary similarities exceeded gender similarities seems to suggest they sought to construct identities linked to the participant relationships and knowledge-creating practices of their fields, rather than those of gender. Professional academic identities are predominantly disciplinary identities.

## Variation in philosophy reviews

Although disciplinary differences were greater than gender differences, there were variations within each discipline which are worth exploring further. Among these are the fact that female philosophers tended to use more interactive features than males and that they were particularly heavy users of transition markers. Males, in contrast, used far more engagement markers and boosters. These different preferences for interactive and interactional forms seem to be related to very different ways of conceptualising argument and crafting persuasion.

Essentially, interactive forms such as transitions are used to signal the arrangement of texts according to the writer's appreciation of the reader's likely knowledge and understandings. They influence the 'reader-friendliness' of a text and mainly involve the control of information flow. This can be seen in this brief example:

(14)

> **Since** Walzer argues that there are competing interpretations of the meanings of social goods, he can justify his own interpretations of these meanings only as interpretations; **nevertheless**, he continues to seek consensus as if his interpretations or the principles he thinks are implied in them are the universally shared and correct ones. **An additional problem** is that he seems to have no critical stance from which to object to society's present principles of justice, **since** they may be grounded on a socially accepted interpretation of the social goods they are used to distribute.

(Female Phil)

Transitions thus represent a working towards a consensus by linking elements of the discourse in ways the reader is likely to best understand and find persuasive, guiding readers by anticipating their likely reactions and needs. They seek to achieve proximity and a close alignment with readers.

In contrast, greater use of *interactional* resources can be seen to represent a very different style of argument, altogether more personal and intrusive, confronting and challenging the reader with a more explicitly committed and engaged stance and expecting more of the reader in working with the writer. Here, for example, the combination of boosters, attitude markers, direct asides to the reader, personal reference and hedges functions to present an individual voice and meet ideas head-on with conviction and clear acceptance of responsibility:

(15)

> This is **almost certainly too weak** an account, for **it fails** to rule out chance coincidences of judgment and motivation. This problem **may be** avoidable by appeal to a more complex pattern of possibilities; however, **I believe** that any moderated account of the disposition to exercise control will run into a **serious** difficulty.
>
> (Male Phil)

> **My only quarrel** with Baker's presentation of her material (the book is **generally very well written** and **as clear as the subject matter permits**) is that **I find here and there a certain carelessness** in her use of logical concepts.
>
> (Male Phil)

Here, then, we see more explicit positioning and attempts by writers to present a more personal, writer-oriented style of argument.

Clearly, both sets of options are available to both men and women, but the distributions over the 56 texts suggest clear gender preferences for these interpersonal choices. The frequency counts imply that these differences are not merely artefacts of analysis, and this interpretation is reinforced by the fact that several informants also raised the possibility that these argument patterns are potentially related to gender identities:

(16)

> Argument is central in our field, but there are different ways to do it … clarity and logic is most valued in the field and it is relatively easy to learn how to write clearly and logically than to forcefully express something, because it only takes more practice to write clearly, but it may involve changing your own personality if you want a battle. I prefer to work twice as hard on plain logical and coherent presentation if I want to convince. When peaceful discussion would do why do you want to fight? It sounds too aggressive and I don't like it. Some men do; they think a philosopher's job is to fight.
>
> (Female Phil interview)

> I won't say men pay less attention to organising their arguments. But I do want to do more than simply set out my views. I also want to convince people and present different views in a way such that some would carry greater force … this is about the philosophical spirit of questioning and arguing.
>
> (Male Phil interview)

Stereotypes contain seeds of lived experience, however, and may even inform the ways individual academics understand their everyday engagement in disciplinary discourses. One male, in fact, attributed an aggressive, combative style to a male predilection for 'verbal battles':

(17)

> Some of those guys, their mind might be like kick-boxers. They just want to show they're the smartest and shut one up and be the boss. I think it is true that a lot of male philosophers are sort of like robot kung fu, they want to have verbal battles with you and see who can win.
>
> (Male Phil interview)

Within the overall patterns of debate in philosophy, therefore, it seems that many female academics work to rhetorically construct an identity based on an even-handed scholarly reasonableness. This is a persona which respects philosophical values of rationality and logic by careful exemplification and coherent analysis of ideas. This differs from the more directly challenging style of debate, more usually adopted by males, and which Bloor (1996) has referred to as 'mind-to-mind combat', where it is assumed that the best way to investigate ideas is to subject them to extreme opposition.

## Variation in biology reviews

In biology we find considerably fewer interpersonal interventions overall, that the male reviewers employed more of almost every metadiscourse feature, and that the cross-gender differences were more marked, particularly in hedges, boosters and transitions.

As I mentioned earlier, transitions aid clarity and reader processing of a text and help writers achieve proximity to their colleagues and disciplines. Once again, these represented the most sizeable inter-gender difference, but unlike the philosophy reviews, these were 86% more common in the texts written by males. This was largely because the male reviewers were more likely to produce pairs of contrasting evaluative comments than women:

(18)

> It is **well** illustrated and there is a **good** glossary, **but** it will **probably** fail to engage.
>
> (Male Bio)

> **Although** I generally found the author's diverse research experiences and first-hand accounts to be a strong aspect of this book, I **sometimes** felt like important research and references from other desert biologists were glossed over or

conspicuously missing from the text and literature citations.

(Male Bio)

Her command of relevant case law, regulations, and legislation is impressive ... She has a tendency, **however**, to downplay the potential benefits of genetics and to focus only on the prospects for harm.

(Male Bio)

More specifically, male reviewers were also more likely than females to engage with the methodological and theoretical bases of the reviewed texts and with the author's argument itself. This more argumentative stance requires greater attention to weighing pros and cons and navigating a route through complex contradictions and alternatives, increasing the need for transitions and for interactional markers of explicit personal involvement to mitigate threats to the book author. Interestingly, closer investigation into the gender of the author being reviewed reveals that many of these more critical and evaluative reviews by males were of books written by other men. While the frequencies are perhaps too small to more than point to a future area for research (just seven texts in each combination gender of reviewer and reviewed writer), concordance patterns suggest in particular that male reviewers used significantly more hedges to evaluate the work of other men:

(19)

Although he wanders freely through an eclectic selection of images and ideas, he **could perhaps** have done more to explore new ground.

(M-review-M Bio)

In my **opinion** there is not enough data or conceptual ideas in most of the chapters for a graduate seminar ...

(M-review-M Bio)

That omission ignores what is **likely to be** a significant component of genetic medicine in this era of genomes and proteomes, and it results in a **rather** skewed consideration of the relative merits of the three alternative frameworks for policy formulation.

(M-review-M Bio)

This kind of male-to-male hedging was mainly used to mitigate personal critical evaluation of a book's content, thereby reducing the face threat of a more direct condemnation (Hyland, 2004a). The less critically engaging stance of female reviewers not only meant that they used far fewer hedges, but also that those they did use were deployed in a different way. This was often to redress the impact of the book's argument on readers, rather than the impact of the criticism on the author:

(20)
>So although readers **might** be horrified by what they see ...
>
>(F-review-M Bio)

>I expect some readers **would** enjoy the multidisciplinary treatment ...
>
>(F-review-F Bio)

>A sceptical reader with even a modicum of expertise in the use of statistics **may** feel uneasy about all these tests that **sometimes** compare ...
>
>(F-review-F Bio)

>Even with the warning that it is not a scholarly book, biologists **might** find themselves shocked by other aspects, if they are not familiar with the genre.
>
>(F-review-M Bio)

In other words, the decision by many male biologists to critically engage with the ideas presented by other males seems to represent a marked choice which needed to be expressed tentatively, particularly as it is impossible in these texts to appeal to experimental evidence for support. For men, the book review is an opportunity in biology to present one's own ideas in opposition to another's, using the argument of the reviewed book to promulgate an alternative perspective without the need for empirical substantiation. While scientists often afford books less importance than in the soft fields and most tend to be written for students, textbooks can be extremely influential in providing a coherently ordered epistemological map of the disciplinary landscape, reducing the multivocality of past texts to a single voice of authority. For this reason they can represent a challenge to the perspectives of other senior academics, who may see a review as a chance to set out their own views.

Reviews are important to disciplinary identity construction. They are highly visible and can be very influential, allowing their writers a public rhetorical platform to signal their allegiance to a particular orientation or group, and to proclaim a position without engaging in the long cycle of inquiry, review and revision involved in a full-length paper. This is, however, an opportunity almost exclusively taken by men reviewing the books of other men, and rarely by females, or male reviewers of female authors. Again, men's position in the field and their need to promote their own ideas and research work may be a possible explanation for this. One female biologist put it like this:

(21)

> I think it might be related to the keen competition between labs and the fact that principal investigators in these labs are mainly male. They may feel it is their responsibility to respond to each other's findings, even if they can't be certain, to promote an active image of their labs and to show other competing labs that they're not ignorant of the issues. You know that people who control grants are aware of what's going on, whether you have something interesting to contribute to the field or not, if anyone is doing similar work as you're doing … maybe women are less likely to be in charge and so don't feel as much need to respond to ideas.
>
> (Female Bio interview)

The competition between male-dominated labs and research groups is frequently intense, particularly as funding, influence and esteem are scarce commodities. The linguistic and rhetorical choices in these reviews reflect something of this competition as writers in biology, just as those in philosophy, construct for themselves a professional identity.

## 8.6 Conclusions on gender and disciplinary identity

This study of interactions in academic book reviews illuminates something of the ways academics participate in and experience the performance of a disciplinary identity and strongly underlines the view that there is no one-to-one relation between gender and language. Instead of uniform patterns of gendered discourse which transcend disciplines, we find multiple relations and meanings cross-cut by the practices and communicative conventions of academic communities. Individual performances of proximity to the field and positioning to colleagues are a consequence of myriad personal experiences. This is not really surprising. An emphasis on rigid differences can lead to an 'essentialist' view of gender: an adherence to polar proclivities or practices which reifies language behaviour and implies a relatively fixed gendered identity. In academic discourse, such a binary position fixes a certain set of traits, such as competition, aggression and so on, as male, for example, and encourages a deterministic view which suppresses space for individual agency and personal choice.

This small study of an important academic genre suggests a more complex picture. An empirical and discourse-based understanding of identity helps reveal something of how dominant cultural understandings of identity categories are both reproduced and undermined by disciplinary practices. In academic communities, authority is exercised by peers, editors, reviewers and other members of one's community over writing, and these influence who gets read, who gets accepted and whose arguments are seen as persuasive. Such constraints contribute to the meanings that can be created and to evaluations of persuasiveness by readers. But while the version of self that will be rewarded may be constrained in this way, individual agency is not eliminated. Identities are not pre-scripted and the unique history of individual encounters with texts gives them the possibility of recombining the options available in their own ways.

As they write, academics draw on a repertoire of voices, bringing to the task their own experiences, purposes and conceptions of self to recombine the options offered by the genre to perform a professional disciplinary identity (Ivanič and Camps, 2001). Our diverse experiences and memberships of overlapping communities, including those of class, ethnicity and gender (Kubota, 2003), influence how we understand our disciplinary participation and how we want to interact with our colleagues in the performance of a professional academic identity. Gender is an important component of our lived experience, and it is unsurprising that it should influence the identities we adopt in our professional writing. The ways men and women use a language, in other words, are not determined by their gender but constructed, negotiated and transformed through social practices informed by particular social settings, relations of power and participation in disciplinary discourses.

# 9 Identity, Disciplinarity and Methodology

At one point in Ian Rankin's detective novel *The Hanging Garden*, a character observes that the problem with conclusions is that they are supposed to be conclusive. Unlike Inspector Rebus, however, who wraps up his cases by assembling pieces of evidence that lead inexorably to some truth, observers of academic discourse are left with loose ends and uncertainty. Any stretch of language allows a variety of plausible interpretations, and often its routinised nature means that users themselves may not always be aware of what they are doing with it. The analyses I've presented in this book have therefore involved trying to assemble coherence from bits of observable data, piecing together potentially polypragmatic and ambiguous tracts of text to see what they reveal about identity as academics and students go about their daily business in universities. My goal has been to show how identity can be made concrete through the exploration of the mundane and the everyday. Some analysts would no doubt do things differently and other observers draw different interpretations from mine, and so I can offer no conclusive conclusions in this final chapter.

I do, however, want to make a few observations to recap the main arguments and pull together some of the trailing threads. I will offer some reflections on three key themes of the book: the connection between writing and identity, the role of disciplinarity and a methodology for exploring each of these. Finally I will comment briefly on the practical value of this kind of work and some possible future directions.

## 9.1  Identity and academic writing

One thread is the idea that academic writing is not just about conveying an ideational 'content': it is also about the representation of self. That is, in arguing our ideas, recounting our achievements, struggling for a course grade, acknowledging our gratitude or applying for a prize, we are also relating to a community of readers and so both giving and 'giving off' information about ourselves. In short, every act of communication is an act of identity because identity is what the writer *does* in a text. It is implicated in the texts we engage in and the linguistic choices we make in creating them on a moment-by-moment basis. What and how we write articulates a performance which says something to others about us.

## Language as choice

The chapters of this book have tried to document some of the ways in which writers accomplish this performance of an academic identity. The analyses underline the idea that language offers us a system of choices for representing ourselves, our allegiances and our ideas in various ways, so the constraints which are imposed by genre and discipline are simultaneously the raw materials which facilitate similarity and difference, compliance and resistance, conformity and idiosyncrasy. I have tried to show that the decisions writers make in doing simple, everyday things with words, things such as modifying a knowledge claim, connecting ideas or putting a link on a homepage, all involve choices which index their membership of a community and their relationship to that community as an individual. So the frequent use of the verb *to be,* the decision to use a first-person pronoun or the preference for identifying over attributive clause types signal something of how the writer wants to be seen by his or her readers.

A point I would like to underline here, and which I have been at pains to argue throughout the book, is that the conventions of academic discourse are not the bars of a prison which force users into a mindless, robotic conformity. It is certainly true, and well documented, that many students and academics alike often find the arcane literacy demands of academic life chillingly impersonal and alienating. The hegemony and authority of these conventions seem intimidating and certainly contrast with the more familiar practices of their home lives. Writers can feel forced to relinquish the congruence of everyday speech based on empathy, activity and solidity for the incongruent, rational anonymity of academic genres. But, and I view things differently from Ivanič, Lillis and others here, they may also see that access to new literacies also admits them into new communities and experiences, offering different ways of understanding the world through abstraction and precision.

Discourses are 'ways of being in the world' (Gee, 1999: 23), and so language choices are always made from culturally available resources. We draw on a repertoire of options in a local context and make judgements about how far successful communication will involve juggling communal and personal voices, subordinating some choices and foregrounding others in expressing positions, while observing proximity to recognised norms. In short, disciplines are human institutions where actions and understandings are influenced by the personal and biographical, as well as the institutional and sociocultural. They are sites where differences in worldview or language usage intersect as a result of the myriad backgrounds and overlapping memberships of participants.

## Threats and opportunities

The peculiar conventions of the academy can certainly threaten an individual's sense of self by overturning familiar practices and discourses, but they are recognised and valued by the particular social groups he or she may be trying to join, or at least attempting to impress. It has to be remembered, however, and made clear to students and novice writers, that these conventions are not monolithic and fixed, determining how writers should represent themselves in their texts. Research into academic writing increasingly shows us how authors exercise choice, and that there is space for the negotiation of identity and for the presence of a writer's external rhetorical experiences. I have tried to show that characteristics such as reputation, seniority, gender and culture mediate the linguistic choices we make and how we use disciplinary resources. I have also argued, however, that academic genres are not blank cheques upon which we can write anything we like.

University genres, like any other, have a constraining power which restricts creativity and places limits on the originality of individual writers. Once we accept that our social and rhetorical goals are best achieved by, say, writing an essay rather than a postcard or lab report, then we will express ourselves in certain more or less predictable ways. The genre does not 'dictate' how or what we write, it enables choices to be made and facilitates expression, but these are made within certain boundaries. Choices are exercised in a context of powerful incentives which give them communicative and social consequences. It is these constraints which make communication possible by marking the borders within which meanings are effective and appropriate in a given context.

Academic discourses, in other words, represent broad frames for managing disputes and constructing agreement on knowledge which have evolved and continue to change in response to shifting contexts and to the repeated adjustments of numerous users. Disciplinary discourses are cultural models which index relationships with others. They take on a hegemonic dimension because sharing these models reflects, recreates and reinforces the discourses which underpin them. However, in the process of using and reproducing texts, actors also elaborate and manipulate them, shaping what they have to say to their own proclivities and preferences within the boundaries of community expectations of how meanings should be conveyed, arguments constructed and relationships negotiated.

## 9.2 Identity and disciplinarity

A second major thread of the book has been that identity is not an individual trait but is ascribed or attributed to an individual by others. As Riley (2007: 87) points out, 'discussing social identity as if it were an intrinsic quality of one person makes about as much sense as discussing the sound of one hand clapping'. While we experience the world from the perspective of an embodied individual, the self is a thoroughly social product, an emergent creation which reveals a quest for coherence and orientation to a social world. It is crammed full of the attitudes of others so that we might more accurately talk of identity *negotiation* than construction.

### Interaction and routinisation

Group membership is meaningful to individuals; it is a shared representation of who we are and has consequences for how we act and interact in the performance of an identity. It gives a sense of belonging and identification with others while enabling us to see outsiders as different. Most importantly, it underpins the habitualisation or routinisation of behaviour, which narrows choices and offers opportunities for reflection and innovation. Our repeated access to certain forms means that we consistently choose within this range. In other words, disciplines provide the resources to construct a relatively stable environment for understanding the way things are and a guide for the way things should be done, indicating both limits and possibilities. Identity, in other words, is an element of context, and it is inseparable from how individuals talk about the world and engage with others. It is this relationship that I have tried to capture in the constructs of proximity and positioning: the ground and field of identity and the ways we negotiate difference from similarity.

The fact is that we just can't claim to be whoever we want to be and get away with it, or not for long anyway, as our identity claims need the support and confirmation of others. Identity is constituted in relationships between people and in the talk that goes on between people. We live our social lives in texts so that in writing and speaking we draw on the resources of our communities to project a certain definition of self for validation by others. This validation is crucial and means that identity is an interactive event enacted repeatedly over time. The idea that the individual and the collective are routinely and inextricably entangled is certainly not original, and not even particularly new. It is prominent in the work of Mead and goes back to Marx, Freud and beyond; however, it seems to be forgotten in conceptions of identity which focus on a reflective, individual self or on fluid and shifting conceptions of identity as discourse roles.

Crucially, identity involves *identification*: so in identifying myself as an applied linguist, for example, I am identifying with a wider category. This identity partly depends on excluding, or at least subordinating, other categories, such as the fact that I am white, middle-aged and male, and so identities exist by virtue of *not being something else* (Hall, 1996). The relationship between individual and community, however, is not entirely straightforward. We all identify with at least one group and these influence how we understand and practise being an academic. Nor is this simply about combining the different identities of these memberships in an *additive* way. We do not just add a gendered identity onto a raced identity on top of a sexual identity and a professional identity and so on. Instead, all forms of identity interact, they impact on one another to mutually constitute an identity in particular local contexts, creating potential tensions and shaping us as uniquely individual people.

## The primacy of discipline

One thing that the analyses in this book point to is the primacy of *discipline* in the professional identities of academics. The various chapters have tried to describe what academics do with language in performing identity work and to identify what influences their decision-making in this process.

In Chapters 4 and 5, I focused on genre and explored some of the ways that *proximity* works in shaping decision-making to constrain the options that writers have in crafting a professional self, looking at acknowledgements, homepages, prize applications and academic bios. Even in these relatively peripheral and more representational genres of the academy, we find a preference for foregrounding particular features of the self and doing this in particular ways. Chapters 6 and 8 highlighted how educational experiences and gender cross-cut disciplinary expectations and practices to show something of how proximity and positioning interact in undergraduate reports and book reviews. In Chapter 7 I focused more on *positioning*, or the ways that authors work with the resources available to them to carve out a distinctive space for a personal self. Here celebrity, or at least seniority or experience, was suggested to be a potentially influential factor in creatively shaping a distinctive identity from the shared practices of disciplinary convention.

In each of these studies, then, the key influence of discipline has been evident. Disciplines provide conceptual frames for organising experiences and carrying out actions, both rhetorical and epistemological, and so steer the actor to choices which construct a representation of self to others. Disciplines offer broad established patterns of practice which are recognised by members and have a certain force as 'the ways things are done'. They are, then, particular combinations of the individual and the collective; a process influenced by proximity and positioning as actors engage in the practical accomplishment of representing themselves in recognisable and valued ways, while at the same time offering them some space for their non-academic experiences. In sum, individual and collective identities are one and the same, created through a dialogue between self and others.

## 9.3 Identity and methodology

A final theme of the book that I want to revisit is the connection between identity and the corpus methodology I have used to study it. Using corpora is a departure in identity studies, distinguished from more familiar methods which analyse conversational turns at talk, unpack political contexts or interpret interview narratives. It is, instead, a view which treats an individual's group identifications as central to the performance of self and sees identity as entirely social, constructed in the repeated interactions of community members in specific contexts of engagement over time.

I believe this method addresses limitations in current ways of conceptualising identity. CA, working within a sociological perspective with limited linguistic tools, for example, is unable to adequately reconstruct the cultural frames that participants might be orienting to in claiming certain identities. CDA on the other hand, is more explicitly informed by a discussion of context, although this is often imposed ad hoc and reflects the analyst's stance rather than the participants' definition of the situation. In the narrative approach, the status we give both the informant's construction and the analyst's interpretations is uncertain. The evidence for identity is what analysts say about what people say about their experiences rather than what individuals actually do. Nor is it clear where the interpretive categories used to explain talk as indexing social categories actually come from, how they relate to each other, and how they are applied to the data (Pavlenko, 2007). Corpora overcome many of the problems by asking different questions and seeing identity as repeated patterns of performance.

## Corpora and their discontents

Using corpora to explore the performance of identity is a novel and, I believe, productive methodology, but corpus approaches also have their critics (e.g. Borsley and Ingham, 2002; Cook, 1998; Widdowson, 2000).

One often-heard criticism (e.g. Widdowson, 2000) concerns representativeness and how far we can claim that the texts selected for analysis actually characterise the population under study: can we generalise from our corpora to make wider statements about the performance of identity in a genre or among a particular group? This question is a serious one and there is little agreement on it. In Chapter 4, for example, my corpus of prize applications is from one university and my sample of acknowledgements from one country. This argument, however, is perhaps less pressing here than when compiling corpora to describe 'a language' more generally (Stubbs, 1996: 232). In cases where the population is huge and constantly changing, representativeness can only be an elusive ideal.

Of course it is true that no corpus can ever be more than a small sample of the writing that people do in a particular genre, yet developing a massive corpus may be counterproductive. Not only does it require additional time and resources in accessing and organising texts, but ever larger corpora can make it difficult to deal with the output. Moreover, a large corpus does not necessarily represent a genre better than a smaller one, particularly if it is used to study high-frequency items. What is more important is that the sample is carefully collected to include a cross-section of the focus texts, and that it provides an adequate quantity of target tokens for the researcher to work with. Narrower studies of particular genres sampled by discipline and writer characteristics help restrict the population and allow us to say rather more about how features are used.

Making generalisations about language use from a corpus will, therefore, always involve some extrapolation and interpretation. But all language study is exploratory and suggestive, and it is, I believe, important just to get on with it and see what we can find. If we are careful in our compilation of texts and consistent in our interpretations, corpora can provide an empirical basis for our investigations and conclusions. They offer a useful starting point for analysis which can yield evidence of proximity to a community and positioning within it, but using frequencies and real examples does not remove intuition and deduction from the process.

Another common criticism is that corpus analyses treat language as an artefact, abstracted from its real context, and that as a result, it is one-dimensional (Baldry, 2000; Borsely and Ingham, 2002). Writers do not sit down to produce concordance lines nor do readers encounter them in research articles or exam scripts, so we lose an understanding of the richness of composing as writers negotiate their immediate writing circumstances. It is certainly true that part of the meaning of a text is how it is encountered and experienced in an authentic context – in a print journal, an expensive hardback monograph, a conference handout or on lined exam paper – and this is not reproduced in a corpus. But are we in a better position, by concentrating on the local setting, to capture the culture and event within which the action of writing is embedded? Texts function communicatively by anticipating particular readers and the reactions of those readers to what is written. In other words, texts respond to, and evoke, an institutional frame which intrudes upon the writer and activates specific language choices. Texts carry traces of how writers understand their readers and their communities, so context, as the writer understands it, is printed on the page.

The issue of abstractness, however, does suggest that we may need to balance corpus data, with its exclusive focus on 'language', with a focus on 'action' if possible. This means 'rematerialising' the features that have been studied to understand how and why language users make the choices they do. Interviews, and particularly discourse-based interviews where respondents are asked to comment on language choices in texts, can help ground patterns of text meanings in the conscious choices of writers. Thus, in Chapter 6 I gathered writers' and readers' views using focus groups and interviews, and in Chapter 7 I assembled the perspectives of my case study writers from a memoir and their responses to my analysis itself.

Every method has limitations and strengths and is suited to addressing particular kinds of questions, and what a corpus does best is tell us what a particular language variety is like. It reveals something of how writers, and speakers, engage in particular acts of communication again and again, and so offers data that is not available in any other way. By examining the genres and meanings writers adopt, we gain a great deal since we can explore the ways writers see their audience and themselves when engaging in academic realities.

## Corpora and habitus

Identity is negotiated between individuals acting in concert, although perhaps not always in harmony, as members of particular social groups. It is constructed from the routine and familiar, and is found in everyday patterns of engagement. As I have noted, texts are about *solidarity*, about uniting community members in a collective endeavour of meaning-making so that claims are made and challenged in recognisable ways. In Bourdieu's terms, our language practices and social behaviours represent a *habitus* or corpus of dispositions, embodied in individuals, and which generate various practices of interaction. These are the seen but largely unnoticed discursive systems which we take for granted and largely operate within. They are the raw materials from which we craft an identity by repeatedly and customarily selecting items from a repertoire of community resources over a range of different occasions of use. Such experience is often concealed from our conscious awareness and hidden from introspection. Intuition is therefore a poor guide to revealing why particular phrasings, words or grammatical patterns are used repeatedly in certain contexts.

As Sinclair (1991), Stubbs (1996) and others have shown, corpus studies reveal that writing is characterised by impressive regularities of pattern with endless variation. In what they include or omit, all texts make assumptions about their readers, shaped by prior texts, by repetitions and by orientations to certain routines or conventions. A corpus approach brings a distributional perspective to linguistic analysis by providing quantitative information about the relative frequency of use of particular elements in different contexts, pointing to systematic tendencies in the selection of meanings. It therefore reduces the burden that is often placed on individual texts (or on intuitions) and dramatically shows how particular grammatical and lexical choices are regularly made.

We learn to participate in our disciplines because we become 'primed' to expect and understand certain patterns of words (Hoey, 2005), whether through training or regular exposure. In the terms I have used here, we are able to adopt a *position* only through our *proximity* to the communicative practices of our disciplines. We become familiar with the ways our teachers, associates and colleagues practise doing biology or philosophy through regular encounters with their discourses. Each feature of language thus has its own distributional patterns and each word its own collocational behaviour which varies across disciplines and genres and which comprises the fabric from which identity is created. The most accessible route to understand disciplinary identities is therefore to explore community preferences for particular rhetorical and linguistic choices.

The various corpus procedures used in this book all observe the idea that through abstracting away from specific examples of writing, we can gather linguistic evidence of consistent rhetorical practices. Frequency counts, collocation and keyness are commonplace and unremarkable corpus techniques available to any analyst with the inclination to use them, but the benefits are well worth the effort. Language use is sensitive to context, and so mapping typicality allows us to uncover what is usual and what is deviant in collections of texts. It helps to reveal evidence of proximity and positioning. Corpus approaches therefore help us see both figure and ground, consistent linguistic choices and individual variations. They reveal how individuals, in constructing knowledge and social relationships, also construct themselves.

## 9.4   Identity and practicalities

One question that remains is whether all this is any more than of passing academic interest. Do identity studies have any practical payoff? Clearly self-help books on identity trade on such practicalities, encouraging us to reflect on who we are and providing strategies for building our self-esteem, sense of purpose and ability to influence others. A book which sees identity as a function of interactive performance, however, must have more modest ambitions. However, the preceding analyses suggest advantages in the professional development of academics, in EAP instruction and in further research into identity.

### Writing for publication

Research shows that academics all over the world are increasingly less likely to publish in their own languages and to find their English language publications cited more often. With the position of universities on league tables and the career prospects of academics now largely dependent on the length of personal bibliographies, submissions to journals have never been greater, and it is not unusual for periodicals to receive over ten times more submissions than they can use. In this context, corpus studies are of potential value as they can reveal features of successful writing to assist academics in publishing their work, particularly in showing how individuals collectively and repeatedly assemble rhetorical indicators of 'who they are'.

The requirements and expectations of academic publishing often seem complex beyond belief with conflicting advice and pressures to fit into a straightjacketing conformity of formal, dense and author-evacuated prose. But good writers are largely people who are better able to imagine how their readers will respond to their texts and envision what their language choices say about themselves. Academic writers, however, are not always clear about the options their disciplines make available to them, the alternatives they have in expressing themselves or the connotations these choices convey. As a result, many are happy to just stick to the conventions and get the job done. Others, however, want to establish a distinctive identity for themselves and strive for a personal 'voice'. Nor is this easier for native English speakers who frequently share many of the difficulties experienced by non-native English speakers (Casanave and Vandrick, 2003). Swales (2004: 56), in fact, argues that the most important distinction in publishing is not between native and non-native English speakers, but

> between experienced or 'senior' researcher/scholars and less experienced or 'junior' ones – between those who know the academic ropes in their chosen specialisms and those who are learning them.

Native English speakers rarely receive help with academic writing during their careers and are often less 'academically bilingual' than many individuals writing English as a second language.

Corpus studies tell us that individual disciplines have different ways of organising ideas and structuring arguments, and that rhetorical features are distributed differently across them (e.g. Biber, 2006; Hyland, 2004a; Hyland and Bondi, 2006). We have seen, for example, that not all disciplines sanction the same degree of authorial presence, that they use different transitions and structuring signals, and that they prefer to frame expertise in different ways. These differences in writers' decision-making are closely related to the social and epistemological practices of the disciplines and as a result represent important ways of signalling a competent disciplinary identity. The kinds of corpus studies discussed in this book can help academics become familiar with the conventions and expectations which operate in particular settings and to see what options are available to them.

I don't want to imply, however, that instruction should simply blindly accommodate writers to the publication machine. Teachers have to ensure that their students are aware of the consequences of their different language choices. The goal, it seems to me, should always be to enhance writer empowerment and agency without disadvantaging their acceptance within their communities. This means providing support for individual understanding and expression within institutional expectations and conventions, following the sort of advice which Kubota (2003: 65) gives to novice writers:

> In my experience, the more the publishing community recognises the credibility of my work, the more I feel empowered to explore alternative ways of expressing ideas. Thus it is advisable for a writer to follow closely the conventions at least in the initial stages of writing for publication in order to gain the cultural capital that will facilitate her or his initiation into the academic community.

This kind of support is provided by an encouraging environment in which writers can reflect on, become aware of, and try out the persuasive options their disciplines make available.

## EAP and writing instruction

Raising students' awareness of the language options available to them in negotiating an identity they feel comfortable with is also important in EAP classes. Once again, teachers can use corpus evidence to help students move beyond the conservative prescriptions of textbooks and style guides and into the preferred patterns of expression of their disciplines. An orientation to instruction based on access to choice through genre teaching and consciousness-raising can help students understand how writing conventions are enabling rather than deterministic. It can reveal the ways that typical patterns provide broad parameters of choice through which they can craft a distinctive self.

The tension between proximity and positioning is a central issue in EAP teaching (e.g. Benesch, 2001; Hyland, 2006). Clearly, an understanding of disciplinary expectations is central to a writer's disciplinary literacy competence and therefore to his or her success as a student or as an academic. For many learners, moreover, this awareness of regularity and structure is not only facilitating, but also reassuring. Conventions provide guidelines for writing in an uncertain domain of practice, which can, however, leave students feeling doubtful about apparent innovations (Chang and Swales, 1999). Although teaching students how they might frame their own meanings in the moulds of disciplinary practice can foster proximity, it ignores the resources for individual positioning and so can crush creativity.

Variation is just as important as similarity, and the notion of generic integrity is therefore an important element of EAP teaching, encompassing the idea that writing involves constraints on allowable configurations rather than the identical reproduction of features. Swales' (1990) notion of *prototypes* and Hasan's (1989) concept of *Generic Structure Potential* suggest that texts spread along a continuum of approximation to core genre examples, with varying options and restrictions operating in particular cases. Our ability to recognise the resemblance of any text to a genre prototype is thus a consequence of exposure to that genre and our experience of using it in specific contexts. Such pedagogies can provide learners with a means of conceptualising their varied experiences with texts and, by highlighting variability, can undermine a view which misrepresents writing as a universal, naturalised and non-contestable way of participating in academic communities. Linking texts and contexts through corpora brings authenticity and evidence to teaching so that instruction is not simply training in reproducing discourse forms but ways of making both constraints and possibilities apparent to students. It can give them opportunities to make choices and to find the ways of writing which are most in harmony with their sense of selves.

In addition to genre approaches, consciousness-raising has proved useful in assisting learners to create, comprehend and reflect on the ways texts work as discourse rather than on their value as bearers of content (e.g. Swales and Feak, 2004). This is a 'top-down' approach to understanding language which encourages writers to see grammatical features as 'the on-line processing component of discourse and not the set of syntactic building blocks with which discourse is constructed' (Rutherford,1987: 104). It therefore focuses on the ways meaning is constructed as part of the overall intentions of writers. This kind of inquiry can take a variety of forms, but most simply it involves training students to read rhetorically and to reflect on the practices they observe and use themselves, thereby learning from an exposure to discourses from a variety of contexts and inquiring into their own literate lives and the literacy practices of others (Johns, 1997).

Exploring texts and the purposes of text users provides a necessary basis for critical engagement with cultural and textual practices, assisting learners to see the impact of different choices. As Bakhtin (1986: 80) has suggested, writers must be able to control the genres they use before they can exploit them. Comparisons of texts and the systematic discussion of language choices are central to consciousness-raising, but so is the development of a metalanguage, or ways of talking and thinking about language, to encourage critical analysis and rhetorical awareness. Texts can therefore be discussed in quite precise and explicit ways and analysed, compared, criticised, deconstructed and reconstructed so that students can find spaces for themselves and the people they want to be.

Focusing on language in this way is a means of encouraging learners to experience for themselves the impact that language choices have on creating meanings. It promotes reflection and the understanding that in constructing their texts writers also construct themselves, assisting them to gain the confidence to speak with independence rather than concealing their authorship behind impersonal uniformity. This understanding does not just provide writers with resources to help them negotiate a valued identity, but is also an important way of creating one's own voice, of speaking with authority and of securing reader support. It is achieved through a sensitivity to the boundaries of appropriateness, to the nuances of particular rhetorical options, and to what these say about the writer. In other words, learning how to manipulate the rhetorical and linguistic options recognised by others increases learners' abilities to carve a space and achieve personal goals.

## Research directions

Finally, I want to say something about where this kind of research might go next. While I have discussed a range of different genres, disciplines and language features in these pages, much of this has been exploratory and programmatic. Clearly some genres, and certainly the research article, have been studied exhaustively and we are familiar with the ways writers build proximity to their disciplines in these genres. Other genres, however, are more or less a blank slate and we know little of how writers are able to create identities for themselves in negotiation with examiners, reviewers, conference organisers, teachers and journal editors in a variety of different contexts. How proximity is constructed in job interviews, responses to journal reviewers, submissions for promotion and applications for grants all offers excellent opportunities for research. Similarly, many disciplines have received only limited attention, with cross-disciplinary writing particularly unrepresented. How identity is negotiated in the practice-based degrees such as nursing, business studies and social work, which span several disciplines, offers interesting possibilities for study.

Beyond proximity, studies of identity need to acknowledge variations and understand how writers are able to make space for their individuality by claiming ownership and bringing creativity to their texts. Genre studies encourage generalisation and perhaps overemphasise similarity by focusing on social purposes, but we need to also find ways of exploring systematic differences in individual cases. In the previous chapters, I have looked at the possible impact of celebrity and experience, of gender and first language, and of seniority and discipline on the ways that individuals negotiate positions in their writing. However, we need to know more about disciplinary norms and the boundaries of possibility. Who can bend generic conventions in academic contexts, how can they do this, and by how much? Keyword comparisons and other detailed studies of individual writers and social groups have great potential for investigating agency within generic norms. I have also ignored diachronic aspects of identity construction and said nothing about the ways that self-representation may change with the experience of success or failure, of age and increasing know-how, or of shifting academic alignments. Nor have I explored how such individual stylistic preferences may contribute to generic innovation and be taken up in a community's practices.

Third, while I have largely emphasised the rhetorical nature of academic texts, it may be helpful to invest more time in exploring contextual issues than I have done here. Investigating the genre networks and activity systems within which individuals participate would seem a fruitful way of revealing individual proclivities which span genres and so define individual positioning more clearly. Another issue is to make use of the more robust methods for analysing multi-modality within both emergent and established genres in order to explain something of the ways in which identity is visually constructed – such as in the layout of homepages and in the formatting of curricula vitae, for example. The expansion of studies into social context also necessarily involves increased attention to the role that readers play in co-constructing identity. The use of interviews, observational and read-aloud responses can help put more flesh on the bones of corpus research into the ways insiders understand language choices.

As identity research continues to expand, it is likely that we can anticipate an ever-increasing broadening of studies beyond written texts to the talk and contexts which surround their production and use, beyond the verbal to the visual, beyond the snapshot to the longitudinal, beyond writing to speech, and beyond tertiary to school contexts. Academic identity remains a rich area of research.

## 9.5    Final words

I began this book by asking how we might relate *discipline* and *identity* in a way which helps us to understand a little more of both concepts, and I hope these connections have become clearer: how the regular orientation to others helps produce both institutional realities and personal identities. Engaging in academic genres is how we demonstrate identities as geologists or linguists, for while we are constructing disciplines and knowledge, we are also constructing ourselves. A disciplinary identity is thus something accomplished on a moment-by-moment basis by employing the symbolic systems valued by a discipline. It is a negotiation of the familiar and the innovative, the group and the individual which works to present a plausible view both of the world and of the self.

Proximity to current conventions helps demonstrate an individual's membership and credibility because repeated patterns of rhetorical behaviour are related to both the epistemologies of a discipline (how it understands knowledge and ways of establishing this) and its social practices (how relationships and activities are sanctioned and conducted). Language choices are significant not only because they help construct communities and knowledge, but because they have deeply personal consequences. But while students often find themselves alienated from these practices and feel forced to become a different sort of person to participate in them, choices are not predetermined or fixed. Experience gives us wriggle-room: the space to negotiate an identity which both makes us 'one-of-them' and offers ways to imprint a personal stance.

Identity continues to be of interest to applied linguists and other social scientists because it sits at the centre of our thinking about the relationship between concrete human behaviour and abstract notions of collectivity and community. It is therefore at the heart of how we can understand scholarly activity and academic disciplines. Language enables us to participate in the collective domain: to build relationships, negotiate alliances, express positions and settle differences, all of which depend on the management of a credible self. It has become a truism of the social sciences that identity is *performed*, and I have argued that one way of understanding identity as performance is to look at how individuals gain the recognition of others through a series of interactive acts of alignment and dissension. The repetitions of institutionalised modes of interaction between actors are therefore not somehow separate from the negotiation of identities, they are the material from which such identities are created. Our growing understanding of how identity works therefore encourages us to search for it in the routinely patterned rhetorical practices of our communities.

# References

Alvesson, M., Lee Ashcraft, K. and Thomas, R. (2008). Identity matters: Reflections on the construction of identity scholarship in organisation studies. *Organization,* 15 (1): 5–28.

Antaki, C. and Widdicombe, S. (eds.) (1998). *Identities in Talk.* London: SAGE.

Appadurai, A. (1996). *Modernity at Large: Cultural Dimensions of Globalization.* Minneapolis: University of Minnesota Press.

Archakis, A. and Papazachariou, D. (2008). Prosodic cues of identity construction: Intensity in Greek young women's conversational narratives. *Journal of Sociolinguistics*, 12 (5): 627–647.

Azar, M. (1997). Concession relations as argumentation. *Text – Interdisciplinary Journal for the Study of Discourse*, 17 (3): 301–316.

Babaii, E. and Ansary, H. (2005). On the effect of disciplinary variation on transitivity: The case of academic book reviews. *Asian EFL Journal*, 7 (3): 113–126.

Bakhtin, M. (1981). *The Dialogic Imagination: Four Essays* (ed. M. Holquist). Austin, TX: University of Texas Press.

Bakhtin, M. (1986). *Speech Genres and Other Late Essays.* Austin, TX: University of Texas Press.

Baldry, A. (2000). *Multimodality and Multimediality in the Distance Learning Age.* Campobasso: Palladino Editore.

Bartholomae, D. (1986). Inventing the university. *Journal of Basic Writing*, 5 (1): 4–23.

Barton, D. and Hamilton, M. (1998). *Local Literacies: Reading and Writing in One Community.* London: Routledge.

Baynham, M. (2006). Performing self, family and community in Moroccan narratives of migration and settlement. In A. de Fina, D. Shiffrin and M. Bamberg (eds.), *Discourse and Identity* (pp. 376–397). Cambridge: Cambridge University Press.

Becher, T. and Trowler, P. (2001). *Academic Tribes and Territories: Intellectual Enquiry and the Culture of Disciplines* (2nd edn.). Milton Keynes: Oxford University Press.

Bechhofer, F., McCrone, D., Kiely, R. and Stewart, R. (1999). Constructing national identity: Arts and landed elites in Scotland. *Sociology*, 33 (3): 515–534.

Belcher, D. (1997). An argument for non-adversarial argumentation: On the relevance of the feminist critique of academic discourse to L2 writing pedagogy. *Journal of Second Language Writing*, 6 (1): 1–21.

Ben-Ari, E. (1987). On acknowledgements in ethnographies. *Journal of Anthropological Research*, 43 (1): 63–84.

Bendle, M. (2002). The crisis of 'identity' in high modernity. *The British Journal of Sociology*, 53 (1): 1–18.

Benesch, S. (2001). *Critical English for Academic Purposes: Theory, Politics, and Practice*. New York: Routledge.

Benwell, B. and Stokoe, E. (2006). *Discourse and Identity*. Edinburgh: Edinburgh University Press.

Berger, P. and Luckman, T. (1967). *The Social Construction of Reality: A Treatise in the Sociology of Knowledge*. London: Anchor.

Bergvall, V. (1999). Toward a comprehensive theory of language and gender. *Language in Society*, 28 (2): 273–293.

Berliner, D. (2002). Educational research: The hardest science of all. *Educational Researcher*, 31 (8): 18–20.

Bhatia, V. K. (1993). *Analysing Genre: Language Use in Professional Settings*. New York: Routledge.

Biber, D. (2006). Stance in spoken and written university registers. *Journal of English for Academic Purposes*, 5 (2): 97–116.

Biber, D. and Finegan, E. (1989). Styles of stance in English: Lexical and grammatical marking of evidentiality and affect. *Text – Interdisciplinary Journal for the Study of Discourse*, 9 (1): 93–124.

Biber, D., Johansson, S., Leech, G., Conrad, S. and Finegan, E. (1999). *Longman Grammar of Spoken and Written English*. Harlow: Longman.

Biglan, A. (1973). The characteristics of subject matter in different scientific areas. *Journal of Applied Psychology*, 57 (3): 195–203.

Bizzell, P. (1989). 'Cultural criticism': A social approach to studying writing. *Rhetoric Review*, 7 (2): 224–230.

Block, D. (2006). *Multilingual Identities in a Global City: London Stories*. London: Palgrave Macmillan.

Blommaert, J. (2005). *Discourse: A Critical Introduction*. Cambridge: Cambridge University Press.

Bloor, T. (1996). Three hypothetical strategies in philosophical writing. In E. Ventola and A. Mauranen (eds.), *Academic Writing: Intercultural and Textual Issues* (pp. 19–43). Amsterdam: John Benjamins.

Bondi, M. (2004). 'If you think this sounds very complicated, you are correct': Awareness of cultural difference in specialized discourse. In C. Candlin and M. Gotti (eds.), *Intercultural Aspects of Specialised Communication* (pp. 53–78). Bern: Peter Lang.

Borsley, R. and Ingham, R. (2002). Grow your own linguistics? On some applied linguists' views of the subject. *Lingua Franca*, 112 (1): 1–6.

Bourdieu, P. (1977). *Outline of a Theory of Practice.* Cambridge: Cambridge University Press.

Bourdieu, P. (1990). Structures, habitus, practices. In P. Bourdieu (ed.), *The Logic of Practice* (pp. 52–65). Stanford, CA: Stanford University Press.

Brubaker, R. (2004). *Ethnicity without Groups.* Cambridge, MA: Harvard University Press.

Bruner, J. (1997). A narrative model of self-construction. In J. Snodgrass and R. Thompson (eds.), *The Self Across Psychology: Self-Recognition, Self-Awareness, and the Self Concept* (pp. 145–161). New York: New York Academy of Sciences.

Burr, V. (1995). *An Introduction to Social Constructionism.* London: Routledge.

Butler, J. (1990). *Gender Trouble: Feminism and the Subversion of Identity.* London: Routledge.

Cadman, K. (1997). Thesis writing for international students: A question of identity?. *English for Specific Purposes*, 16 (1): 3–14.

Caldas-Coulthard, C. and Iedema, R. (eds.) (2008). *Identity Trouble: Critical Discourse and Contested Identities.* London: Palgrave Macmillan.

Cameron, D. (1992). Not gender differences but the differences gender makes: Explanation in research on sex and language. *International Journal of the Sociology of Language*, 94 (1): 13–26.

Cameron, D. (1995a). Rethinking language and gender studies: Some issues for the 1990s. In S. Mills (ed.), *Language and Gender: Interdisciplinary Perspective* (pp. 31–44). London: Routledge.

Cameron, D. (1995b). *Verbal Hygiene.* London: Routledge.

Cameron, D. (2000). *Good to Talk?.* London: SAGE.

Cameron, D. (2001). *Working with Spoken Discourse.* London: SAGE.

Cameron, D. (2006). *On Language and Sexual Politics.* London: Routledge.

Cameron, D. (2007). *The Myth of Mars and Venus: Do Men and Women Really Speak Different Languages?.* Oxford: Oxford University Press.

Canagarajah, A. S. (1999). *Resisting Linguistic Imperialism in English Teaching.* Oxford: Oxford Universtity Press.

Casanave, C. and Vandrick, S. (eds.) (2003). *Writing for Scholarly Publication.* Mahwah, NJ: Lawrence Erlbaum Associates.

Chandler, D. (1998). Personal homepages and the construction of identities on the web. Paper presented at Aberystwyth Post-International Group Conference on

*Linking Theory and Practice: Issues in the Politics of Identity, 9–11 Sept. 1998,*
*University of Wales.*

Chandler, D. and Roberts-Young, D. (1998). The construction of identity in the personal homepages of adolescents. Retrieved 12/8/2011 at: www.aber.ac.uk/media/Documents/short/strasbourg.html.

Chang, Y. Y. and Swales, J. (1999). Informal elements in English academic writing: Threats or opportunities for advanced non-native speakers?. In C. N. Candlin and K. Hyland (eds.), *Writing: Texts, Processes and Practices* (pp. 145–167). London: Routledge.

Clancy, P. M. (1986). The acquisition of communicative style in Japanese. In B. Schieffelin and E. Ochs (eds.), *Language Socialization Across Cultures* (pp. 213–250). Cambridge: Cambridge University Press.

Clark, B. (1987). *The Academic Life: Small Worlds, Different Worlds.* Princeton, NJ: The Carnegie Foundation for the Advancement of Teaching.

Coates, J. (1989). Gossip revisited: Language in all-female groups. In J. Coates and D. Cameron (eds.), *Women in Their Speech Communities* (pp. 94–121). London: Routledge.

Cohen, A. P. (1985). *The Symbolic Construction of Community.* London: Routledge.

Connor, U. and Upton, T. (2004). The genre of grant proposals: A corpus linguistic analysis. In U. Connor and T. Upton (eds.), *Discourse in the Professions: Perspectives from Corpus Linguistics* (pp. 235–256). Amsterdam: John Benjamins.

Conrad, S. and Biber, D. (2001). Adverbial marking of stance in speech and writing. In S. Hunston and G. Thompson (eds.), *Evaluation in Text: Authorial Stance and the Construction of Discourse* (pp. 56–73). Oxford: Oxford University Press.

Cook, G. (1998). The uses of reality: A reply to Ronald Carter. *ELT Journal,* 52 (1): 57–63.

Cooley, C. (1964). *Human Nature and the Social Order.* New York: Shocken Books.

Cortazzi, M. and Jin, L. (1996). Cultures of learning: Language classrooms in China. In H. Coleman (ed.), *Society and the Language Classroom* (pp. 169–206). Cambridge: Cambridge University Press.

Coulthard, M. (2008). By their words shall ye know them: On linguistic identity. In C. Caldas-Coulthard and R. Iedema (eds.), *Identity Trouble: Critical Discourse and Contested Identities* (pp. 143–155). London: Palgrave Macmillan.

Coulthard, M. and Johnson, A. (2007). *An Introduction to Forensic Linguistics: Language in Evidence.* London: Routledge.

Crismore, A., Markkanen, R. and Steffensen, M. (1993). Metadiscourse in persuasive writing: A study of texts written by American and Finnish university students. *Written Communication,* 10 (1): 39–71.

Cronin, B. and Overfelt, K. (1994). The scholar's courtesy: A survey of acknowledgement behaviour. *Journal of Documentation*, 50 (3): 165–196.

Cronin, B., McKenzie, G. and Rubio, L. (1993). The norms of acknowledgement in four humanities and social sciences disciplines. *Journal of Documentation*, 49 (1): 29–43.

Daiute, C. and Lightfoot, C. (eds.) (2004). *Narrative Analysis: Studying the Development of Individuals in Society*. Thousand Oaks, CA: SAGE.

Davies, B. and Harré, R. (1990). Positioning: The discursive production of selves. *Journal for the Theory of Social Behaviour*, 20 (1): 43–63.

Day, D. (1998). Being ascribed, and resisting, membership of an ethnic group. In C. Antaki and S. Widdicombe (eds.), *Identities in Talk* (pp. 151–170). London: SAGE.

Day, R. and Gastel, B. (2006). *How to Write and Publish a Scientific Paper* (6th edn.). Cambridge: Cambridge University Press.

De Vel, O., Corney, M., Anderson, A. and Mohay, G. (2002). Language and gender author cohort analysis of e-mail for computer forensics. In the second Digital Forensic Research Workshop (DFRWS), Syracuse, New York, USA.

Dillon, G. (1981). *Constructing Texts: Elements of a Theory of a Composition and Style*. Bloomington: Indiana University Press.

Ding, H. (2007). Genre analysis of personal statements: Analysis of moves in application essays to medical and dental schools. *English for Specific Purposes*, 26 (3): 368–392.

Donald, J. (1990). University professors' views of knowledge and validation processes. *Journal of Educational Psychology*, 82 (2): 242–249.

Dressen-Hammouda, D. (2008). From novice to disciplinary expert: Disciplinary identity and genre mastery. *English for Specific Purposes*, 27 (2): 233–252.

Drew, P. and Heritage, J. (1992). *Talk at Work: Interaction in Institutional Settings*. Cambridge: Cambridge University Press.

Duranti, A. and Goodwin, C. (eds.) (1992). *Rethinking Context: Language as an Interactive Phenomenon*. Cambridge: Cambridge University Press.

Eckert, P. and McConnell-Ginet, S. (1992). Think practically and look locally: Language and gender as community-based practice. *Annual Review of Anthropology*, 21: 461–490.

*Economist, The* (editorial) (1996). Acknowledgents: Gratitude that grates. 340: 83.

Edwards, D. and Stokoe, E. (2004). Discursive psychology, focus group interviews, and participants' categories. *British Journal of Developmental Psychology*, 22 (4): 499–507.

Ehrlich, S. (1997). Gender as social practice: Implications for second language acquisition. *Studies in Second Language Acquisition*, 19 (4): 421–446.

Elliott, A. (2007). *Concepts of the Self* (2nd edn.). Cambridge: Polity Press.

Elliott, W. and Valenza, R. (1991). *Was the Earl of Oxford the True Shakespeare?*

*A Computer-Aided Analysis*. Available at: http://shakespeareauthorship.com/elval.html.

Faigley, L. (1986). Competing theories of process: A critique and a proposal. *College English*, 48 (6): 527–542.

Fairclough, N. (1992). *Discourse and Social Change*. Cambridge: Polity Press.

Fairclough, N. (1995). *Critical Discourse Analysis: The Critical Study of Language*. London: Routledge.

Fairclough, N. (2003). *Analysing Discourse: Textual Analysis for Social Research*. London: Routledge.

Flynn, E. (1988). Composing as a woman. *College Composition and Communication*, 39 (4): 423–435.

Foucault, M. (1972). *The Archaeology of Knowledge*. London: Tavistock.

Foucault, M. (1981). The order of discourse. In R. Young (ed.), *Untying the Text: A Post-Structuralist Reader* (pp. 48–78). Boston: Routledge.

Francis, B., Robson, J. and Read, B. (2001). An analysis of undergraduate writing styles in the context of gender and achievement. *Studies in Higher Education*, 26 (3): 313–326.

Garfinkel, H. (1967). *Studies in Ethnomethodology*. Englewood Cliffs, NJ: Prentice Hall.

Gee, J. (1999). *An Introduction to Discourse Analysis*. New York: Routledge.

Gee, J. (2004). *Situated Language and Learning: A Critique of Traditional Schooling*. New York: Routledge.

Geertz, C. (1973). *The Interpretation of Cultures*. New York: Basic Books.

Geertz, C. (1988). *Works and Lives: The Anthropologist as Author*. Stanford, CA: Stanford University Press.

Georgakopoulou, A. (2006). Small and large identities in narrative (inter)action. In A. de Fina, D. Shiffin and M. Bamberg (eds.), *Studies in International Sociolinguistics: Vol. 23. Discouse and Identity* (pp. 83–102). Cambridge: Cambridge University Press.

Gergen, K. J. and Thatchenkery, T. J. (1996). Organisation science as social construction: Postmodern potentials. *The Journal of Applied Behavioral Science*, 32 (4): 356–377.

Ghadessy, M. (ed.) (1999). *Text and Context in Functional Linguistics*. Amsterdam: John Benjamins.

Giddens, A. (1991). *Modernity and Self-Identity: Self and Society in the Late Modern Age*. Cambridge: Polity Press.

Gilbert, G. and Mulkay, M. (1984). *Opening Pandora's Box: A Sociological Analysis of Scientific Discourse*. Cambridge: Cambridge University Press.

Gilbert, S. F. (1995). Introduction: Postmodernism and science. *Science in Context*, 8 (4): 559–561.

Giles H. and Coupland, N. (1991). *Language: Contexts and Consequences*. Pacific Grove, CA: Brooks/Cole.

Goffman, E. (1971). *The Presentation of Self in Everyday Life.* Harmondsworth: Penguin Books.

Goffman, E. (1975). *Frame Analysis: An Essay on the Organization of Experience.* Harmondsworth: Penguin Books.

Goffman, E. (1981). *Forms of Talk.* Philadelphia: University of Pennsylvania Press.

Gong, G. and Dragga, S. (1995). *A Writer's Repertoire.* New York: HarperCollins.

Goodwin, C. (1987). Forgetfulness as an interactive resource. *Social Psychology Quarterly*, 50 (2): 115–130.

Gosden, H. (1993). Discourse functions of subject in scientific research articles. *Applied Linguistics*, 14 (1): 56–75.

Gray, J. (1993). *Men Are from Mars, Women Are from Venus.* New York: HarperCollins.

Greatbach, D. and Dingwall, R. (1998). Talk and identity in divorce mediation. In C. Antaki and S. Widdicombe (eds.), *Identities in Talk* (pp. 121–132). London: SAGE.

Groom, N. (2005). Pattern and meaning across genres and disciplines: An exploratory study. *Journal of English for Academic Purposes*, 4 (3): 257–277.

Grossberg, L. (2011). Will work for cultural studies. *Communication and Critical/Cultural Studies*, 8 (4): 425–432.

Gumperz, J. (1982). *Discourse Strategies.* Cambridge: Cambridge University Press.

Gupta, A. and Ferguson, J. (eds.) (1997). *Culture, Power and Place: Explorations in Critical Anthropology.* Durham, NC: Duke University Press.

Hadden, S. and Lester, M. (1978). Talking identity: The production of 'self' in interaction. *Human Studies*, 1 (4): 331–356.

Hall, S. (1996). Introduction: Who needs identity?. In S. Hall and P. Du Gay (eds.), *Questions of Cultural Identity* (pp. 1–17). London: SAGE.

Halliday, M. A. K. (1994). *An Introduction to Functional Grammar* (2nd edn.). London: Edward Arnold.

Halliday, M. A. K. (1998). Things and relations: Regrammaticising experience as technical knowledge. In J. R. Martin and R. Veel (eds.), *Reading Science* (pp. 185–235). London: Routledge.

Halliday, M. A. K. and Martin, J. R. (1993). *Writing Science: Literacy and Discursive Power.* London: The Falmer Press.

Halliday, M. A. K., McIntosh, A. and Strevens, P. (1964). *The Linguistic Sciences and Language Teaching.* London: Longman.

Hanlein, H. (1999). *Studies in Authorship Recognition: A Corpus-Based Approach.* Frankfurt am Main: Peter Lang.

Hasan, R. (1989). The structure of a text. In M. A. K. Halliday and R. Hasan (eds.), *Language, Context and Text: Aspects of Language in a Social Semiotic Perspective* (pp. 52–69). Oxford: Oxford University Press.

Heath, S. B. (1991). The sense of being literate: Historical and cross-cultural features. In R. Barr, M. L. Kamil, P. B. Mosenthal and P. D. Pearson (eds.), *Handbook of Reading Research. Vol. II* (pp. 3–25). New York: Longman.

Herbert, R. K. (1990). Sex-based differences in compliment behaviour. *Language in Society*, 19 (2): 201–224.

Heritage, J. (1984). *Garfinkel and Ethnomethodology*. Cambridge: Polity Press.

Heritage, J. and Clayman, S. (2010). *Talk in Action: Interactions, Identities, and Institutions*. Oxford: Wiley-Blackwell.

Herring, S., Johnson, D. and DiBenedetto, T. (1995). 'This discussion is going too far!': Male resistance to female participation on the Internet. In K. Hall and M. Bucholtz (eds.), *Gender Articulated: Language and the Socially Constructed Self* (pp. 67–96). New York: Routledge.

Hess, M. (2002). A nomad faculty: English professors negotiate self-representation in university Web space. *Computers and Composition*, 19 (2): 171–189.

Hester, S. and Francis, D. (2001). Is institutional talk a phenomenon? Reflections on ethnomethodology and applied conversation analysis. In A. McHoul and M. Rapley (eds.), *How to Analyse Talk in Institutional Settings: A Casebook of Methods* (pp. 206–218). London: Continuum.

Hester, S. (1998). Describing 'deviance' in school: Recognizably educational psychological problems. In C. Antaki and S. Widdicombe (eds.), *Identities in Talk* (pp. 133–150). London: SAGE.

Hinkel, E. (1999). Objectivity and credibility in L1 and L2 academic writing. In E. Hinkel (ed.), *Culture in Second Language Learning and Teaching* (pp. 90–108). Cambridge: Cambridge University Press.

Hoey, M. (2005). *Lexical Priming: A New Theory of Words and Language*. London: Routledge.

Holland, D. and Skinner, D. (1987). Prestige and intimacy: The cultural models behind American's talk about gender types. In D. Holland and N. Quinn (eds.), *Cultural Models in Language and Thought* (pp. 78–111). New York: Cambridge University Press.

Holmes, J. (1988). Paying compliments: A sex-preferred positive politeness strategy. *Journal of Pragmatics*, 12 (4): 445–465.

Holmes, J. (1995). *Women, Men and Politeness.* London: Longman.

Holmes, J. (2006). Workplace narratives, professional identity and relational practice. In A. de Fina, D. Shriffin and M. Bamberg (eds.), *Studies in Interactional Sociolinguistics: Vol 23. Discourse and Identity* (pp. 166–187). Cambridge: Cambridge University Press.

Hunston, S. (1993). Evaluation and ideology in scientific writing. In M. Ghadessy (ed.), *Register Analysis: Theory and Practice* (pp. 57–73). London: Pinter Publishers.

Hunston, S. (2002). *Corpora in Applied Linguistics.* Cambridge: Cambridge University Press.

Hunston, S. and Thompson, G. (eds.) (2001). *Evaluation in Text: Authorial Stance and the Construction of Discourse.* Oxford: Oxford University Press.

Hyland, F. and Hyland, K. (2001). Sugaring the pill: Praise and criticism in written feedback. *Journal of Second Language Writing,* 10 (3): 185–212.

Hyland, K. (1998a). *Hedging in Science Research Articles.* Amsterdam: John Benjamins.

Hyland, K. (1998b). Persuasion and context: The pragmatics of academic metadiscourse. *Journal of Pragmatics,* 30 (4): 437–455.

Hyland, K. (2001a). Bringing in the reader: Addressee features in academic articles. *Written Communication,* 18 (4): 549–574.

Hyland, K. (2001b). Humble servants of the discipline? Self-mention in research articles. *English for Specific Purposes,* 20 (3): 207–226.

Hyland, K. (2002a). Directives: Argument and engagement in academic writing. *Applied Linguistics,* 23 (2): 215–239.

Hyland, K. (2002b). What do they mean? Questions in academic writing. *Text – Interdisciplinary Journal for the Study of Discourse,* 22 (4): 529–557.

Hyland, K. (2002c). Authority and invisibility: Authorial identity in academic writing. *Journal of Pragmatics,* 34 (8): 1091–1112.

Hyland, K. (2003). Dissertation acknowledgements: The anatomy of a Cinderella genre. *Written Communication,* 20 (3): 242–268.

Hyland, K. (2004a). *Disciplinary Discourses: Social Interactions in Academic Writing.* Ann Arbor, MI: University of Michigan Press.

Hyland, K. (2004b). Disciplinary interactions: Metadiscourse in L2 postgraduate writing. *Journal of Second Language Writing,* 13 (2): 133–151.

Hyland, K. (2004c). Graduates' gratitude: The generic structure of dissertation acknowledgements. *English for Specific Purposes,* 23 (3): 303–324.

Hyland, K. (2005a). *Metadiscourse: Exploring Interaction in Writing.* London: Continuum.

Hyland, K. (2005b). Stance and engagement: A model of interaction in academic discourse. *Discourse Studies,* 7 (2): 173–192.

Hyland, K. (2006). *English for Academic Purposes: An Advanced Resource Book.* London: Routledge.

Hyland, K. (2008). As can be seen: Lexical bundles and disciplinary variation. *English for Specific Purposes,* 27 (1): 4–21.

Hyland, K. (2009). *Academic Discourse: English in a Global Context.* London: Continuum.

Hyland, K. (2010). Community and individuality: Performing identity in applied linguistics. *Written Communication*, 27 (2): 159–188.

Hyland, K. (2011). The presentation of self in scholarly life: Identity and marginalization in academic homepages. *English for Specific Purposes*, 30 (4): 286–297.

Hyland, K. and Bondi, M. (eds.) (2006). *Academic Discourse across Disciplines*. Bern: Peter Lang.

Hyland, K. and Diani, G. (eds.) (2009). *Academic Evaluation: Review Genres in University Settings*. London: Palgrave MacMillan.

Hyland, K. and Tse, P. (2004a). Metadiscourse in academic writing: A reappraisal. *Applied Linguistics*, 25 (2): 156–177.

Hyland, K. and Tse, P. (2004b). 'I would like to thank my supervisor': Acknowledgements in graduate dissertations. *International Journal of Applied Linguistics*, 14 (2): 259–275.

Hyland, K. and Tse, P. (2005). Evaluative *that* constructions: Signaling stance in research abstracts. *Functions of Language*, 12 (1): 39–63.

Hyland, K. and Tse, P. (2007). Is there an 'academic vocabulary'?. *TESOL Quarterly*, 41 (2): 235–253.

Ivanič, R. (1998). *Writing and Identity: The Discoursal Construction of Identity in Academic Writing*. Amsterdam: John Benjamins.

Ivanič, R. and Camps, D. (2001). I am how I sound: Voice as self-representation in L2 writing. *Journal of Second Language Writing*, 10 (1–2): 3–33.

Ivanič, R. and Simpson, J. (1992). Who's who in academic writing. In N. Fairclough (ed.), *Critical Language Awareness* (pp. 141–173). London: Longman.

Jefferson, G. (2004). Glossary of transcript symbols with an introduction. In G. H. Lerner (ed.), *Conversation Analysis: Studies from the First Generation* (pp. 13–31). Amsterdam: John Benjamins.

Jenkins, R. (2008). *Social Identity* (3rd edn.). London: Routledge.

John, S. (2009). Using the revision process to help international students to understand the linguistic construction of the academic identity. In M. Charles, D. Pecorari and S. Hunston (eds.), *Academic Writing: At the Interface of Corpus and Discourse* (pp. 272–290). London: Continuum.

Johns, A. M. (1997). *Text, Role and Context: Developing Academic Literacies*. Cambridge: Cambridge University Press.

Johnson, D. and Roen, D. (1992). Complimenting and involvement in peer reviews: Gender variation. *Language in Society*, 21 (1): 27–57.

Juola, P. and Baayen, R. H. (2005). A controlled-corpus experiment in authorship identification by cross-entropy. *Literary and Linguistic Computing*, 20 (Suppl): 59–67.

Kaufer, D. and Geisler, C. (1989). Novelty in academic writing. *Written Communication*, 6 (3): 286–311.

Kiely, R., Bechhofer, F., Stewart, R. and McCrone, D. (2001). The markers and rules of Scottish national identity. *The Sociological Review*, 49 (1): 33–55.

Killingsworth, M. J. and Gilbertson, M. K. (1992). *Signs, Genres, and Communication in Technical Communication*. Amityville, NY: Baywood.

Kirsch, G. (1993). *Women Writing the Academy: Audience, Authority, and Transformation*. Carbondale & Edwardsville: Southern Illinois University Press.

Knorr-Cetina, K. (1981). *The Manufacture of Knowledge*. Oxford: Pergamon Press.

Kolb, D. A. (1981). Learning styles and disciplinary differences. In A. Chickering (ed.), *The Modern American College* (pp. 232–255). San Fransico, CA: Jossey Bass.

Koppel, M., Argamon, S. and Shimoni, A. R. (2002). Automatically categorizing written texts by author gender. *Literary and Linguistic Computing*, 17 (4): 401–412.

Koutsantoni, D. (2009). Persuading sponsors and securing funding: Rhetorical patterns in grant proposals. In M. Charles, D. Pecorari, D. and S. Hunston (eds.), *Academic Writing: At the Interface of Corpus and Discourse* (pp. 37–57). London: Continuum.

Kraus, W. (2000). Making identity talk. On qualitative methods in a longitudinal study. *FQS* (*Forum: Qualitative Social Research*), 1 (2), Art. 15.

Kress, G. (2010). *Multimodality: A Social Semiotic Approach to Contemporary Communication*. London: Routledge.

Kress, G. and van Leuwen, L. (1996). *Reading Images: The Grammar of Visual Design*. London: Routledge.

Kroskrity, P. (ed.) (2000). *Regimes of Language: Ideologies, Polities, and Identities*. Santa Fe, NM: School of American Research Press.

Kubota, R. (2003). Striving for original voice in publication?: A critical reflection. In C. Casanave and S. Vandrick (eds.), *Writing for Scholarly Publication: Behind the Scenes in Language Education* (pp. 73–83). Mahwah, NJ: Lawrence Erlbaum Associates.

Kuckartz, U. (1998). *WinMAX: Scientific Text Analysis for the Social Sciences*. Thousand Oaks, CA: Scolari.

Kuhn, T. (1977). *The Essential Tension: Selected Studies in Scientific Tradition and Change*. Chicago: The University of Chicago Press.

Kuo, C-H. (1999). The use of personal pronouns: Role relationships in scientific journal articles. *English for Specific Purposes*, 18 (2): 121–138.

Laclau, E. (1990). *New Reflections on the Revolution of Our Time*. London: Verso.

Laclau, E. and Mouffe, C. (1985). *Hegemony and Socialist Strategy: Towards a Radical Democratic Politics*. London: Verso.

Lage, H., Heitmann, D., Cingolani, R., Grambow, P. and Ploog, K. (1991). Center-of-mass quantization of excitons in GaAs quantum-well wires. *Physical Review B*, 44 (12): 6550–6553.

Lakoff, G. (2002). *Moral Politics: How Liberals and Conservatives Think.* Chicago: The University of Chicago Press.

Lakoff, R. (1975). *Language and Woman's Place.* New York: Harper & Row.

Lantolf, J. P. (1999). Second culture acquisition: Cognitive considerations. In E. Hinkel (ed.), *Culture in Second Language Teaching and Learning* (pp. 28–46). Cambridge: Cambridge University Press.

Lave, J. and Wenger, E. (1991). *Situated Learning: Legitimate Peripheral Participation.* Cambridge: Cambridge University Press.

Lawler, S. (2008). *Identity: Sociological Perspectives.* Cambridge: Polity Press.

Lea, M. and Street, B. V. (2000). Student writing and staff feedback in higher education: An academic literacies approach. In M. Lea and B. Stierer (eds.), *Student Writing in Higher Education: New Contexts* (pp. 32–46). Buckingham: Society for Research into Higher Education and Open University Press.

Lemke, J. (1994). Science, masculism and the gender system. Paper given at University of Delaware, USA.

Lemke, J. (1995). *Textual Politics: Discourse and Social Dynamics.* London: Taylor and Francis.

Lester, J. (2005). *Writing Research Papers* (11th edn.). New York: Pearson.

Lillie, J. M. (1998). Cultural uses of new, networked information and communication technologies: Implications for US Latino identities (Master's thesis). School of Journalism and Mass Communications, University of North Carolina at Chapel Hill, NC, USA.

Lillis, T. (2001). *Student Writing: Access, Regulation, Desire.* London: Routledge.

Lin, A. M. Y. (2000). Resistance and creativity in English reading lessons in Hong Kong. *Language, Culture and Curriculum*, 12 (3): 285–296.

Lin, A. M. Y. (2008). The identity game and discursive struggles of everyday life: An introduction. In A. M. Y. Lin (ed.), *Problematizing Identity: Everyday Struggles in Language, Culture and Education* (pp. 1–10). Mahwah, NJ: Lawrence Erlbaum Associates.

Lindholm-Romantschuk, Y. (1998). *Scholarly Book Reviewing in the Social Sciences and Humanities.* London: Greenwood Press.

Luke, C. and Gore, J. (1992). Women in the academy: Strategy, struggle and survival. In C. Luke and J. Gore (eds.), *Feminisms and Critical Pedagogy* (pp. 192–210). New York: Routledge.

Lutz, C. (1995). The gender of theory. In R. Behar and D. Gordon (eds.), *Women Writing Culture* (pp. 249–266). Berkeley: University of California Press.

Lynch, C. and Strauss-Noll, M. (1987). Mauve washers: Sex differences in freshman writing. *English Journal*, 76 (1): 90–94.

Lynch, M. (1985). *Art and Artifact in Laboratory Science: A Study of Shop Work and Shop Talk in a Research Laboratory.* London: Routledge Revivals.

Mahlberg, M. (2007). Clusters, key clusters and local textual functions in Dickens. *Corpora*, 2 (1): 1–31.

Markus, H. and Kitayama, S. (1991). Culture and the self: Implications for cognition, emotion, and motivation. *Psychological Review*, 98 (2): 224–253.

Markus, H. and Nurius, P. (1986). Possible selves. *American Psychologist*, 41 (9): 954–969.

Martin, J. R. (2001). Beyond exchange: APPRAISAL systems in English. In S. Hunston and G. Thompson (eds.), *Evaluation in Text: Authorial Stance and the Construction of Discourse* (pp. 142–175). Oxford: Oxford University Press.

Martin, J. R. and White, P. (2005). *The Language of Evaluation: Appraisal in English*. London: Palgrave Macmillan.

Martínez, I. A. (2001). Interpersonality in the research article as revealed by analysis of the transitivity structure. *English for Specific Purposes*, 20 (3): 227–247.

Matalene, C. (1985). Contrastive rhetoric: An American writing teacher in China. *College English*, 47 (8): 789–808.

Mathews, G. (2000). *Global Culture/Individual Identity: Searching for a Home in the Cultural Supermarket*. London: Routledge.

Mauranen, A. (2001). Reflexive academic talk: Observations from MICASE. In R. Simpson and J. Swales (eds.), *Corpus Linguistics in North America: Selections from the 1999 Symposium* (pp. 165–178). Ann Arbor, MI: University of Michigan Press.

Mauranen, A. (2006). Speaking the discipline: Discourse and socialisation in ELF and L1 English. In K. Hyland and M. Bondi (eds.), *Academic Discourse Across Disciplines* (pp. 271–294). Bern: Peter Lang.

Mead, G. H. (1934). *Mind, Self and Society: From the Standpoint of a Social Behavorist*. Chicago: The University of Chicago Press.

Miller, H. (1995). The presentation of self in electronic life: Goffman on the Internet. Paper presented at Embodied Knowledge and Virtual Space Conference, Goldsmiths' College, University of London, UK.

Mishler, E. (2006). Narrative and identity: The double arrow of time. In A. de Fina, D. Schiffrin and M. Bamberg (eds.), *Studies in Interactional Sociolinguistics: Vol. 23. Discourse and Identity* (pp. 30–47). Cambridge: Cambridge University Press.

Moore, T. (2002). Knowledge and agency: A study of 'metaphenomenal discourse' in textbooks from three disciplines. *English for Specific Purposes*, 21 (4): 347–366.

Murray, M. (2003). Narrative psychology. In J. Smith (ed.), *Qualitative Psychology: A Practical Guide to Research Methods* (pp. 111–131). London: SAGE.

Myers, G. (1992). Textbooks and the sociology of scientific knowledge. *English for Specific Purposes*, 11 (1): 3–17.

Norton, B. (2000). *Identity and Language Learning: Gender, Ethnicity and Educational Change*. Harlow: Pearson.

Odell, L., Goswami, D. and Herrington, A. (1983). The discourse-based interview: A procedure for exploring the tacit knowledge of writers in non-academic settings. In P. Mosenthal, L. Tamor and S. A. Walmsley (eds.), *Research on Writing: Principles and Methods* (pp. 221–236). New York: Longman.

Ohta, A. S. (1991). Evidentiality and politeness in Japanese. *Issues in Applied Linguistics*, 2 (2): 211–238.

Olsson, J. (2004). *Forensic Linguistics: An Introduction to Language, Crime and the Law*. London: Continuum.

Orteza y Miranda, E. (1996). On book reviewing. *Journal of Educational Thought*, 30 (2): 191–202.

Parks, M. and Archley-Landas, T. (2003). Communicating self through personal homepages: Is identity more than screen deep?. Paper presented at the Annual Conference of the International Communication Association, San Diego, CA, USA.

Pavlenko, A. (2007). Autobiographic narratives as data in applied linguistics. *Applied Linguistics*, 28 (2): 163–188.

Podgórecki, A. (1997). *Higher Faculties: A Cross-National Study of University Culture*. Westport, CT: Praeger.

Pomerantz, A. (1986). Extreme case formulations: A way of legitimizing claims. *Human Studies*, 9 (2–3): 219–229.

Prelli, L. (1989). *A Rhetoric of Science: Inventing Scientific Discourse*. Columbia: University of South Carolina Press.

Ramanathan, V. and Atkinson, D. (1999). Individualism, academic writing and ESL writers. *Journal of Second Language Writing*, 8 (1): 45–75.

Rheingold, H. (1995). *The Virtual Community: Finding Connection in a Computerized World*. London: Minerva.

Richards, K. (2006). *Language and Professional Identity*. London: Palgrave Macmillan.

Riessman, C. K. (2008). *Narrative Methods for the Human Sciences*. London: SAGE.

Riley, P. (2007). *Language, Culture and Identity: An Ethnolinguistic Perspective*. London: Continuum.

Robson, J., Francis, B. and Read, B. (2002). Writes of passage: Stylistic features of male and female undergraduate history essays. *Journal of Further and Higher Education*, 26 (4): 351–362.

Rorty, R. (1979). *Philosophy and the Mirror of Nature*. Princeton, NJ: Princeton University Press.

Rubin, D. and Greene, K. (1992). Gender-typical style in written language. *Research in the Teaching of English*, 26 (1): 7–40.

Ruiying, Y. and Allison, D. (2003). Research articles in applied linguistics: Moving from results to conclusions. *English for Specific Purposes*, 22 (4): 365–385.

Rutherford, W. (1987). *Second Language Grammar: Learning and Teaching*. London: Pearson.

Sacks, H. (1995). *Lectures on Conversation. Vol. II* (ed. G. Jefferson). Oxford: Wiley-Blackwell.

Salager-Meyer, F. M., Ariza, A. A. and Zambrano, N. (2003). The scimitar, the dagger and the glove: Intercultural differences in the rhetoric of criticism in Spanish, French and English medical discourse (1930–1995). *English for Specific Purposes*, 22 (3): 223–247.

Schleef, E. (2008). Gender and academic discourse: Global restrictions and local possibilities. *Language in Society*, 37 (4): 515–538.

Scollon, R. (1991). Eight legs and an elbow: Stance and structure in Chinese English compositions. In *Launching the Literacy Decade: Awareness into Action. Proceedings of the Second North American Conference on Adult and Adolescent Literacy: Multiculturalism and Citizenship* (pp. 1–14). Toronto: International Reading Association.

Scollon, R. (1994). As a matter of fact: The changing ideology of authorship and responsibility in discourse. *World Englishes*, 13 (1): 33–46.

Scollon, R. and Scollon, S. (1981). *Narrative, Literacy and Face in Interethnic Communication*. Norwood, NJ: Ablex.

Scott, M. (2007). *WordSmith Tools 5.0*. Oxford: Oxford University Press.

Scott, M. and Tribble, C. (2006). *Textual Patterns*. Amsterdam: John Benjamins.

Shotter, J. (1993). *Conversational Realities: Constructing Life through Language*. London: SAGE.

Sinclair, J. (1991). *Corpus, Concordance, Collocation*. Oxford: Oxford University Press.

Sinclair, J. (1999). A way with common words. In H. Hasselgård and S. Oksefjell (eds.), *Out of Corpora: Studies in Honour of Stig Johansson* (pp. 157–179). Amsterdam: Rodopi.

Skeggs, B. (2004). *Class, Self, Culture*. London: Routledge.

Somers, M. (1994). The narrative constitution of identity: A relational and network approach. *Theory and Society*, 23 (5): 605–649.

Spack, R. (1997). The rhetorical construction of multilingual students. *TESOL Quarterly*, 31 (4): 765–774.

Starfield, S. and Ravelli, L. (2006). 'The writing of this thesis was a process that I could not explore with the positivistic detachment of the classical sociologist': Self and structure in *New Humanities* research theses. *Journal of English for Academic Purposes*, 5 (3): 222–243.

Storer, N. and Parsons, T. (1968). The disciplines as a differentiating force. In E.

B. Montgomery (ed.), *The Foundations of Access to Knowledge* (pp. 101–121). Syracuse: Syracuse University Press.

Street, B. V. (1995). *Social Literacies: Critical Approaches to Literacy in Development, Ethnography and Education*. New York: Pearson.

Stubbs, M. (1996). *Text and Discourse Analysis: Computer-Assisted Studies of Language and Culture*. Oxford: Blackwell.

Stubbs, M. (2001). *Words and Phrases: Corpus Studies of Lexical Semantics*. Oxford: Blackwell.

Stubbs, M. (2005). Conrad in the computer: Examples of quantitative stylistic methods. *Language and Literature*, 14 (1): 5–24.

Swales, J. (1990). *Genre Analysis: English in Academic and Research Settings*. Cambridge: Cambridge University Press.

Swales, J. (1996). Occluded genres in the academy: The case of the submission letter. In E. Ventola and A. Mauranen (eds.), *Academic Writing: Intercultural and Textual Issues* (pp. 45–58). Amsterdam: John Benjamins.

Swales, J. (1998). *Other Floors, Other Voices: A Textography of a Small University Building*. Mahwah, NJ: Lawrence Erlbaum Associates.

Swales, J. (2004). *Research Genres: Explorations and Applications*. Cambridge: Cambridge University Press.

Swales, J. (2009). *Incidents in an Educational Life*. Ann Arbor, MI: University of Michigan Press.

Swales, J. and Feak, C. (2000). *English in Today's Research World: A Writing Guide*. Ann Arbor, MI: University of Michigan Press.

Swales, J. and Feak, C. (2004). *Academic Writing for Graduate Students: Essential Tasks and Skills* (2nd edn.). Ann Arbor, MI: University of Michigan Press.

Swales, J. and Malczewski, B. (2001). Discourse management and new episode flags in MICASE. In R. Simpson and. J. Swales (eds.), *Corpus Linguistics in North America* (pp. 145–164). Ann Arbor, MI: University of Michigan Press.

Tadros, A. (1993). The pragmatics of text averral and attribution in academic texts. In M. Hoey (ed.), *Data, Description, Discourse* (pp. 99–114). London: HarperCollins.

Tajfel, H. (ed.) (1982). *Social Identity and Intergroup Relations*. Cambridge: Cambridge University Press.

Tang, R. and John, S. (1999). The 'I' in identity: Exploring writer identity in student academic writing through the first person pronoun. *English for Specific Purposes*, 18 (1): S23–S39.

Tannen, D. (1994). *Talking from 9 to 5: How Women's and Men's Conversational Styles Affect Who Gets Heard, Who Gets Credit, and What Gets Done at Work*. New York: William Morrow.

ten Have, P. (2007). *Doing Conversation Analysis: A Practical Guide* (2nd edn.). London: SAGE.

Thompson, G. (2001). Interaction in academic writing: Learning to argue with the reader. *Applied Linguistics*, 22 (1): 58–78.

Thompson, G. and Ye, Y. (1991). Evaluation of the reporting verbs used in academic papers. *Applied Linguistics*, 12 (4): 365–382.

Thoms, L. and Thelwell, M. (2005). Academic home pages: Reconstruction of the self. *First Monday*, 10 (12).

Tognini-Bonelli, E. (2001). *Corpus Linguistics at Work*. Amsterdam: John Benjamins.

Tse, P. and Hyland, K. (2008). 'Robot Kung fu': Gender and the performance of a professional identity. *Journal of Pragmatics*, 40 (7): 1232–1248.

Turkle, S. (1997). *Life on the Screen: Identity in the Age of the Internet*. New York: Simon and Shuster.

Turner, J. C. (1987). *Rediscovering the Social Group: A Self-Categorization Theory*. Oxford: Blackwell.

Van Dijk, T. A. (2008). *Discourse and Context: A Sociocognitive Approach*. Cambridge: Cambridge University Press.

Vološinov, V. N. (1973). *Marxism and the Philosophy of Language* (L. Matejka and I. R. Titunik, trans.). New York: Seminar Press.

Vygotsky, L. S. (1978). *Mind in Society: The Development of Higher Psychological Processes*. Cambridge, MA: Harvard University Press.

Wells, G. (1992). The centrality of talk in education. In K. Norman (ed.), *Thinking Voices: The Work of the National Oracy Project* (pp. 283–310). London: Hodder and Stoughton.

Wengraf, T. (2001). *Qualitative Research Interviewing: Biographic Narrative and Semi-Structured Methods*. London: SAGE.

Wertsch, J. (1991). *Voices of the Mind: A Sociocultural Approach to Mediated Action*. Cambridge, MA: Harvard University Press.

Whitley, R. (1984). *The Intellectual and Social Organisation of the Sciences*. Oxford: Oxford University Press.

Widdicombe, S. (1998). Identity as an analyst's and a participant's resource. In C. Antaki and S. Widdicombe (eds.), *Identities in Talk* (pp. 191–206). London: SAGE.

Widdowson, H. (1998). The theory and practice of Critical Discourse Analysis. *Applied Linguistics*, 19 (1): 136–151.

Widdowson, H. (2000). On the limitations of linguistics applied. *Applied Linguistics*, 21 (1): 3–25.

Wignell, P., Martin, J. R. and Eggins, S. (1993). The discourse of geography: Ordering and explaining the experiential world. *Linguistics and Education*, 1 (4): 359–391.

Winter, E. and Woolls, D. (1996). Identifying authorship in a co-written novel. An internal report for the University of Birmingham, UK.

Wodak, R. (1997). Critical Discourse Analysis and the study of doctor–patient interaction. In B-L. Gunnarsson, P. Linell and B. Nordberg (eds.), *The Construction of Professional Discourse* (pp. 173–200). London: Longman.

Wodak, R. and Chilton, P. A. (eds.) (2005). *A New Agenda in (Critical) Discourse Analysis*. Amsterdam: John Benjamins.

Wodak, R., de Cillia, R., Reisigl, M. and Liebhart, K. (1999). *The Discursive Construction of National Identity*. Edinburgh: Edinburgh University Press.

Wortham, S. (2000). Interactional positioning and narrative self-construction. *Narrative Inquiry*, 10 (1): 157–184.

Wortham, S. and Gadsden, V. (2006). Urban fathers positioning themselves through narrative: An approach to narrative self-construction. In A. de Fina, D. Schiffrin and M. Bamberg (eds.), *Studies in Interactional Sociolinguistics: Vol. 23. Discourse and Identity* (pp. 314–341). Cambridge: Cambridge University Press.

Wynn, E. and Katz, J. (1997). Hyperbole over cyberspace: Self-presentation and social boundaries in Internet home pages and discourse. *The Information Society*, 13 (4): 297–327.

Young, L. and Harrison, C. (2004). Introduction. In L. Young and C. Harrison (eds.), *Systemic Functional Linguistics and Critical Discourse Analysis* (pp. 1–11). London: Continuum.

Zimmerman, D. H. (1998). Identity, context and interaction. In C. Antaki and S. Widdicombe (eds.), *Identities in Talk* (pp. 87–106). London: SAGE.

# Name Index

# Subject Index

abstraction, 17, 60, 132, 133, 184, 208

accommodation, 17

acknowledgements, 63, 67, 74–82, 100, 211, 213

affinity space, 16

agency, 14, 22, 37, 45, 53, 54, 56, 79, 91, 106, 119, 123, 148, 156, 172, 183, 206, 218, 221

alienation, 20, 133

alignment, 8, 9, 11, 14, 35, 37, 43, 54, 57, 60, 82, 84, 85, 87, 105, 118, 169, 200, 221, 223

applied linguistics, xx, 18, 64, 68, 71, 76, 104, 107, 108, 116, 118, 159, 163–165, 167, 169, 171, 174

appropriation, 20, 36, 72

argument conventions, 28, 30

assertion, 52, 74, 77, 102, 153, 154, 170, 174, 183

attitude, 8, 15, 35, 42, 54, 64, 72, 84, 85, 132, 160, 164, 166, 171–175, 178, 189, 190, 210

attitude markers, 42, 190, 191, 197, 200

attributive types, 121, 125

authority, 20, 30, 80, 92, 130, 135–137, 142, 143, 149, 150, 152–154, 156, 185, 189, 192, 194, 204, 206, 208, 220

authorship studies, 61

biographical statement / academic bio, 102–129

biology, xiii, 2, 64, 65, 76, 140, 141, 188, 196, 197, 202, 204, 205, 216

boasting, 86

book reviews, 106, 180, 186–205, 212

boosters, 190, 191, 193–195, 197, 200, 206

bricolage, 90

business studies, xxi, 64, 76, 140, 141, 221

Cameron, Deborah, 67, 156, 158, 160–183, 186, 190

chemistry, 57, 184

code gloss, 190, 191, 196

collective identity, 10, 38, 39, 154

collocation, 60, 65, 67–70, 158, 160, 165, 166, 216

community, 1–22, 23, 25, 27, 35–45, 59–68, 72, 74, 82, 84–116, 126–139, 156–187, 194, 206–222

community of practice, 2

concordance, 69, 70, 72, 159, 160, 165, 172, 203, 214

conference presentation, 6, 91, 121, 123

conflict, 41, 130, 133, 137, 148, 150, 153

conformity, 23, 27, 31, 130, 156–159,